THE WATCH

A TWENTIETH-CENTURY STYLE HISTORY

THE WATCH

A TWENTIETH-CENTURY STYLE HISTORY

ALEXANDER BARTER

PRESTEL
MUNICH · LONDON · NEW YORK

CONTENTS

FOREWORD

The journey of the twentieth-century watch is one that says as much about the collective need to know time as it does about people's personality or social position. From the very beginnings of the watch more than five hundred years ago, its aesthetic style and form have been almost as important as the mechanics within. Time and our ever growing need to know it, to possess it, to capture it – and yes, even, if possible, to stop it – never grows old.

Two hundred years ago the ownership of a watch was largely restricted to the wealthy. However, new mass-production techniques developed during the second half of the nineteenth century brought about a democratisation of the watch that placed it within reach of the wider population. Such advances had coincided with the expansion of the railways and socio-economic changes, which made accurate time-telling increasingly of importance to the general public. At the start of the twentieth century, the pocket watch was the only common form of portable timekeeper, but the realities of modern warfare would soon render the pocket watch all but obsolete, superseded by a more practical means of telling time: the wristwatch.

Wristwatches are very personal objects; worn on the body rather than concealed in a pocket, they have a connection with their owner and at the same time are exposed for all to see. Having proved themselves practical in the trenches of the First World War, in the years that followed, watchmakers were quick to recognise the marketing potential that this new form of mass-market timepiece could offer. The 1920s and '30s would be a period of extraordinary experimentation and development that would witness the emergence of a range of new styles and forms. An entrepreneurial spirit mixed with an advanced and highly organised industry ensured that the Swiss quickly came to dominate the manufacture of high-end wristwatches, to the detriment of their counterparts in Britain and America. Developments were not led solely by trends in fashion; the two world wars would also impact watch design and influence civilian-issue watches of later years. In a similar way, technological and stylistic elements that were developed for specific users or tasks – whether for aviators or astronauts, mountaineers or divers – would in turn influence the design and production of watches for everyday use.

In the fifty-year period that followed the end of the First World War, Swiss makers enjoyed an almost unbroken and unprecedented period of growth and prosperity. However, this would come to an end during the 1970s as vast numbers of inexpensive, highly accurate electronic quartz watches from Japan and America began to flood the international market, seemingly heralding the death of the mechanical watch. By the early 1980s, speculation was rampant in Switzerland about the demise of the Swiss mechanical watch. Most sobering was the rumour that the Swiss would destroy the machinery necessary to manufacture mechanical mechanisms and would instead install the technology required to make quartz movements.

Indeed, many Swiss watch companies and thousands of jobs disappeared entirely in the fallout of what became known as the Quartz Crisis. Yet all was not lost, and thanks to the determination of certain key players, other watch houses would be born, reborn or successfully amalgamated and reorganised to ensure their futures. A few of the most famous and historic watch houses would emerge from the crisis bruised but ultimately more resilient – following a period of reflection and recalibration, it became clear that demand for and marketing of the fine watch depended on the continued use of mechanical rather than quartz movements.

In the immediate aftermath of the Quartz Crisis, appreciation of vintage wristwatches began to grow in an unprecedented way. Suddenly, pocket watch collectors who had once spurned vintage wristwatches translated their knowledge of the field into the foundation of a new and distinct collecting category. Driven partly by nostalgia and partly by what appeared to be the end of a horological chapter, this new enthusiasm for the vintage wristwatch in turn engendered an explosion of interest among the wider public, further fuelling the collector's market. In the early 1980s, auction houses such as Sotheby's began to devote entire sections of their watch auctions to the sale of wristwatches, and within a few short years the market matured. The success enjoyed by the vintage market spread to contemporary makers, inspiring them to achieve heights of design and quality that helped lead to an overall market renaissance in the last two decades of the twentieth century.

The mechanical watch's renaissance not only benefited existing brands, but it also led to the establishment of new independent watchmakers who were buoyed by the growth in demand for fine and innovative mechanical timepieces. First and foremost among the independents was the English maker George Daniels. Daniels believed that he could create a new type of mechanical movement, one that could take on the quartz watch. The result was the co-axial escapement. Daniels worked for more than twenty years to gain acceptance for his device, eventually achieving the first successful commercialisation of a new escapement in over two hundred years. Daniels sold his patented design to Omega, who launched their first line of co-axial watches in 1999. Such was Daniels's genius and tenacity that he would inspire a new generation of talented watchmakers.

The twentieth century was a period of dramatic, fast-paced change in many arenas, and one in which the watch was transformed into almost every conceivable shape and form. Decade by decade, this book reveals the fascinating story of the stylistic development of the most personal of timekeepers, the watch.

DARYN SCHNIPPER
CHAIRMAN, SOTHEBY'S INTERNATIONAL
WATCH DIVISION

LEFT George Daniels, made in 1970.
An 18 ct yellow gold twin-barrel
one-minute tourbillon watch with
spring-detent chronometer escapement
and retrograde hour hand
Diameter 62 mm

AUX *Fabriques* DE *Genève*

HORLOGERIE
BIJOUTERIE

JOAILLERIE
ORFÈVRERIE

SPÉCIALITÉ
POUR
MARIAGES

ENVOI
FRANCO
du Catalogue
sur demande

R. Hem.

E. BILLARD
8 Rue Grosse Horloge
LA ROCHELLE

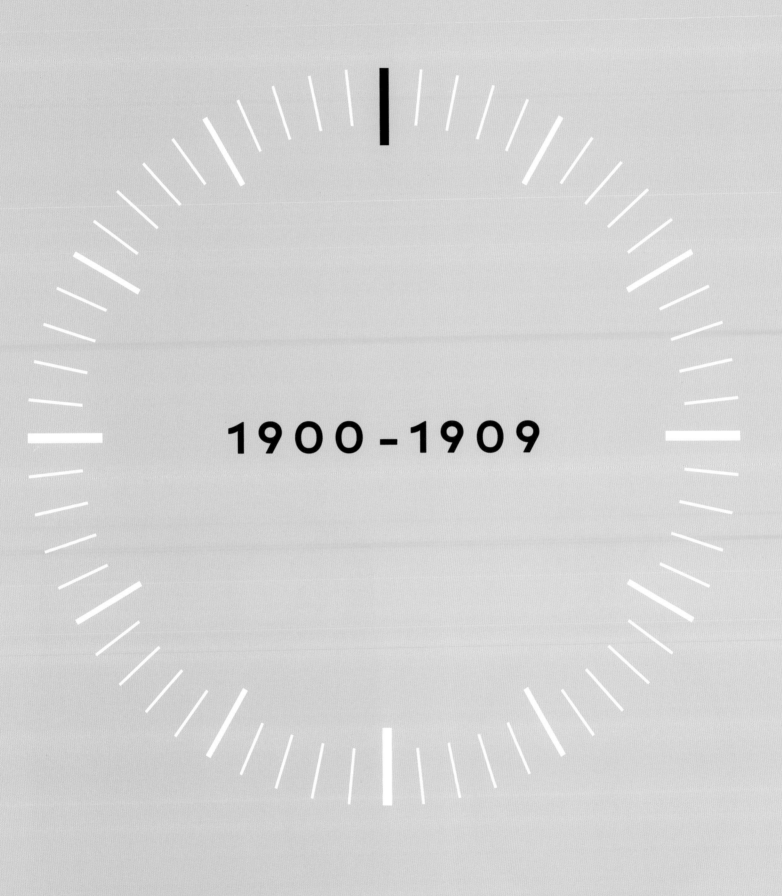

1900 - 1909

THE 1900s

The proliferation of the classically styled pocket watch of the early 1900s has rather unfairly tarnished the general perception of this period as one of plain design that occasionally verges towards the dour. By the last quarter of the nineteenth century, the mass production of cheap yet reliable watches by firms such as Roskopf in Switzerland had, for the first time, placed the portable timepiece within the grasp of almost all members of society.[1] Yet it was techniques developed during the second half of the nineteenth century in the United States that had truly transformed the market, dramatically increasing the availability of affordable, good-quality watches; by 1886, for example, Elgin of Illinois were manufacturing a thousand watch movements per day.[2] Meanwhile, Waltham, that great behemoth of American watchmaking, had developed technology for the mass production of precision watches that was adapted and adopted by factories in Switzerland, Japan and England.[3] In addition to their higher-quality watches, from the late 1870s, some American manufacturers began producing so-called 'dollar'

watches,[4] their movement plates stamped out of sheet metal and their dials frequently made of paper. As a consequence of the sheer volume of production during the last quarter of the nineteenth century, survival rates of the 'textbook' pocket watch from this era are far higher than for any previous period. The fact that a significant proportion of these follow similar forms and styles has certainly gone a long way to colour the way in which we think about the watch of the early twentieth century.

Yet the watch has always been a diverse creature, never immune to the influence of changing fashions. At the luxury end of the market, watchmakers had collaborated for centuries with enamellers and jewellers to produce timepieces of exceptional beauty. No period of watchmaking could be unaffected by the influence of the decorative arts, and it is therefore unsurprising that the impact of the Belle Époque and Art Nouveau filtered into the watch designs of the early 1900s.

Niello work, chasing and engraving and a wide range of decorative enamel techniques were used during this

BELOW, LEFT Waltham, c. 1908.
A gold-filled open-faced lever watch
(cal. 19¼‴ size 16)
Diameter 51 mm

BELOW, RIGHT Breguet, c. 1900.
A silver and niello half-hunting-cased
lever watch
Diameter 51 mm

OPPOSITE Patek Philippe, sold in 1902.
A silver open-faced lever watch, the case
back chased and engraved with irises,
daffodils and a dragonfly (cal. 19‴)
Diameter 51 mm

period. The use of translucent enamel was especially popular, and this was often applied above an engine-turned gold case back to form impressive, wave-like patterns that added a sense of depth and grandeur to a watch. The image below shows an Omega watch made in 1905 that has a case back composed of concentrically chased and engraved borders of laurel wreaths, these naturalistically overlapping the solid green enamel ring that separates them. Surrounding the central medallion, and framed by solid white enamel borders, a turquoise enamel has been applied over an engine-turned ground. This watch has elements of the classical and is certainly heavily influenced by the Belle Époque style. The dial remains traditional, with a decoratively engine-turned centre and a satin-finished chapter ring that carries the black Arabic numerals. Raised, openwork chased decoration also fitted well with the aesthetics of the Art Nouveau movement. In the Patek Philippe watch shown opposite, leaves and branches of mistletoe are naturalistically worked above a case back of enamel

in tones of blue, green and yellow. The mistletoe berries are represented by pearls, and the decoration continues across the case to include the original matching brooch to which the watch is attached.

Traditional decorative techniques that had been used for decades continued to be employed within ornamental schemes. During the first decade of the twentieth century, for example, the London watchmakers Jump & Sons created some exceptionally beautiful pocket watches that paid homage to the style Abraham-Louis Breguet had established in Paris at the end of the eighteenth and beginning of the nineteenth centuries – these included highly finished dials with multiple engine-turned finishes. Illustrated on page 14 is an example of Jump's work that dates to 1904. The watch has a silver dial with combinations of engine-turned decoration to give depth and contrast to the finish, and the Roman numerals are engraved and filled on a high-sheen, satin-finished chapter ring. Above the twelve o'clock position an aperture shows the phases of the moon, while a smaller window at six o'clock displays the date.

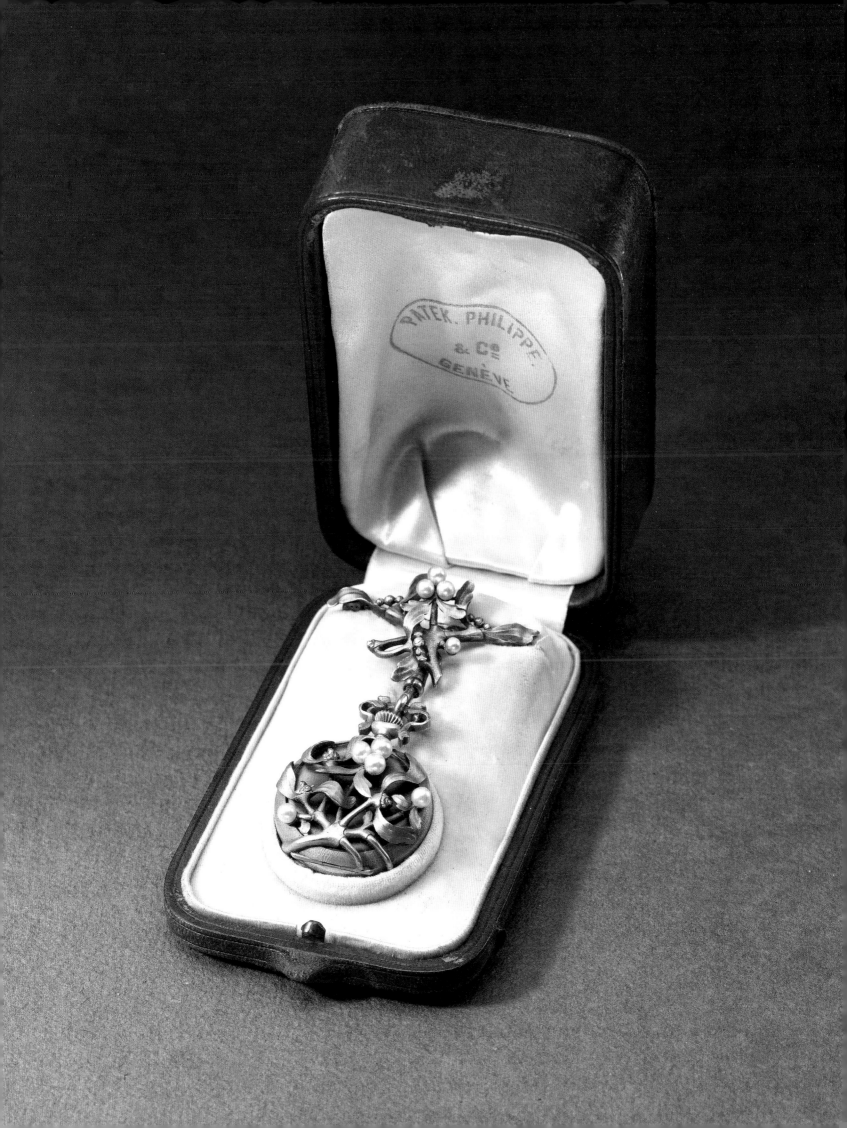

Although the pocket and pendant styles were the dominant forms of watch during the first decade of the twentieth century, other genres were also available. Lapel watches, for example, could be fitted to a jacket, the dial poking through the button hole while the main body of the watch remained concealed from view. Button and lapel-form watches continued to be popular for a number of years, the majority with plainer cases often made from gunmetal. It was also during these years that the wristwatch began to emerge as a distinct genre of timepiece.

The wristwatch was still not a clearly defined category at the turn of the twentieth century. In general, the application of a bracelet to a watch was a form of decorative enhancement, the bangle or bracelet often being set with enamels, precious stones and pearls, or having decoratively chased and engraved gold panels and links. Almost exclusively the preserve of wealthy women, bracelet watches had appeared intermittently throughout the nineteenth century but were relatively few and far

between, seemingly failing to capture the public imagination. Patek Philippe, for example, produced a bangle-form bracelet watch in 1868, yet the Patek Philippe Archives make no further reference to bracelet or wristwatches until the turn of the century.[5]

The image opposite right shows a yellow gold, platinum and diamond-set bracelet watch that dates to about 1900. An ornate and highly decorative wristwatch, this very much follows the nineteenth-century pattern of the bracelet watch as an object of jewellery, where the timepiece itself is almost incidental. The watch head is of a style similar to decorative pendant watches of the period and was clearly not intended for everyday use. To the bezel are engraved gold floral swags, and these are interspersed with black enamel panels heightened with painted white flowers. The gold bracelet is composed of laurel wreaths interlaced with diamond-set bows and connected by enamel panels with theatrical scenes painted in grisaille. The movement was made by the Swiss watchmaker Henri Sandoz & Fils, while the

BELOW, LEFT Unsigned, c. 1905.
A ladies' platinum, gold, emerald, seed
pearl and diamond-set wristwatch
Total length 140 mm

BELOW, RIGHT Henri Husson and Henri
Sandoz & Fils, c. 1900.
A ladies' yellow gold, platinum, enamel
and diamond-set wristwatch, the bracelet
with panels painted in grisaille
Diameter 26 mm, total length 185 mm

exceptional bracelet and case were executed by the French jeweller and metalworker Henri Husson.

As more women entered the workplace, so the wristwatch became an ever more useful means of tracking time throughout the day. Such wristwatches, intended for a working life, had no need to be overly decorative; being first and foremost objects of utility, they were usually adaptations of small pocket watches. Shown below is a pink gold ladies' wristwatch. Made in Switzerland, the watch was exported to the UK and has English import hallmarks for the year 1909. The design is derived from the small pendant watches that were popular at the end of the nineteenth and beginning of the twentieth centuries and is of typical half-hunter form. The cover is glazed to the centre, and this is surrounded by a pink guilloché enamel chapter ring with blue enamel Roman numerals and an inner minute track. As the watch is not designed to be suspended from a brooch or chain, there is no pendant or bow. The winding crown is relatively flat but with a knurled edge to allow the watch to be easily wound. Pressing the crown towards the case releases

a catch, causing the cover to spring open to reveal a white enamel dial that is calibrated to the edge with slim black Roman numerals and a red twelve o'clock. To the edge of the dial, the minutes are calibrated in black. The hands are made from blued steel and the hour hand has a double taper; this means that when the cover is closed, the first spade-form taper indicates to the hours engraved in blue to the cover, and when the cover is opened and time viewed on the white enamel dial, the secondary taper at the tip of the hour hand indicates hours to the dial's black Roman numerals. Rather than requiring the crown to be pulled out to adjust the time, the watch incorporates an earlier form of adjustment whereby a fingernail may be inserted to press the small pusher to the case side, just beneath the crown, which itself is protected by rounded shoulders. With this button pressed in, the crown can then be used to turn the hands. To enable a wrist strap to be fitted to the watch, gold wire has been shaped and soldered to the case to form lugs.

While the early 1900s continued to see the wristwatch genre as almost solely designed for women, some

BELOW Swiss, unsigned, with London import hallmarks for 1909. A 9 ct pink gold half-hunting cased ladies' wristwatch with cylinder movement (cal. 10.5‴) Diameter 27.5 mm

precedents for men's wristlets had already been set and would develop, albeit very slowly, as the decade advanced. The Swiss maker Girard-Perregaux was among the first to produce wristwatches in series. In 1879, at a trade fair in Berlin, Kaiser Wilhelm I approached Girard-Perregaux to produce a watch that could be fixed to the wrist using a strap. These wristwatches, designed for the Kaiser's naval officers, were to be fitted with a grille over the crystal to protect the glass. Following production of a prototype in 1880, two thousand examples were reportedly ordered. Sadly, none are known to survive, but their description would suggest a style not dissimilar to watches used by soldiers during the First World War.[6] In 1904, Eterna patented the design of a wristwatch case under Swiss patent 29974.[7] In the same year, Louis Cartier supplied his pioneering aviator friend Alberto Santos-Dumont with a wristwatch that could be easily used to consult the time while at the controls of his plane. Although no trace of the original survives, it is believed to have been the inspiration for the Santos II, which was developed in 1908 and marketed commercially as the Santos-Dumont

three years later (see image p. 34).[8] The significance of the Santos lay in the fact that it was specifically designed as a wristwatch – rather than being adapted from a pocket watch – with special 'lugs' that formed an integral part of the case design and held the wrist strap in place.

As the 1900s turned to the 1910s, it was the wristwatch that stood on the cusp of transformation. The advent of the First World War would be the most influential driver of this change by proving the wristlet's practicality to a wider audience. Experimentation with the form and shape of the wristwatch would lead to more decorative and varied dial designs. In Switzerland, the dominance of precision watchmaking had firmly taken root and the Alpine country's reputation for the production of luxury watches was well established. Improved production techniques increased the output of 'complication' watches, placing chronographs, repeaters and calendar watches within reach of a broader clientele.

DECORATING WITH ENAMELS

The enhancement of the watch's case and dial with enamel decoration has a long and rich history, one that is largely dominated by Swiss and French artisans. During the first quarter of the nineteenth century, Switzerland witnessed the rise of spectacular enamel miniaturists, and during the latter part of that century it was an exceptionally talented enamel portraitist, John Graff (1836–1903), who dominated in this field. Executing works for important families throughout Europe and beyond, it is Graff's portraits of the Maharajahs of India that are among the most evocative and captivating of this genre. Naturalistically painted, the portraits of the Maharajahs are often embellished with precious stones, in some cases applied to the necklaces and earrings that the sitters are shown to be wearing.

By the turn of the twentieth century, a broad range of decorative enamel techniques were being employed to enhance the cases of watches. Shown opposite is a gold pocket watch of Art Nouveau design that has an ivory dial and a further ivory panel inset to the case back.

Each panel is painted in muted polychrome enamel tones and depicts classical figures in a freer, almost Pompeiian style. The panels are attributed to the French miniaturist Fernand Paillet (1850–1918). A pupil of Albert-Ernest Carrier-Belleuse, Paillet's sitters included a number of American socialites and the novelist Edith Wharton. Paillet's reputation led to the artist receiving commissions from the Parisian jeweller Boucheron as well as Tiffany, New York. The image on page 20 (bottom) shows a pendant watch made by Verger Frères for Tiffany with panels signed by Paillet. Of oval form, this watch has a border of pearls and, like the pocket watch discussed above, is set with ivory panels to the front and back, both of which are painted, once again, in similarly muted tones and depict neoclassical figures and putti.

Brighter and more vibrant enamel decoration was executed by using the technique of cloisonné. The image on page 20 (top) illustrates a polychrome cloisonné-enamel-decorated watch case supplied by the Swiss maker Longines to their Berlin agent in 1903. This is typical

BELOW Seeland, with enamel-painted portrait miniature by John Graff, c. 1890. An 18 ct yellow gold, enamel, ruby- and diamond-set hunting-cased lever watch, the enamel portrait depicting Maharaja Pratap Singh of Orchha Diameter 51 mm

OPPOSITE Unsigned Swiss movement, c. 1900. An 18 ct yellow gold open-faced lever watch with miniature enamel-painted ivory panels attributed to Fernand Paillet Diameter 46 mm

ABOVE Longines, made in 1903.
An 18 ct gold and cloisonné enamel
open-faced lever watch (cal. 18.89)
Diameter 48 mm

RIGHT Verger Frères for Tiffany & Co.,
with ivory panels signed by Fernand
Paillet, c. 1905–10.
An 18 ct white gold, diamond- and
pearl-set pendant lever watch with
miniature enamel-painted ivory panels
Length 37 mm

of a style of watch decoration that had been applied to cases in varying forms throughout much of the previous century. The dial is traditional in design, with a gold ground, and the centre is engraved with stylised flowers.

Pendants and brooches in the form of insects, especially beetles, were a popular style of novelty watch. These watches had articulated wings that were released via a catch positioned at the base or head of the beetle's body. The wings themselves were invariably decorated with translucent enamels over a chased and engraved ground to give them a naturalistic appearance, and the abdomen and legs of the beetles were usually realistically rendered. Diamonds and enamels were often inlaid to further enhance the decorative scheme, and the eyes of the beetles were frequently set with rubies or other coloured stones. At the head of the beetle, the forelegs and antennae were formed into a framework onto which the pendant's chain could be affixed.

Watches in the form of spheres (often referred to as *boule de Genève*), gourds or eggs had been popular during the last quarter of the nineteenth century and continued to be fashionable in the early part of the twentieth. These watches could be suspended from a chain or

brooch and would hang with the watch's dial facing downwards – a discreet way of carrying the time. Many of these watches incorporated a bezel winding system whereby the watch was wound by turning the top half of the case; a small button could then be depressed in the side of the case to allow the hands to be adjusted. They were decorated with varying combinations of enamels, pearls, diamonds and other precious stones, their chains and pendants regularly styled to match.

COMPLICATION WATCHES

Although seemingly in terminal decline, the English watch was still a force to be reckoned with at the beginning of the twentieth century. Makers such as Charles Frodsham were continuing to produce watches of exceptional quality. The watch shown below, made by Frodsham in 1902, has a superb movement with one-minute tourbillon, split-seconds chronograph and minute repetition. The dial, with its creamy, off-white enamel, wonderfully lustrous in appearance, is typically English in style and was made by T. J. Willis, one of the finest dial makers. There was no holding back with the use of gold: the 63 mm diameter case is large and heavy – satisfyingly so when held in the palm of the hand – and the covers are substantial, broad and thick, unapologetically adding to its heft. To the right-hand case side, a repeating slide will chime the hours, quarters and minutes past each hour when activated. Partially recessed into the band, the slide is protected by the channel in which it sits, and its action is both solid and purposeful. The pusher to adjust the hands is also protected, positioned in the case side close

to one o'clock and just to the right of the pendant: a fingernail can be used to press the pusher in the middle of its protective shoulders while turning the crown with one's other hand to adjust the time. The crown at the top can be depressed to start the chronograph running, releasing both central chronograph hands; pressing the pusher above eleven o'clock will stop one of the seconds hands while the other continues – this allows the timing of two events begun at the same time but finishing at different intervals. One other rather ingenious feature is the so-called 'thief-proof' bow: the ring that would hold the chain swivels on the pendant, a design intended to prevent a pickpocket from easily wrenching the watch off its chain, this being much easier to do when the pendant is fixed.

One of Frodsham's great patrons was the Morgan banking family in the USA. In 1854, Junius Morgan became a business partner in the English branch of the banking house George Peabody & Co. It was while living in England that Junius began a tradition of purchasing

BELOW Charles Frodsham, hallmarked 1902.
An 18 ct yellow gold open-faced one-minute tourbillon watch with minute repetition, split-seconds chronograph and 60-minute register
Diameter 63 mm

BELOW Charles-Henri Meylan, c. 1900.
An 18 ct yellow gold open-faced lever
watch with perpetual calendar, moon
phases, split-seconds chronograph
and minute repetition
Diameter 54 mm

Frodsham watches for himself and as gifts for family, friends and employees. The tradition was continued by Junius's son, John Pierpont Morgan (1837–1913), and in turn his own son, John Pierpont Morgan Jr (1867–1943). The watch shown here is one of a group of approximately 25 pieces made between 1897 and 1931 that the Pierpont Morgans commissioned from Frodsham's to give as gifts to partners and employees of the Morgan firm in recognition of their outstanding achievement. Known as the 'Morgan calibres', these watches all featured the same specifications as the present example. Immensely expensive, the watches were sold for between £200 and £300 and at the time were among the most costly and complex English production watches available.[9] The inner cuvette (cover) of this watch is engraved 'W.G.H. from J.P.M.', recording that the watch was given by John Pierpont Morgan Sr to the American banker William Gould Harding.[10] Later, from 1916 to 1922, Harding would serve as the second chairman of the US Federal Reserve.

Watches with additional functions such as calendars, chronographs and repeaters became increasingly popular towards the end of the nineteenth century. The Swiss were already dominant in this field, and developing new and innovative forms of the complication watch became one of the industry's driving forces in the first half of the twentieth century.

Shown here is a fine-quality watch by Charles-Henri Meylan of Le Brassus, Switzerland. Made about 1900, the watch has a perpetual calendar with an additional indication for the phases of the moon. The perpetual calendar function will self-adjust for the varying lengths of the months and is also designed to allow for the extra day at the end of February in a leap year. This watch also incorporates a split-seconds chronograph and minute repetition. It is certainly one of the more complex watches of the era, yet the style and layout of its dial and case are fairly typical of the period, and similar watches were made, albeit in relatively small numbers, by the major watch houses.

While most watches that displayed the day, date and month in combination used subsidiary dial displays, such as those found on the Meylan watch just mentioned, dials with 'windows' displaying the calendar were also available. The watch shown below, which is unsigned, dates to about 1890–1900. The enamel dial has one long aperture to display the day, date and month, which are all engraved on separate discs mounted to the top-plate of the movement. Although a clear and highly legible form of calendar display, the traditional subsidiary dial remained dominant until the development of the calendar wristwatch. As the popularity of calendar wristwatches grew in the second and third quarters of the twentieth century, the aperture form of calendar display proved an essential method of space-saving and a means of ensuring greater clarity on the smaller dial of a wristwatch.

Innovations by watchmakers such as the Swiss firm Le Phare meant that, by 1910, the complication watch was no longer the sole preserve of a wealthy elite. The development of new equipment by Le Phare under its Dixi brand enabled the more efficient production of repeaters, chronographs and calendar watches, which allowed the firm to offer good-quality complication watches at a considerably lower price than its competitors at the higher end of the market.[11]

RIGHT Anonymous, c. 1890–1900.
An 18 ct gold open-faced lever watch with linear triple-calendar display and aperture for moon phases
Diameter 50 mm

OPPOSITE Le Phare, c. 1905.
A 14 ct pink gold hunting-cased triple-calendar quarter-repeating chronograph watch with moon phases
Diameter 57.5 mm

TIME ZONES

At the beginning of the twentieth century, the relevance of the current time in different world locations was beginning to be of significance for business and politics. As the expansion of the railway network gathered pace in North America, Europe and India during the mid-nineteenth century, the establishment of standard time became increasingly important. Historically, towns and cities had kept their own local time based on solar time, and this meant that there were enormous discrepancies in the times held by different towns and cities even within the same country. With rail journeys passing through growing numbers of towns, the difference between railway time and local time was not only bewildering but dangerous, with accidents caused by confusion over running schedules. In 1884 the International Meridian Conference was held in Washington, DC, with 26 nations represented. An overwhelming majority voted to establish Greenwich, in London, as the prime meridian. The establishment of the prime meridian led directly to the formation of a standardised system of 24 times zones used around the world, each zone covering 15 longitudinal degrees and representing 1 hour. At the same time, communications were undergoing a revolution, with subsea cables now stretching across the Atlantic – already in 1866, time signals were being sent from Greenwich's Royal Observatory to Harvard University in Cambridge, Massachusetts.

Watches with world time indications began to appear relatively soon after the 1884 Meridian Conference. The Swiss watch illustrated opposite dates to about 1900 and is a typical example of a double-dialled watch of the period displaying different time zones. Both dials are white enamel and this example is marked to the front 'Greenwich Time', with the added complications of full calendar and moon phases. To the back of the watch, a further white enamel dial is divided into seven subsidiary dials for time indication in New York, St Petersburg, Calcutta, Melbourne, Vienna, Berlin and Paris. The watch is fitted with an array of adjusting pushers to the side of the case to control, via the top crown, the adjustment of the different time zones and the calendar indications.

This example was clearly intended for the British market, but examples were made with different cities marked to the main dial and with London then taking the place of one of the smaller subsidiary dials to the back. It must have been an extraordinary sensation for the owner, when the watch was new, to be holding a watch that displayed time simultaneously across the globe, surely altering their perception of the world.

OPPOSITE Swiss, c. 1900.
An 18 ct yellow gold double-dialled watch with multi-time-zone indication, triple calendar and moon phases
Diameter 54 mm

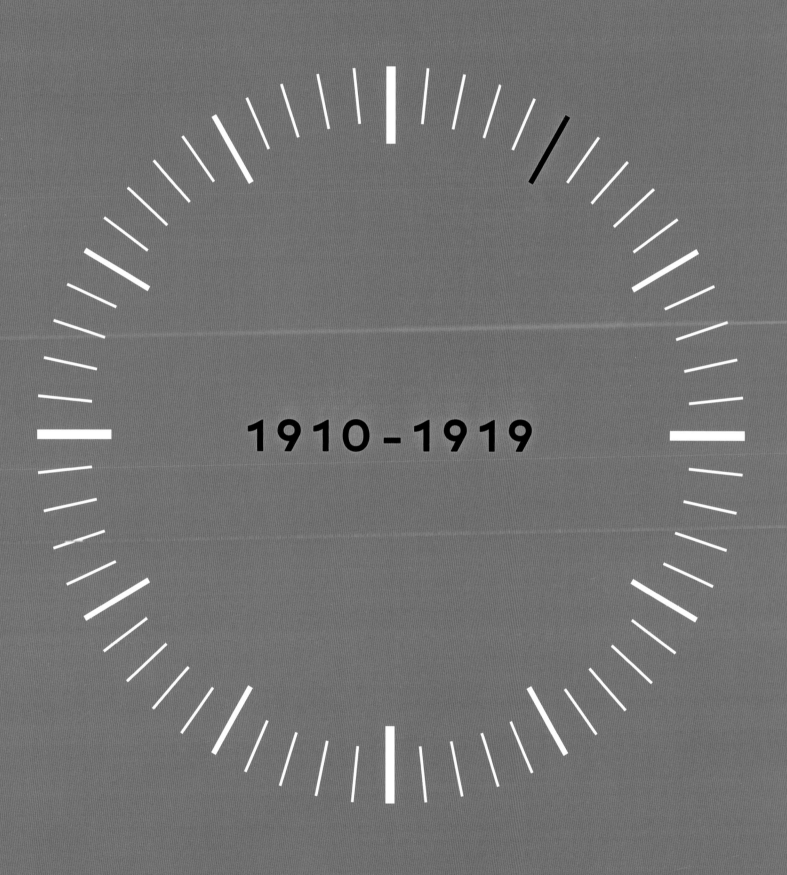

1910–1919

THE 1910s

As the new decade opened, designs and formats that had been popular at the turn of the century continued to appear and formed the staple of many catalogues and retailers' window displays. However, a shift had begun. The continuing popularity of the pendant watch and the slow but gradual rise of the wristwatch encouraged experimentation with shape and form. Traditionally the pocket watch was circular in shape, for practical reasons – the movement's major parts, comprising wheels, balance and spring barrel, were all round; the dial was circular to allow the hands to navigate each minute division equally; and the case was round, not only to evenly follow the watch's components but also to slide easily and smoothly into a pocket. What better way to modernise and individualise a watch than by changing its form?

Manufacturers of wristwatches were quick to capitalise on the design possibilities offered by this relatively new time-telling medium, and shaping was an important means to diversify their ranges. The natural curvature of the forearm meant that a wristwatch could be designed both for comfort and aesthetics. Rectangular, lozenge- and barrel-form cases were among the earliest designs to appear, and these shapes were further enhanced when curved, giving a sleek design that would also fit comfortably to the wrist.

Enlarged numerals are a notable feature of many wristwatches from the 1910s. In part this is due to the thickly applied, luminous radium numerals that were increasingly prevalent during the period. In the newly shaped wristwatches, numerals were also stretched to fill the dial space or even the bezel of a watch. A large proportion of early wristwatches were produced with subsidiary dials for seconds, usually located at the six o'clock position but occasionally offset at nine o'clock. However, many wristwatches were manufactured without seconds indication, especially those with smaller dials. Examples of wristwatches with centre seconds are relatively unusual from this period. One of the earliest Rolex wristlets to have been produced with a centre seconds indication is shown on page 32 (bottom left).

Hallmarked for 1914, this watch is otherwise typical of the period, with a silver hinged case and white enamel dial.

The classic hunting-cased and open-faced pocket watches of the 1910s were little changed, and their forms were transferred to early wristwatches, most notably those used during the First World War. However, the demand for slim dress watches, particularly those with enamel decoration, was rising. An example by Movado is shown opposite (top); this gold watch, which dates to about 1915, has an especially finely rendered case back with translucent grey enamel over engine-turned, chased and engraved decoration. To the centre of the case back, the bust of a Roman centurion is shown in profile, surrounded by wonderful engine-turning bordered with a laurel wreath. Watches with polychrome enamel-painted covers also continued to be produced, depicting flora, landscapes, townscapes and portraiture. It was pendant watches for ladies that often displayed the most creativity in terms of design and decoration, and this period witnessed the perfect melding of the jeweller's and watchmaker's arts to produce timepieces of exquisite beauty.

Although few defined wristwatch models appeared during this era, Cartier commercially released their Santos model in 1911,[1] and this was followed, in 1912, by Movado, who registered a patent for their own pioneering wristwatch, the Polyplan (Swiss patent 60 360, 7 June 1912). The Polyplan was one of the first wristwatch models by any company to feature a movement specifically designed for it, rather than incorporating a calibre that had previously been used in a pocket or pendant watch. Rectangular or tonneau-form (barrel-shaped), the Polyplan was an elongated, curved watch designed to fit the natural shape of the wrist. At the time of its introduction, the Polyplan would have appeared both modern and distinctive in design, clearly an item of wristwear and not merely a modified pocket or pendant watch strapped to the arm. However, the most remarkable aspect of the watch was its movement, the Movado calibre 400. Designed on three planes (hence 'Polyplan'), the calibre had a flat central section incorporating the going train, and to either end the movement was chamfered downwards at a 25-degree angle. The top end of the movement consisted of a mechanism for winding and hand-setting, while, ingeniously, the lowest-angled portion held the balance, which was mounted and connected to the watch's train

BELOW, LEFT Rolex, with London import hallmarks for 1914.
A silver hinged-cased centre seconds wristwatch
Diameter 34 mm

BELOW, RIGHT Movado Polyplan, with London import hallmarks for 1918.
A sterling silver curved, tonneau-form wristwatch (cal. 400)
Length 44 mm

OPPOSITE, TOP Movado, c. 1915.
A slim 18 ct yellow gold open-faced lever watch with opaque white and translucent grey guilloché enamel (cal. 580)
Diameter 47 mm

OPPOSITE, BOTTOM Longines, retailed by L. Kramer & Co., Cairo, 1912.
An 18 ct yellow gold hunting-cased lever watch with polychrome enamel-painted scenes (cal. 11.87)
Diameter 48 mm

via an angled section of the pallet lever. Measuring 38 mm in length, 15.2 mm in width and with a depth of 4.5 mm, the movement design was a 'reversed' calibre – the wheel train side of the movement and balance were visible to the underside of the dial, which in turn resulted in the underside of the movement being largely composed of a plain backplate. This arrangement allowed for a slightly larger balance (crucial for enhanced precision) as well as a reduction in movement depth. Polyplans were made in their original form from 1912–17.[2] It would seem that production was hampered by the expense and difficulty of producing the specially made calibre. Nevertheless, Movado appears to have continued experimenting with the model, and a further patent for the Polyplan was registered in 1929. Perhaps a little ahead of its time, the Polyplan was an important early step in the development of the wristwatch and demonstrated the potential of mass-produced watch models specifically designed for wrist wear, not mere adaptations of pocket watches.

By the end of the decade, the innovative spirit of the Art Deco era was creating a renaissance in watch design. The successful mass-production techniques achieved during the second half of the nineteenth century had been in danger of relegating the pocket watch to a mere object of utility, yet by the 1920s the watch in all its forms had been firmly catapulted into an arena of glamour and fashion. The importance of personal timekeeping in the modern world had opened new opportunities for watch manufacturers. Through innovation and variety of design, the watch's case and dial could be tailored for specific activities or occasions, thereby encouraging multi-watch ownership. The rise of the wristwatch had also begun, its importance in the field during the First World War having transformed society's perception of the bracelet watch: its popularity and proliferation among returning soldiers meant that its visibility had greatly increased. In December 1917 the *Horological Journal* noted: 'the wristlet watch, little used by the sterner sex before the war, but now to be seen on the wrist of nearly every man in uniform and of many men in civilian attire'.[3] It is perhaps telling that 1917 also saw the development of Cartier's Tank wristwatch, which the firm would release to the market before the close of the decade, in 1919, and which would become one of the most successful watch designs of the twentieth century. As the 1920s opened, the steady rise in production of the wristwatch would gather pace, drawing innovation and creativity from a range of pioneers.

BELOW Cartier Santos, commercially introduced during the 1910s.
An 18 ct yellow gold wristwatch
Width 25mm

OPPOSITE, TOP Patek Philippe, sold in 1912.
An 18 ct yellow gold tonneau-form wristwatch, the bezel with stretched dark blue enamel Roman numerals
Length 33.5 mm

OPPOSITE, BOTTOM Cartier Tank, c. 1919.
A platinum, gold and diamond-set rectangular wristwatch
Length 28 mm

PENDANT WATCHES

Throughout the 1910s there was an exuberant experimentation in the style and design of the watch, and it was through the ladies' pendant watch that these developments found their greatest expression. French artisans were especially influential during this era, working with enamels, rock crystal and onyx as well as diamonds and other precious stones to embellish the cases of watches. Jewellery makers would frequently buy in movements to complete watches themselves, as well as working to commission from watch houses, often to fulfil special orders.

The images opposite illustrate an 18 ct yellow gold, enamel, ruby- and diamond-set hexagonal pendant watch that the Swiss watchmaker Longines supplied to their agent in Paris, the firm Hauser-Zivy, on 15 June 1910. The case was made for Longines by the Parisian jeweller Joseph Vergely. Vergely, who had made his name working at Cartier, had a particular talent for creating unusual watch cases. The hexagonal case with its teardrop-shaped, diamond-set pendant loop puts one

in mind of a hand-held boudoir mirror; the case back is decorated with translucent blue-grey enamel over an engine-turned gold base, which creates wonderful, wave-form patterns. The central panel is similarly decorated in green guilloché enamel, centred with a neoclassical woman painted in white enamel and surrounded by a border set with rose-cut diamonds. The sides of the case are channel-set with calibré-cut rubies. The neoclassical figures that appeared on pendant watches during this period were often painted in similarly muted tones to the Longines watch just mentioned; however, they could also be sculpted. Shown below is a watch by the French jeweller Georges Fouquet. The square-shaped case is made from onyx, and the back is inset with a rock crystal panel that is carved and engraved with a neoclassical figure and surrounded by a border of single-cut diamonds.

Elaborate diamond settings were greatly favoured. The watch illustrated on page 38, signed by Haas Neveux & Cie, is typical of intricately framed pendant watches

BELOW Haas Neveux & Cie, c. 1910.
A gold, platinum, guilloché enamel and
diamond-set pendant lever watch
Width 33 mm

BELOW Cartier, c. 1911.
A platinum, guilloché enamel and
diamond-set pendant watch, the case
back with a pear-shaped diamond
surrounded by old European and
single-cut diamonds
Length 89 mm

OPPOSITE Cartier, c. 1915.
A ladies' gold, guilloché enamel,
diamond- and cabochon emerald-set
wristwatch
Diameter 27 mm

ABOVE Cartier, c. 1917.
A ladies' platinum, gold and diamond-set
tonneau-form wristwatch
Length 30 mm

of the 1910s. Similar watches were made by a number of makers, including Patek Philippe and Cartier. The range and variety of pendant watches made by Cartier during this period is astonishing; at their most opulent, these were dazzling items of jewellery into which the convenience of a watch had been added.

Decorating with enamels and diamonds was by no means restricted to the pendant watch. One of the earliest Cartier wristwatch designs is shown opposite. This ladies' wristwatch closely follows the established designs of the pendant watch, its front bezel heightened with translucent light blue enamel over engine-turned gold. A border of rose-cut diamonds surrounds the dial, while the dial itself is silver and also decorated with engine turning. Of course, being a wristwatch – where the reverse is not designed to be viewed – the back is of gold but has a plain, polished finish. The design and form of gem-set wristwatches could be further enhanced by the development of the shape and form of the lugs. The image above illustrates a Cartier wristwatch that, although influenced by the designs of pendant watches, is a distinct wristwatch shape with lugs of fancy form.

ACTUAL SIZE

COMPLICATION WATCHES

OPPOSITE, TOP Audemars Piguet, made
in 1912.
A small platinum open-faced lever watch
with minute repetition (cal. 9½‴ SMV
#61)
Diameter 25 mm

OPPOSITE, BOTTOM LEFT
Detail of movement backplate

OPPOSITE, BOTTOM RIGHT
Detail of movement under-dial

BELOW H. Moser & Cie, c. 1915.
A silver wristwatch with day and date
indication
Diameter 36 mm

The miniaturisation of the watch movement has long
been a means by which the watchmaker can demonstrate
their skill and talent. However, it is in scaling down
the size of the complication movement that the limits
of the watchmaker's art are truly tested.

The images opposite show a remarkably small
minute-repeating watch. The movement was made
by Audemars Piguet in 1912, and the watch was
subsequently sold to P. Schuch in Vienna in 1914.
Incredibly, the movement is just 21.4 mm in diameter
and 3.11 mm in height, and this tiny area has to
incorporate not only the standard time-telling function
but, additionally, one of the most complex mechanisms
in horology: the minute repeater. Chiming on demand
the hours, quarters and minutes past the hour, using two
hammers on two gongs, the successful miniaturisation
of its parts was an extraordinary achievement.

The significance of this type of movement lay in the
possibility it allowed the watchmaker to manufacture
extremely complex movements that would fit into the

small size of a wristwatch case. Success in miniaturising
other forms of complication movements had included
the perpetual calendar and split-seconds chronograph.
In 1898–99, Victorin Piguet & Cie developed a small
(27 mm diameter) perpetual calendar ébauche for Patek
Philippe that was later completed and cased as a wristwatch
in 1925, in the process becoming the earliest known
perpetual calendar wristwatch. In 1903, Victorin Piguet
& Cie also supplied Patek Philippe with a similarly sized
movement incorporating a split-seconds chronograph,
which Patek Philippe subsequently finished and sold as
a wristwatch in the 1920s (see pp. 68–69). Watches such
as these would form the basis for future development
of the complication wristwatch.

Although demand for complication wristwatches
was extremely small during the 1910s, examples do exist.
The image below illustrates a rare and early calendar
wristwatch, made by H. Moser & Cie in about 1915.
A long aperture to the dial of the watch displays the days
of the week, while an outer ring is calibrated in red for

the date; the case is made in silver and has large hoop-form lugs. Repeating wristwatches are also known from this period. Between 1908 and 1918 Audemars Piguet produced and sold five wristwatches that incorporated minute repetition. Intriguingly, in 1910 the London retailer Guignard commissioned Audemars Piguet to produce a wristwatch with a 10-*ligne* (22.6 mm diameter) movement that incorporated both minute repetition and chronograph functions. It seems that the project was halted at the outbreak of the First World War and it remains unclear whether the watch was ever completed.[4] Had the watch been finished, it would have been an incredibly important example of an early complication wristwatch.

Development and refinement of the complication pocket watch continued apace during the decade, and pocket watches with chronograph, calendar and/or repeating functions were readily available. However, the ambitions of the most talented watchmakers led to the production of ever more innovative and complex watches.

Unique pieces were created that tested the skills of the finest horologists and acted not only as advertisements of a brand's prowess but as a springboard for further development. Some of these watches were specially ordered, and increasingly so by the industrialists and entrepreneurs of North America.

In 1914, Patek Philippe produced an exceptional and unique double-dialled pocket watch for George Thompson, an English-born entrepreneur who had emigrated to the United States in the 1880s. This piece (shown here) perfectly illustrates the advantages of the pocket-sized complication watch over its smaller, wrist-sized cousin. By dividing the watch into two dials, this example is able to combine the functions of a split-seconds chronograph and a perpetual calendar while maintaining the utmost clarity in its displays. To the front, time is shown in hours and minutes, with a subsidiary dial for seconds. Beneath the twelve o'clock position, a further subsidiary dial is calibrated for 30 minutes in order to record the minutes elapsed while

the chronograph function is running – this minute-registering dial, being calibrated only to its lower half, does not interfere with the hours indicated above. The dial to the watch's reverse is solely dedicated to a perpetual calendar, with subsidiary dials indicating days of the week, months of the year and date, together with a further dial which is combined with an aperture for the age and phase of the moon. In addition to the visual functions, the watch also incorporates a minute-repeating function, activated via a slide to the case side. A pusher through the crown sets the two central chronograph hands running; an additional button to the shoulders of the case may be used to 'split' the seconds, thereby enabling the timing of two simultaneous events. The movement, which was developed for Patek Philippe by Victorin Piguet & Cie, is exceptional in its complexity, execution and finishing. Especially remarkable is the fact that the watch is not great in size, measuring 54 mm in diameter and with a depth of 15 mm (excluding the glasses). George Thompson was an accomplished mathematician and it was perhaps this interest that fired his enthusiasm for mechanical complexity and ultimately led to the commission for this watch. One can imagine the satisfaction Thompson must have derived from the clarity of the design, which masked the incredible engineering beneath its two dials.

Ever more complex pocket watches would continue to excite and amaze in the decade to follow, and the production of wristwatches with mechanical complications would begin an inexorable rise that would reach its apotheosis in the 1940s and '50s, during the golden age of vintage watch production.

EARLY WRIST CHRONOGRAPHS

Although some wrist chronographs were advertised during the opening decade of the 1900s, the wider commercial production of this genre did not begin to evolve until the 1910s. The majority of early chronograph wristwatches were made with relatively large movements of 40–45 mm in diameter. These were traditional pocket watch movements and therefore the cases of these wrist chronographs were oversized. With the majority of early wristwatches being of sober design and modest proportions, the market for large-sized chronograph wristlets was presumably rather limited, and production would have been aimed at customers who had specific requirements, such as aviators. Some of the earliest wrist chronographs were little more than pocket watches with bows soldered to either side of the case to act as fastenings for the wrist strap, the dials with their calibrations frequently shifted 90 degrees counter-clockwise to adjust to the wristwatch format.

The oversized chronograph wristwatch by Omega illustrated opposite measures 46 mm in diameter and was made in 1917. The movement is an 18-*ligne* (40.6 mm) calibre, and the watchmaker had already advertised a model almost identical to this one in 1913. Cased in silver, the watch has a traditional pocket watch shaping to the case, with hinged closures to the bezel and case back and corresponding lips for ease of opening. Simple wire attachments form the lugs onto which the wrist strap may be secured. The dial is white enamel with black Arabic numerals; the two subsidiary dials to the left are for constant seconds and, to the right, a 15-minute register measures minutes elapsed while the chronograph is running. Divisions of just 15 minutes are relatively unusual. Chronographs that featured minute registers were more usually calibrated for 30 or occasionally 60 minutes. As only 15 minutes are displayed, there is space for each increment to be individually marked with its corresponding minute numeral, rather than simply being represented by linear dashes. The pink gilt activation pusher for the chronograph is wide but relatively sleek and is positioned below six o'clock. Many early chronograph wristwatches, such as that by H. Moser & Cie shown here, incorporated their activation pusher through the winding crown. By using a movement that entirely separated the crown and pusher, as well as using slim wire lugs to affix the wrist strap, the overall design is minimal and utilitarian.

BELOW H. Moser & Cie, c. 1915. A 14 ct yellow gold single-button chronograph wristwatch with enamel dial and 30-minute register Diameter 43 mm

RIGHT AND BELOW Omega, made in 1917.
A silver single-button chronograph
wristwatch with enamel dial and
15-minute register (cal. 18''' P CHRO)
Diameter 46 mm

WATCHES OF THE FIRST WORLD WAR

The earliest forms of production wristwatches were very closely based on the 'bassine' pocket watch form – a traditional casing comprising a hinged back with rounded edge and a rounded bezel that retained the watch's crystal. Unlike a pocket watch, the wristlet dispensed with the pendant and bow to which the suspension chain was traditionally secured; instead lugs were added, onto which a wrist strap could be affixed. These lugs were often simple metal wire loops that were soldered onto the watch case, although larger, hinged hoops that were stylistically similar to the traditional pocket-watch bow were often affixed instead.

Of course, the wristwatch's dial had to be configured a little differently to the open-faced pocket watch. The traditional open-faced pocket watch displayed the numeral for twelve o'clock beneath the winding crown – that is, the three o'clock position on a standard wristwatch dial. Although some early advertisements show a number of wristwatches with the twelve o'clock position located beneath the crown, it seems that there was a general acceptance, early on, that the wristwatch required a realignment of the dial's configuration to compensate for its differing format – indeed, it is highly likely that at least some of those wristwatches advertised with the twelve o'clock located beneath the crown were pocket-watch stock that the manufacturers were themselves converting for sale as wristlets. To avoid confusion, it was not uncommon for manufacturers of early wristwatches to mark the twelve o'clock numeral in its 'new' position with a different colour – usually red, but occasionally blue. This practice was already common on watches of non-standard configuration, for example sphere watches and lapel watches, where the twelve o'clock position would not be immediately apparent at a quick glance without some form of highlight.

During the First World War, when communication and synchronised timekeeping were essential for operations, the practicality of the wristwatch ensured that this timekeeping genre gained the acceptance among men that it had lacked for so long. Requiring only a quick glance to the wrist rather than fumbling in a pocket, the advantages were obvious. Writing in March 1916, the chairman of H. Williamson Ltd noted, 'It is said that one soldier in every four wears a wristlet watch, and the other three mean to get one as soon as they can. Wristlet watches are not luxuries ... [and] have been selling in the greatest quantities for many months past.'[5]

The silver watch illustrated above is typical of the earliest style of wristwatch made for men. This watch is hallmarked for the years 1911–12, and the case's shape and the white enamel dial are both of traditional pocket

OPPOSITE, TOP Swiss, unsigned
movement, case with London import
hallmarks for 1911.
A silver hinge-cased wristwatch
with enamel dial and lever movement
Diameter 34 mm

OPPOSITE, BOTTOM Borgel cased Swiss
movement with London import hallmarks
for 1914.
A silver wristwatch with shrapnel guard,
black enamel dial and luminescent
numerals and hands
Diameter 35 mm

RIGHT Borgel cased Swiss movement
with Glasgow import hallmarks for 1915.
A 9 ct yellow gold wristwatch in early
damp-proof case, the enamel dial with
luminescent numerals and hands
Diameter 34 mm

BELOW Harrods advertisement
reproduced in *Punch* on 24 April 1918

watch style. Thick silver wire is attached to the case as the framework on which to attach a slim leather wrist strap. A good-quality Swiss lever movement is incorporated. To change the hands, a small pusher below the winding crown is depressed using a fingernail, and this simultaneously disengages the winding mechanism and activates the hand-setting mechanism – turning the winding crown while the pusher is depressed allows the time to be set. Numerous similar watches were used by soldiers in the First World War.

Early wristwatches of this style were far from robust, often having thin metal cases of gold or silver, and while 'shrapnel' grilles (see p. 48 bottom) could be added to help protect a delicate watch glass, one of the main issues was the lack of protection the casing afforded its movement. With friction-fitted, hinged closures, there was no real protection against knocks or the ingress of dirt or moisture, the enemies of the mechanical movement. Also, in the darkness of the trenches, an unilluminated watch dial was next to useless at night. Watches aimed at officers included models with their hands and hour markers painted with radium for luminescence and cases constructed to provide some protection against ingress of water. The image on page 49 (top) illustrates a gold officer's style watch from 1915. This watch has a white enamel dial with bold, radium-painted Arabic numerals and hands, which together would have provided a highly visible display at night. The watch's case was made by Borgel, a Swiss company specialised in the production of dust- and damp-proof cases. Rather than a traditional hinged case with a cover and bezel that 'snapped' shut, the Borgel case's main body was made from a single piece of gold or silver into which the dial and its movement were fitted and secured with a screw-down bezel. This design dramatically reduced the chance of moisture or dirt entering the watch and thereby greatly increased the watch's reliability. By the middle of the decade, so-called 'unbreakable' crystals were available. Made from celluloid, this form of glazing could replace the fragile glass and dispense with the need for a separate shrapnel cover.

Despite these attempts to protect the wristwatch, it remained an inherently delicate object. Its smaller size compared to the pocket watch, combined with the harsh conditions in which it had to perform, meant that in many instances the pocket watch would have been a more reliable timekeeper. Other solutions that were available included a large leather band with an integrated pocket-watch holder – the one illustrated here is typical. Allowing for slight shrinkage due to age, the leather casing would have measured just under 60 mm in width. This example houses a pocket watch with a diameter

of 44 mm. At this size, the pocket watch was able to accommodate a substantial movement, in this instance a 16-*ligne* (36 mm diameter) movement that was of good quality and relatively robust. The watch's case is made from gunmetal and has a protective cuvette (hinged cover) directly over the movement, in addition to the case back itself. This provided some 4.5 mm of stepped rims, which allowed some protection from the ingress of dirt and moisture (though it was by no means water-resistant). The leather holder itself lent further protection for the watch, enveloping the bezel, and when new must have provided a fairly tight seal around the watch's case, again limiting the ability of dirt or moisture to enter.

Pocket watches were, of course, also used in the traditional manner during the First World War, concealed in a jacket or coat and secured with a chain. Those made specially for military use invariably followed the same pattern of design as the luminescent wristwatch, with bold radium numerals painted on enamel dials. Indeed, although the popularity of the wristwatch among the troops was increasing, substantial orders for 'military' pocket watches were still being made at the end of the war. In 1918, the American Expeditionary Forces ordered several thousand open-faced pocket watches with chronograph function from Vacheron Constantin. The order stipulated that each should have luminous numerals and hands, while the cases were to be made of oxidised silver.

These is no doubt that the First World War transformed the perception of the wristwatch. A general reticence among men to wear a wristwatch had been dispelled by the widespread use of the strap watch during the conflict. Many men returning from the front continued to wear wristwatches after the war, and although the pocket watch would still dominate Swiss exports for the next ten to fifteen years, the tide was beginning to turn in the wristlet's favour.

DEFIES THE ELEMENTS!

THE ROLEX OYSTER

THE ALEXANDER CLARK COMPANY, LTD.,

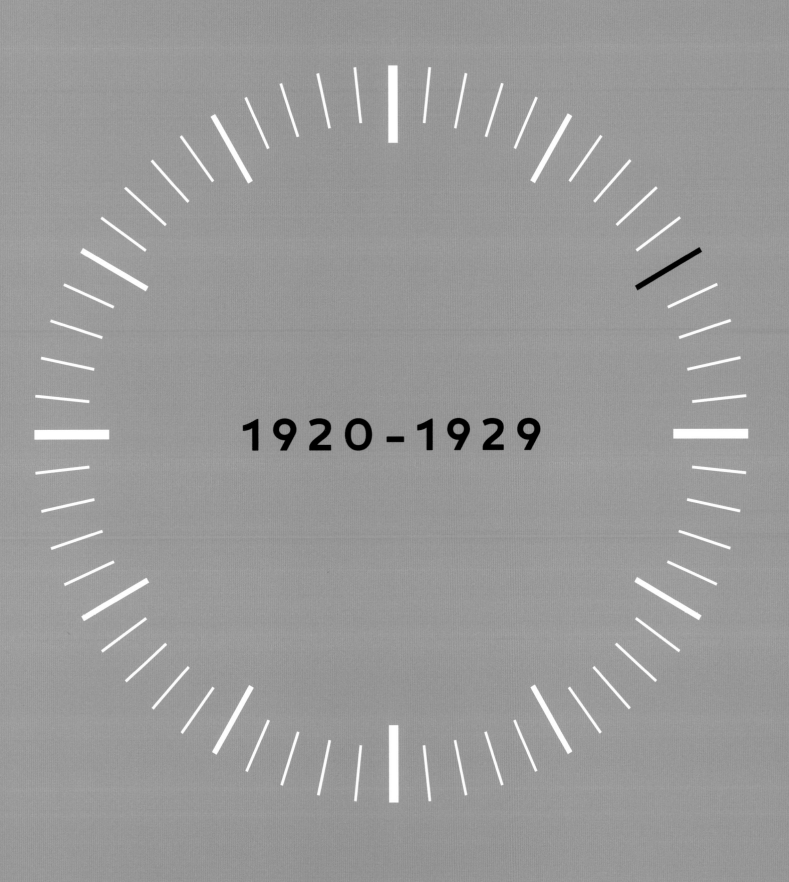

1920–1929

THE 1920s

No longer merely confined to the pocket, the watch had been liberated and suddenly its application appeared to be everywhere. In addition to the rise of the wristlet, watches began to be integrated into all manner of objects, from pencils and steering wheels to lipstick and cigarette cases. The watch's form was evolving and developing into designs that would influence the portable timepiece's style for decades to come. An increasingly diverse choice of watches resulted in a far broader range of consumers having the means to express their own tastes. Watches were becoming a symbol of modernity itself, and fashion was increasingly playing its part.

Many within the industry still regarded the wristlet as little more than a gimmick: to them, exposing a delicate mechanical item on the wrist was anathema. Indeed, the introduction in the mid-1920s of avant-garde models such as wristwatches in the shape of car radiator grilles may well have served to further the naysayer's argument that the wristwatch was little more than a passing fad. Innovation was therefore key during the decade – the wristlet had to prove itself indispensable. To achieve this, practicality was essential: the wristwatch had to be reliable and durable. For some horological entrepreneurs, the ultimate goal was to waterproof, shock-proof and automate the wristwatch. However, designing novel and

interesting case shapes was also key to winning over a new wave of buyers. The newly established styles of rectangular and tonneau-shaped wristwatches naturally lent themselves to the Art Deco period. In 1921 Cartier released their Tank Cintrée, a supremely elegant wristwatch with an elongated, slim rectangular case that was curved to naturally follow the contour of the wrist.

During the 1920s, Patek Philippe produced some extraordinary wristwatches for the Brazilian retailer Gondolo & Labouriau. Usually with large dimensions – and in many instances dramatically oversized for the period of production – these watches featured square, rectangular, tonneau or round cases. The majority had silvered metal dials with engraved tracks for the minutes and hours, which were filled with black enamel paint. Among the most dramatic of the period are those with large, curved rectangular cases and dials featuring stretched Arabic numerals and semi-circular dial signatures. While the external stylistic elements were by no means exclusive to Patek Philippe, the perfection of this form of wristwatch design was honed by the company during this period, and many of the motifs incorporated are to be found recurring time and again across a variety of watch brands right up to the present day. Patek Philippe's relationship with Gondolo &

BELOW, LEFT Dunhill, hallmarked 1929. A 9 ct yellow gold cigarette case with inset lighter and watch
Length 116 mm, width 77 mm

BELOW, RIGHT Mido Bugatti, made in 1925. An 18 ct yellow gold wristwatch in the form of a Bugatti car radiator grille
Width 24 mm

OPPOSITE Patek Philippe, made in 1928. An 18 ct yellow gold wristwatch with enamel dial, curved screw-set lugs and hinged case
Diameter 33 mm

OVERLEAF, LEFT Cartier Tank Cintrée, first introduced during the 1920s. A platinum curved rectangular wristwatch with platinum bracelet, movement by the European Watch & Clock Co.
Length 47 mm

OVERLEAF, RIGHT Patek Philippe Chronometro Gondolo, sold by Gondolo & Labouriau in 1924. An 18 ct yellow gold oversized, curved rectangular wristwatch (cal. 12′′′)
Length 49 mm

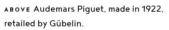 Audemars Piguet, made in 1922, retailed by Gübelin.
A platinum and yellow gold cushion-form perpetual calendar open-faced lever watch with moon phases (cal. 17SVF)
Width 43 mm

RIGHT Cartier Éclipse, c. 1929.
An 18 ct yellow gold and enamel shutter-form purse watch
Length 46 mm

BELOW, LEFT Cartier, c. 1926.
A platinum, gold, enamel and rock crystal octagonal-shaped open-faced lever watch with movement by the European Watch & Clock Co.
Width 46 mm

BELOW, RIGHT Léon Hatot, made in 1927.
An 18 ct yellow and white gold curved octagonal wristwatch
Length 38 mm

Labouriau was an immensely important one – during this period, almost a third of the watchmaker's total production made its way to the Rio de Janeiro retailer.[1]

By the mid-1920s, wristwatch production still only accounted for around a third of all Swiss watch exports. Mechanically complex movements displaying all manner of functions were increasingly in demand, and it was the pocket watch's size that allowed it to dominate in this area. The 1920s also saw the development of an alternative portable timepiece, the so-called purse watch. The purse watch was developed for use by both men and women, and the concept created an infinite number of decorative possibilities, with ingenious forms of sliding, hinged and sprung openings designed both to please the user and impress the casual observer.

The decade witnessed an increasing variety in the materials and decorative techniques employed by makers. A great range of metals were used, including platinum as well as coloured golds in tones of yellow, pink, white and even green. Enamels, precious and semi-precious stones, corals, seed pearls, mother-of-pearl and rock crystal were all incorporated for their decorative merits. Cases were often engraved with geometric patterns, occasionally infilled with enamel highlights. As metal dials grew in popularity, so variation in their finish began to increase – in addition to elaborately configured numerals, some might be executed with contrastingly toned sections to their surface or enhanced with engine-turned decoration.

All this energy and creativity led to a boom in watch production. In 1920, some 13.7 million completed watches and movements were exported from Switzerland, and by 1929 this figure had reached almost 21 million.[2] But with great expansion came great risk. On 29 October 1929 the Wall Street Crash arrived, and with it came the beginning of the Great Depression. Swiss watchmakers were heavily exposed; the watch revolution seemed in danger of screeching to a halt.

JEWELLERY WATCHES

Nothing evokes the opulence of the Art Deco period more than its jewellery. The image below shows an astonishing platinum, diamond and synthetic ruby pocket watch. Made by Longines, the watch was delivered to the maker's agent in Mexico on 9 June 1921. The delicate filigree hands and gently stylised Arabic numerals could place the watch almost anywhere in the first twenty years of the twentieth century. Yet the case, its unapologetically clean lines dazzling with 4.65 carats of pavé-set diamonds, accented with synthetic ruby hour markers, is the epitome of 1920s glamour. The wonderful enamel dial is painted in grisaille with a sculptural rendition of a classical maiden riding a lion, all against a crimson background. To the sides of the case, a crisp Greek key motif is engraved, a design element applied time and again to watch cases during the Art Deco period.

Cartier's influence on Art Deco design is, of course, legendary. At the defining Exposition Internationale des Arts Décoratifs et Industriels Modernes held in Paris from April 1925, Cartier exhibited some 150 pieces of jewellery, among them fifteen watches, all of which were executed using a wealth of materials, including jade, coral, onyx, lapis, rock crystal, diamond, platinum and gold.[3] The images opposite illustrate a highly unusual trapezoid-form pendant watch made by Cartier. The watch has an unmistakable Art Deco appearance with overtones of the then popular Egyptian revival style. Cased in platinum, the bezel is white enamel inlaid with stretched gold Roman numerals, all beneath a blazing sun. The dial focuses on function, with each hour marker pointing to its corresponding gold numeral. The contrast with the case back is startling – a plain, trapezoid onyx panel surrounded by glittering pavé-set diamonds follows through to the matching pendant, which is formed of a broad onyx and diamond-link chain. Cartier manufactured many sensational gem-set watches throughout the Deco period, including some magnificently stylised bracelet watches, often to special commission. One spectacular example is the ladies' wristwatch commissioned in the mid-1920s by the Marquesa de San Carlos de Pedroso

BELOW Longines, retailed by Diener Hermanos, Mexico City, in 1921. A platinum, enamel, diamond- and synthetic ruby-set open-faced lever watch (cal. 10.85) Diameter 41 mm

OPPOSITE Cartier Egyptian, c. 1929. A platinum, onyx and diamond-set trapezoid-form pendant lever watch with movement by the European Watch & Clock Co. Length 36 mm; 140 mm including chain

OPPOSITE, TOP Cartier, c. 1920.
A slim platinum and sapphire-set
open-faced lever watch with movement
and case by the European Watch & Clock Co.
Diameter 45 mm

OPPOSITE, BOTTOM Vacheron Constantin,
with case by Verger Frères, made in 1927.
A white gold, yellow gold, champlevé
enamel and diamond-set ladies' wristwatch
(cal. RA 8‴ 15/12)
Width 20 mm, length 70 mm

ABOVE Cartier, c. 1925.
A platinum, coral, enamel and diamond-
set rectangular ladies' wristwatch with
movement by the European Watch
& Clock Co.
Length 36 mm

of Biarritz (shown above). The watch is made in platinum
and decorated with coral, enamel and diamonds. Typical
of Cartier's attention to detail, the design of the folding
clasp has also been carefully considered, with gold exposed
to the wearer's skin and only stark black enamel visible to
the outside while worn.

Around the middle of the decade, a fashion for ladies'
wristwatches with panels or sections that stretched away
from the watch's dial began to emerge. Forming an almost
hybrid case/bracelet arrangement, the panels dramatically
elongated the length of the watch case and allowed a larger
surface area upon which intricate decorative schemes
could be developed with coloured enamels, diamonds
and other precious stones.

Jewellery watches could also be subtle. The vogue for
extra-slim pocket or dress watches saw the development
of 'highlighted' case sides. A recessed channel cut into
the sides of a watch case could be filled with calibré-cut
stones, most often diamonds but occasionally other
precious gems such as sapphires. Dress watches of this
style are beautifully refined: from the front an apparently
plain timepiece devoid of adornment, yet a slight tilt brings
a flash of colour.

JUMP HOUR AND WANDERING HOUR WATCHES

Innovation was not restricted to style and decoration alone; indeed, the 1920s witnessed experimentation with the display of time itself. One of the most dramatic Art Deco twists on telling time was the production of the so-called 'jump hour' or 'digital display' watch. Examples of watches with dials displaying the time in apertures had been made for more than three hundred years, yet the reapplication of this style of time telling during the 1920s seemed to embrace the very ethos of the period with its confident modernity.

During the decade, a variety of jump hour models appeared. In 1926 Breguet patented one of the most unusual forms of this genre. Known as a 'wandering' jump hour watch, the dial was composed of a central disc with engine-turned arrow (see image below left), the tip of which contained an aperture that displayed the hours. As time advanced, so the central disc revolved, taking the hours around the circumference of the dial and pointing to the minutes as it passed. Upon reaching the top of the hour, the hour disc jumped forwards to

reveal the next hour in the arrow's aperture. An ingenious display made more for show than practicality, the jump hour watch is a challenging timepiece to tell the time by in low light or with strained eyes; this is perhaps particularly so in the aforementioned example: with the hours whizzing around the edge of the dial, one may easily be confounded by whether the hour shown is an upside-down 9 or 6, or perhaps an 8 or 5 in the low light. While not the best watch for making a surreptitious glance at the time during a long evening's entertainment, it certainly was the watch to bring out to impress your host.

An arguably more user-friendly example of the jump hour watch, combining an aperture for hours with a traditional central hand for minutes, was offered by a variety of companies. However, the most commercially exploited form of the digital display watch was that which showed both the hours and minutes (and increasingly during the following decade, seconds) through apertures to the watch's cover. The action of these watches was achieved by modifying the movement plate in the

BELOW, LEFT Haas Neveux & Cie, c. 1925.
An 18 ct white, yellow and pink gold jump
hour wristwatch
Width 26.5 mm

BELOW, RIGHT Audemars Piguet,
delivered in 1926 to the retailer Bittmann
in St Moritz.
An 18 ct white gold jump hour lever watch
with minute repetition and simple calendar
displayed linearly, the back opening to
reveal a glazed aperture to display the
moon phases and movement (cal. 18′′′
SMV#2)
Diameter 48 mm

traditional under-dial area to incorporate discs calibrated
with the hours and minutes. This latter form of jump
hour watch removed the need for an exposed glass dome
above the dial, the watch's cover instead forming a grille
under which a glazed insert would protect the revolving
time discs.

Although some early examples of the jump hour
wristwatch featured decorative cases – that shown
below left, for example, has bands of yellow and pink
gold applied to the white gold case – this genre of watch
is usually plain and stark, the focus being solely the
shape of the case and the time apertures themselves.
As we have already seen, such 'window' forms of display
were also well suited to calendar indications. The image
below right shows an extraordinarily complex pocket
watch made by Audemars Piguet in the mid-1920s.
This watch not only has apertures for the hours and
minutes, but a linear, three-aperture display calendar
for the day, date and month. Like the hours and minutes,
the three calendar indications are each displayed on separate
discs. On depression, a pusher mounted in the winding
crown opens the case back to reveal the movement, which
is displayed beneath a glazed cuvette (cover); between
the movement and the cuvette, the phases of the moon
are shown in an aperture. Concealing the moon phases
in this manner ensures the stark, monochromatic design
of the watch's time and calendar display is uninterrupted.
To the watch's left side one can just see a slide: rather
brilliantly, this is also a minute repeating watch. In the
half-light, a vexed user, unable to see the time clearly,
may merely activate the slide and the time will be crisply
chimed to the nearest minute.

CALENDARS AND CHRONOGRAPHS

Watches with mechanical complications gained greatly in popularity during the 1920s. The famously competitive watch commissioning of industrialists James Ward Packard of Ohio and Henry Graves Jr of New York, from watchmakers such as Patek Philippe and Vacheron Constantin, led to the production of some of the most complex watches ever seen. Almost every conceivable function was developed, from tidal indications to star charts. However, for the majority of wealthy purchasers, the favoured complications were calendars, chronographs and repeaters, incorporated either individually or in combination.

Calendar wristwatches appeared only infrequently during the 1920s. Although there was no reason why the wristwatch medium should restrict the production of calendar models, their smaller size and delicacy when compared to the traditional pocket watch was certainly an issue. Cost was a further factor, and this, combined with the fact that the pocket watch's dial was a larger, more convenient canvas on which to view complex indications, would have been among the reasons so few were produced during the decade. Indeed, if we put ourselves in the mind of the buyer purchasing an expensive calendar watch in the 1920s, the pocket watch must have seemed the logical

format to choose – the calendar wristwatch, by contrast, perhaps appearing dangerously akin to a gimmick.

The image opposite illustrates an intriguing wristwatch. Exhibiting one of the most beautiful designs from the early period of wristwatch production, this timepiece was originally sold by the Swiss retailer Gübelin. The watch displays a so-called 'simple' calendar: while the calendar will advance each day, unlike an annual or perpetual calendar it will not take into account differences in the length of the month, requiring the user to adjust the date at the end of those months with fewer than 31 days. Made by Audemars Piguet, the watch was specially ordered by Gübelin, whose signature appears to the dial, case and movement. Particularly arresting, however, is the inscription to the outside case back (shown right), which, beneath the original owner's name, reads: 'This is the first calendar wrist watch ever made by us and I believe it to be the only one in existance [sic]. E. Gübelin, Lucerne 1924 Switzerland.' It is extraordinarily rare to find a statement of this type engraved on a wristwatch and it serves to show quite how special this wristwatch was considered to be in 1924. Mr Barr, the original owner, no doubt immensely enjoyed showing the watch to his friends and acquaintances.

ABOVE AND OPPOSITE Audemars Piguet, sold by Gübelin, Lucerne, in 1924. An 18 ct white gold simple calendar rectangular wristwatch with moon phases (cal. 10 HPVM) Length 28 mm, width 24.5 mm

BELOW, LEFT Audemars Piguet, made in 1925. A platinum open-faced split-seconds chronograph lever watch with 30-minute register and minute repetition (cal. 18 SMCRV) Diameter 46 mm

Today we are used to the idea of limited-edition and unique wristwatches within the collector's market, yet this watch demonstrates that cachet was already associated with a special wristwatch. Gübelin clearly found a demand for such watches among its clientele, and in the years following the sale of this wristwatch the firm ordered several further examples from Audemars Piguet.

Extremely mechanically complex, the split-seconds chronograph is considered one of the three most challenging complications in watchmaking. Designed to time events commencing simultaneously but concluding at different times, the split-seconds mechanism employs two central chronograph seconds hands, usually controlled by two push-buttons in the case side – although occasionally with a single button activation to start, stop and reset the chronograph and an additional pusher above or below for activating the split. One hand, the fly-back, can be stopped to register one event's duration and then, in turn, be reactivated to resynchronise with the chronograph hand; this will allow, for instance, the

timing and registering of an intermediary stage, and thus the lengths of multiple events can be recorded. This complication proves extremely useful during sporting events with multiple competitors, whether it be a horse race, a car race or the hundred-metre dash.

Illustrated here is a Patek Philippe that is believed to be the earliest known split-seconds chronograph to have been born as a wristwatch (rather than converted from a pocket watch) and is also, therefore, one of the most mechanically complicated early wristwatches ever made. Production of the movement began in 1903, but the watch was not completed and sold until 1923. The watch was bought on 13 October 1923 by Attilio Ubertalli, the seventh president of Turin's Juventus football club.[4] It seems highly likely, therefore, that Ubertalli approached Patek Philippe with a special request for a split-seconds chronograph wristwatch and that Patek took the opportunity to complete this piece specially for the customer.

The 18 ct yellow gold case is of bassine style, one of the earliest wristwatch case designs to have been used. Clearly

greatly influenced by the traditional pocket watch case, there is a hinged bezel and back as well as a traditional cuvette. An enamel dial is used, again a classical feature, but this is of course orientated for use as a wristwatch (the twelve o'clock being at 90 degrees to the crown, rather than next to it as one would expect on an open-faced pocket watch). Straight, screw-set lugs hold the leather strap in place and are typical of the early wristwatch lug form known as the 'officer' style.

The movement was made for Patek Philippe by the specialist chronograph manufacturer Victorin Piguet & Cie and is remarkably slim, especially in consideration of the depth required to accommodate the chronograph/split mechanism and its bridge work; the movement's diameter is a mere 28 mm. Cased, the watch has a diameter of 33.1 mm and is 11.1 mm thick. Such is the complexity and expense of the split-seconds chronograph that while standard chronograph wristwatches would quickly gain in popularity during the succeeding decades, the chronograph wristwatch with split seconds would remain a relatively rare variant for almost the entire twentieth century.

SECURING THE WATCH CASE

Protecting the watch movement from water and dirt had long been a challenge for both watch and case maker. At sea, where navigation relied on the accuracy of marine chronometers and other marine timekeepers, protective cases had been developed to minimise the potentially corrosive effects of the salty elements. In the 1870s, the English maker Herbert Blockley began selling so-called traveller's or explorer's pocket watches. These were designed for use on land, and in some cases at sea in the form of 'deck' watches. Cased in silver, these watches had plain covers, yet rather than the traditional friction-fitted case backs and bezels, the watches had screw-down bezels and backs; significantly, the watches also had a protective cap that entirely covered and screwed down over the winding crown. Gaskets made of leather were used to ensure a tight seal for the bezel, crown cap and case back.

The watch by Usher & Cole illustrated here was originally sold to the Admiralty for use as a deck watch in March 1893, for £18 10s. However, Usher & Cole's surviving workbooks show that the watch was repurchased by them in May 1929, converted to a traveller's watch and resold a month later, in June 1929. Interestingly, the records note it was repurchased for £6 and resold for £18 10s.[5] Usher & Cole was a partnership formed in 1869 by Joseph Usher and Richard Cole. The firm produced some exceptional timepieces, and the fact that the movement of this watch was deemed worthy of reuse some 37 years after its original completion is testament to its quality. This is particularly notable when one considers that the watch was specifically being reused as a traveller's watch and would have been intended for use on expeditions, where a reliable and accurate timepiece was of critical importance – the Royal Geographical Society had, for example, ordered a fleet of traveller's watches for use on polar and African expeditions, where the watches would be exposed to extreme climates.[6]

For the makers of wristwatches, the protection of the crown was still problematic in the 1920s. The use of a screwed cap over the winding crown of a wristlet must have been perceived as clumsy and impractical, especially

given the relatively small size of early wristwatches. In Switzerland, Borgel's patented case design provided some level of water-resistance, and examples of watches with Borgel cases continued to be made throughout the 1920s. However, the problem with these remained the winding crown: this relied on close metal-to-metal adherence without the use of gaskets, and the separate 'pin-set' mechanism used to adjust the hands on many versions of these cases also provided potential weak points where moisture or dirt might enter, especially after some years of use. Other experimental watches were made during the period, one of the most interesting being the hermetic watch.

The hermetic watch shown opposite has London import hallmarks for 1925 and was retailed by the Reading-based company Botly & Lewis. The sterling silver case was made by Jean Finger and follows Finger's 1921 patented design (Swiss patent 89276, published 2 May 1921). Featuring a double case, the watch's inner case is plain and made in three pieces with friction-fitted, snap-on bezel and back. This inner case is hinged into

the outer and has a pronounced lip beneath the crown to enable it to be easily 'swung out' for winding and hand-setting. The outer case is made of two parts, a solid body and separate screw-down bezel; this latter has a knurled finish for the owner's fingers to grip when opening and closing the watch. In theory this was an excellent way to protect the watch, providing an acceptable seal, yet it was also a rather fiddly daily exercise to open and wind the watch, and continued use eventually led to wear of the bezel's thread, thereby compromising its seal.

Finger's patent was not the only one for a hermetic-style wristwatch of this design. A very similar design by Frederick Gruen (US patent 1,303,888, filed 29 May 1918) was granted on 20 May 1919 for an almost identical case construction. Interestingly, an arrangement appears to have been made between Jean Finger and Rolex, for in 1923 Hans Wilsdorf of Rolex was granted British patent 197208 for a hermetic case of identical design to Finger's, and Rolex subsequently put a model based on these designs into production.[7]

THE ROLEX OYSTER

Early attempts at successfully waterproofing the wristwatch were invariably thwarted by the winding crown. Producing a tight, water-resistant seal by the use of gaskets in combination with the screw closure of the watch's front and back was a relatively straightforward procedure, so long as precision machinery was used. The crown was a different matter, for in order for it to be acceptable to the buying public it had to be practical, easy to use and aesthetically pleasing. Rolex's solution was a screw-down crown. On 28 September 1926, Rolex registered the 'Oyster' name; today the Oyster is as synonymous with the Rolex name as the brand's crown logo. The patenting and application of the Oyster method transformed the company's future and has been one of the most successful and influential wristwatch designs ever conceived.

The solution of a screw-down crown may appear an obvious one, yet it was a challenging feature to incorporate. A regular winding crown is fixed to its stem, and when 'at rest' against the watch case, the crown and its stem are always engaged in the winding position. While the standard winding crown can be free-wheeled backwards without engaging the watch's winding, if you are to screw down a crown, the crown and its stem must be disengaged from the winding system, both for its unscrewing and screwing down. In the Oyster watch, the crown itself screws onto a tube which is fitted to the watch case – this provides a hermetic seal. When the crown is unscrewed it springs away from the body of the watch, simultaneously activating the winding system, which allows the user to wind up the watch. Pulling the crown out will then allow the user to set the hands as normal. When the crown is pushed back to the case, the winding is disengaged and the crown can be screwed back onto its case tube. Without this disengagement, if the watch were already fully wound, the stem or mainspring could be broken by force when the crown was screwed back onto its tube. The Oyster solution was both reliable and practical, allowing the watch to be wound and set easily, with only the simple and quick

BELOW, LEFT Rolex Oyster, hallmarked 1928.
A sterling silver cushion-form wristwatch with enamel dial and screw-down crown, bezel and case back (cal. 9½''' Prima)
Width 33 mm

BELOW, RIGHT Rolex Oyster, retailed by Armstrong, Manchester, c. 1927.
An 18 ct yellow gold octagonal wristwatch with screw-down crown, bezel and case back (cal. 9½''' Observatory Quality)
Width 32 mm

additional step of screwing and unscrewing the crown before and after use.

The first Oysters were formed of three main case parts, plus the crown. The body of the watch had a screw-down bezel (holding the crystal) and screw-down case back with lead gasket. It has been noted by various researchers that the original patent for the Rolex Oyster crown is identical to one filed in October 1925 by Paul Perregaux and Georges Perret.[8] It seems that Hans Wilsdorf, Rolex's founder and ever the horological entrepreneur, recognised the importance of their invention and acquired the rights to the design.

The Oyster design was able to be adapted in order to take advantage of the popularity of the 'shaped' wristwatch, and early models included cushion and octagonal designs. Indeed, so long as the watch's case had its Oyster crown and a solid body with circular screw-down bezel and case back, its actual shape had the potential to be extremely varied; advantageously, this also set it apart from the traditional circular cases of its hermetic predecessors by Borgel, Finger and others.

Wilsdorf was utterly convinced by the potential of the Oyster and vast sums were spent on its promotion. This included newspaper advertisements extolling the brilliance of the design and even corporate sponsorship. On 7 October 1927, Mercedes Gleitze became the first British woman to swim the English Channel. Throughout the event, Gleitze wore a Rolex Oyster, and on 24 November 1927 Rolex took out a full-page advertisement on the front of the *Daily Mail* newspaper that included an announcement declaring the perfect performance of their watch during Gleitze's swim. Clever shop displays were also used: in 1927 Rolex began issuing its retailers with branded goldfish bowls, a Rolex Oyster wristwatch suspended within.

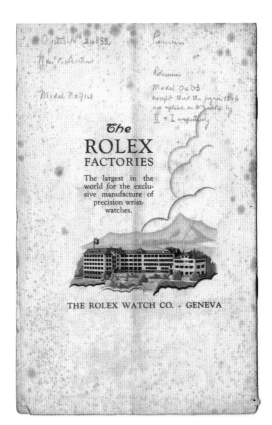

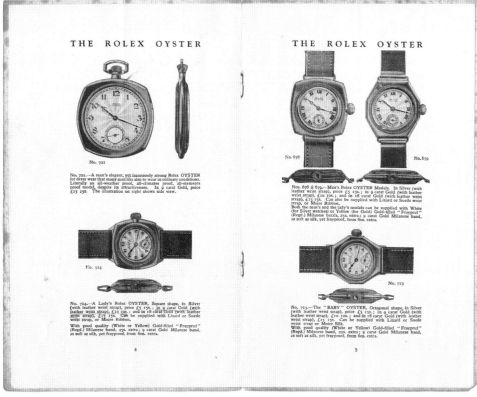

THE MOVADO ERMETO

Undoubtedly the most famous, varied and commercially successful purse watch, the Ermeto comprises an inner watch case protected within a shell of outer sliding covers. The Ermeto name was derived from the Greek meaning 'sealed' and thus emphasised the watch's resistance to dirt and moisture. Patented in Germany on 12 October 1926 (DRP no. 443 555) by Huguenin Frères of Le Locle, Switzerland, Movado acquired the rights to market the Ermeto the same year.[9]

At a time when the wristwatch was still to gain universal acceptance, the Ermeto offered a striking alternative. This was a watch that was modern and stylish but which did not involve wrist wear and could be safely stowed in a bag or pocket, perfectly protected within its outer shell. The sliding covers provided a canvas of infinite decorative possibilities, ideally suited to the Art Deco period, allowing the user to express their individuality. Movado produced a wide range of models, their covers variously finished with decorative engraving or ornamental enamel motifs, translucent enamels over engine turning or, most frequently, lacquers, exotic leathers and shagreen. The perfect travelling companion, the Ermeto was also available with an integrated hinged stand that allowed the watch to be placed on a desk or bedside table, those with luminous numerals becoming an especially useful night clock.

In 1928 Movado released their ingenious 'automatic' case winding system. As the sliding covers were opened, a pinion on the winding stem was engaged, which automatically turned the winding crown and wound the watch. An ingenious piece of horological engineering, each opening and closing of the case was designed to provide four hours of running time – the user was therefore only required to open their watch six times a day in order to power it for 24 hours.

Such was the brilliance of the Ermeto's design that Movado were able to offer a compelling argument to the potential buyer. An early advertisement for the model explained: 'The round watch and wrist watch ... take a shock like a car without tyres. The "Ermeto" with its modern simplicity of line, winds itself. It is suspended in an air-cell, protected by smash-proof outer cases. No unnecessary protruding winder, exposed glass, or possibility of overwinding. The "Ermeto" is safe in any pocket or handbag.'[10]

Made in 1929, the example illustrated below is the smallest of Movado's purse watch range and is known as the Ermeto 'Baby'. Originally designed as a model to integrate into ladies' handbags, the Baby was quickly added to the general Ermeto range. The present example is one of the earliest made by Movado and has a sterling silver case with black-lacquered sliding covers. The silvered dial has a frosted, matt finish, there are raised Arabic numerals and outer minute track, and blued steel hands. The movement is Movado's calibre 11 and incorporates the 'automatic' case winding system mentioned above. Calibre 11 was the original Ermeto Baby movement and the forerunner of the calibre 575.

Over the years, the Ermeto was made with a variety of different case and dial designs and became one of the company's most recognised and iconic pieces. The artist Andy Warhol, who was a great fan of Movado, owned at least six different versions of the Ermeto from a wide range of periods.

ERMETO

MOVADO

AUTOMATIC WINDING

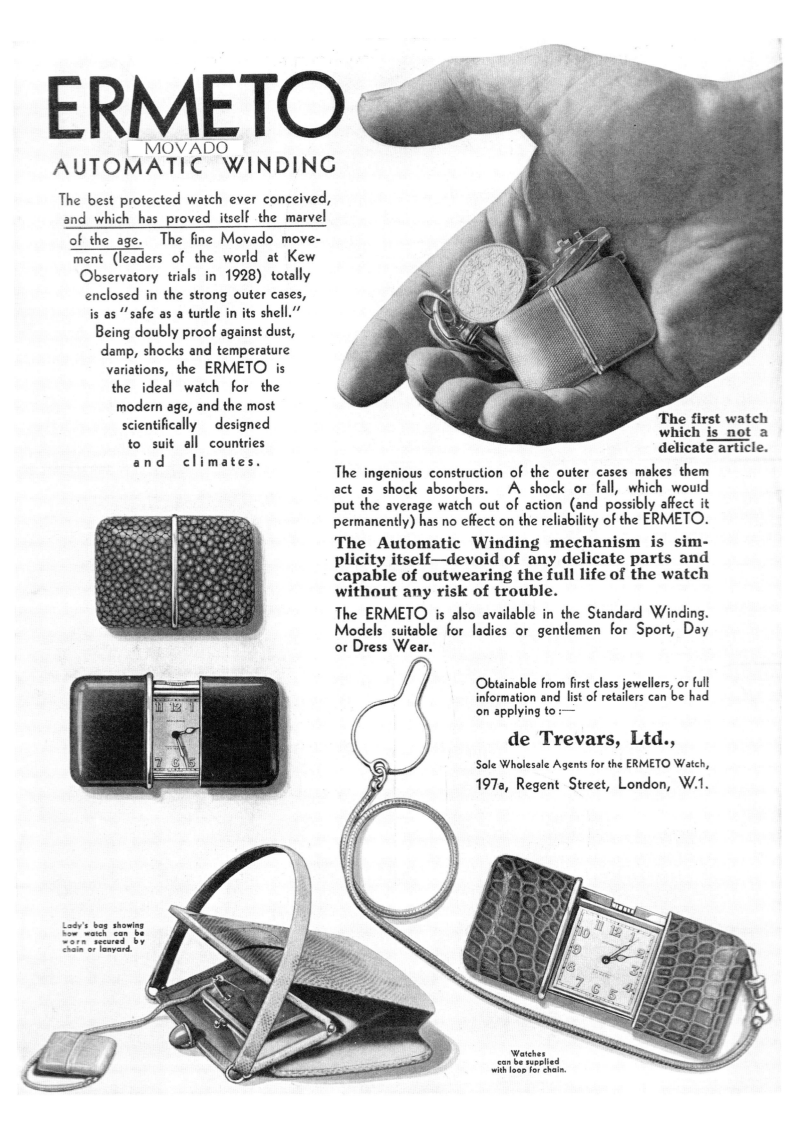

The best protected watch ever conceived, and which has proved itself the marvel of the age. The fine Movado move-ment (leaders of the world at Kew Observatory trials in 1928) totally enclosed in the strong outer cases, is as "safe as a turtle in its shell." Being doubly proof against dust, damp, shocks and temperature variations, the ERMETO is the ideal watch for the modern age, and the most scientifically designed to suit all countries and climates.

The first watch which **is not** a delicate article.

The ingenious construction of the outer cases makes them act as shock absorbers. A shock or fall, which would put the average watch out of action (and possibly affect it permanently) has no effect on the reliability of the ERMETO.

The Automatic Winding mechanism is sim-plicity itself—devoid of any delicate parts and capable of outwearing the full life of the watch without any risk of trouble.

The ERMETO is also available in the Standard Winding. Models suitable for ladies or gentlemen for Sport, Day or Dress Wear.

Obtainable from first class jewellers, or full information and list of retailers can be had on applying to :—

de Trevars, Ltd.,

Sole Wholesale Agents for the ERMETO Watch, 197a, Regent Street, London, W.1.

Lady's bag showing how watch can be worn secured by chain or lanyard.

Watches can be supplied with loop for chain.

INTRODUCING THE AUTOMATIC WRISTWATCH

The invention of the perpetual or 'automatic' watch is generally ascribed to the Swiss watchmaker Abraham-Louis Perrelet (1729–1826). In the 1770s Perrelet developed a system by which a pocket watch would self-wind, using the motion of the owner's body to 'charge' its mainspring and thereby power the watch. This revolutionary concept was quickly exploited by other watchmakers and further developed by, among others, Abraham-Louis Breguet and Louis Recordon. At the time, watches were wound by means of a key, and the somewhat cumbersome nature of this arrangement meant that an automatic watch had the potential advantage of allowing people to dispense with a fiddly daily routine.

Problems with reliability and no doubt concern among some that this technology might fail to ensure the watch was kept wound and on time seem to have hampered the widespread adoption of the perpetual pocket watch. Keyless winding systems, which dispensed with the need for a key and allowed a watch to be wound via a crown, were developed in earnest during the first half of the

nineteenth century, with Adrien Philippe (of Patek Philippe fame) transforming the medium in 1842. The convenience and reliability afforded by the keyless winding system made the requirement for an automatic solution of seemingly minor importance.

Today the automatic watch may be considered primarily for its convenience, yet the idea of a wristwatch that wound itself was, for the early pioneers, also one of protection and enhancement of the movement's performance (if a mainspring is kept fully wound, its power remains much more consistent, helping the movement achieve greater accuracy). While the pocket watch lay relatively well protected in one's pocket, the wristwatch was exposed to a barrage of potential hazards, from water and dirt to knocks and bashes. If one were able to protect the delicate mechanical movement from the ingress of dirt and moisture, reliability, accuracy and longevity could, potentially, be greatly enhanced. Early wristwatch cases tended to follow the designs of pocket watches, but the former's friction-fitted bezels and

BELOW Recordon, Spencer & Perkins, London, c. 1780.
An early pedometer-wound (automatic) watch movement, made according to British patent no. 1249 of 1780. The motion of the large silver oscillating weight wound the mainspring
Diameter (cased) 52 mm

case backs were generally thinner than the latter's and therefore provided little protection against the elements; furthermore, their winding crowns provided a tube into the movement through which water could potentially flow.

John Harwood was an English watchmaker convinced by the potential of the automatic wristwatch. His research and experimentation, in part carried out with his business partner Harry Cutts, began after the First World War. His experience in the trenches had shown Harwood the convenience of the early wristwatch, but also demonstrated its failure to withstand exposure to the elements and rugged wear on the wrist. In 1923, having secured funding, Harwood applied for a Swiss patent (no. 106583, granted 1 September 1924) for his automatic movement system. This was formed of a pivoted weight moving backwards and forwards around the movement, buffering off springs and winding the watch in a hammer-like action. Quite apart from the automatic system itself, Harwood's genius also lay in the development of a hand-setting system that dispensed with the need for either a button/crown or key,

meaning that the entire movement could be encased and, potentially, hermetically sealed. Ingeniously, the hands were set by turning the bezel of the watch.

Harwood approached, among others, Schild SA, a Swiss movement manufacturer who went on to commercially develop Harwood's watches together with Fortis. By mid-1929, Harwood watches were being acclaimed on both sides of the Atlantic and were available at hundreds of prestigious outlets. Blancpain manufactured watches with Harwood's movements for the French market, and in the USA watches with Harwood's movements were sold by the Perpetual Selfwinding Watch Company.[11] The future of the Harwood watch seemed assured, yet the vagaries of history dealt a crushing blow. On Tuesday 29 October 1929, the Wall Street Crash heralded a cataclysmic economic depression. This, coupled with the high production costs of the Harwood watches and the delicacy of their movements, saw the venture quickly unravel, and the Harwood Self-Winding Watch Company ceased trading in 1931,[12] filing for bankruptcy in December the following year.

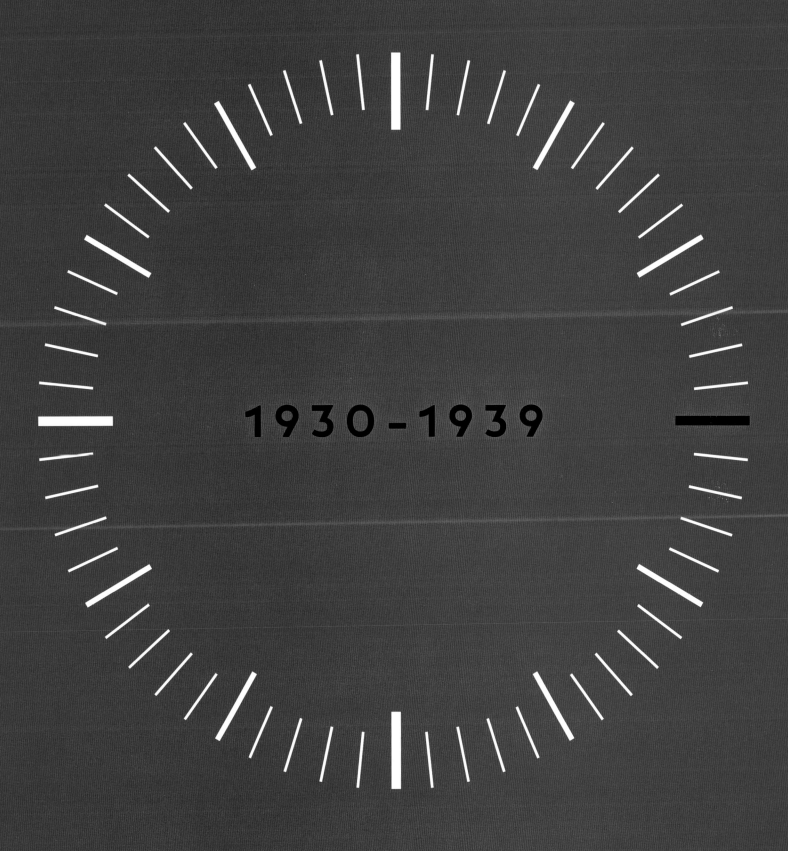

1930 – 1939

THE 1930s

The effects of the Wall Street Crash and its aftermath were dramatic for the Swiss watch industry. From a height of almost 21 million watches exported in 1929, shipments crashed to a little over 16 million in 1930 and just above 8 million in 1932.[1] Despite this seemingly cataclysmic turn of events, the 1930s proved, from the outset, to be one of the most inventive and creative decades for watchmaking in the whole of the twentieth century. Many icons of twentieth-century watch design made their entrance in the first few years of the decade, including LeCoultre's Reverso, 1931; Rolex's Oyster Perpetual of 1931–34; Patek Philippe's Calatrava, 1932; and the Cadenas by Van Cleef & Arpels, 1935. These watches would be joined by an array of other novel designs as the decade progressed.

Despite the early failure of the pioneering automatic wristwatch company of John Harwood, watchmakers still vied with one another to produce a commercially successful watch that could wind itself. A host of solutions were proffered, some rather outlandish, including whole movements and dials that whizzed back and forth on runners within a case. Waterproofing the watch remained another important area of development. The popularity of rectangular watches challenged many case makers to experiment with waterproofing the 'shaped' watch. Omega provided one solution in the form of the 'Marine' case, which was introduced in 1932; several others would follow.

Watches with their time shown in apertures, rather than via a traditional analogue dial, were increasingly prevalent, especially during the first half of the 1930s. However, while they were made and sold in relatively large numbers at the less expensive end of the market, they remained relatively few and far between at the higher end. Other forms of unusual time display included a series of watches made by Verger Frères for Vacheron Constantin. Known as *bras-en-l'air*, literally 'arms in the air', these watches used figures, animals or objects to indicate the time. The images opposite illustrate two examples of these watches, with a design of a magician applied to the centre of one and an American eagle to the other. They were operated via a pusher to the left case side which, when depressed, would cause the magician's arms or eagle's legs to be raised; these would then indicate the time – to the left, the hours and to the right, the minutes.

ABOVE Patek Philippe Calatrava Ref. 96, made in 1937.
A steel circular wristwatch with flat bezel
Diameter 31 mm

OPPOSITE, TOP Verger Frères for Vacheron Constantin, c. 1930.
An 18 ct white and yellow gold lever *bras-en-l'air* watch (cal. RA 17‴ 15/12)
Diameter 48 mm

OPPOSITE, BOTTOM Verger Frères for Vacheron Constantin, c. 1930.
An 18 ct white and yellow gold lever *bras-en-l'air* watch (cal. RA 17‴ 15/12)
Diameter 48 mm

An increase in sporting and leisure activities during this period offered watchmakers enormous marketing opportunities and led to the production of specially designed cases that afforded greater protection for movements and glasses. LeCoultre's Reverso (see p. 88) was but one way of protecting the watch's glass from shattering during ball games. Grilles and shutters were also deployed in a bid to reduce the risk of glass breakages during everyday life, although these latter forms were often so intricate and ingenious that one cannot help but wonder if the primary purpose was to impress rather than protect.

Tailored models were also developed for use in aviation and motor racing. Watches that were specially designed to be worn on the side of the wrist began to appear; often featuring deeply curved cases, these watches allowed the wearer to see the time more easily while steering their motor car. Chronographs for timing and calculating were produced in ever growing numbers, assisting navigators and motor racing organisers but

also, by glamorous association, increasing demand among the wider public.

Case materials were also evolving. Platinum, although difficult to work due to its strength, is extremely hard-wearing and for this reason exceptionally well suited to the case of the wristwatch, and a few such models for men continued to appear at the higher end of the market. The availability of steel-cased watches grew greatly during the 1930s – until this period, the difficulty of producing and working cases in high-grade anti-corrosion steel that could be worn next to the skin meant that the vast majority of fine watches had been manufactured in silver and gold. Steel's strength and hardness meant that it was an excellent option for use on an exposed wrist, where the durability of the watch case was a matter of great importance. Steel was also extremely well suited to the designs of the 1930s: the sharper lines and decorative facets and chamfers popular during the period were able to retain their clarity of form for considerably longer when applied to a steel case, compared to those made

in the softer metals of gold or silver. The other clear advantage, in a time of austerity, was the cost of steel versus that of precious metals. As an option, steel allowed manufacturers to increase their range, offering models in a variety of different case metals at correspondingly varying prices, potentially expanding their customer base. The trend for mixed-metal cases, which had grown in popularity during the 1920s, continued to develop throughout the 1930s – steel bodies with yellow or pink gold panels and/or caps, for example, helped enhance and vary case design. Such mixing of metals was also frequently seen in solely precious metal cases, where combinations of white and yellow golds proved particularly popular. At the most exclusive end of the market, contrasting sections of platinum and yellow or pink gold might also be used. Rectangular cases were well suited to such treatments, and the popularity of this form during the 1930s saw a great diversity of oblong styles emerge, many with stepped sides in steel or a combination of metals in differing colours.

RIGHT Vacheron Constantin,
made in 1930.
An 18 ct yellow and white gold
rectangular wristwatch
Length 32 mm

Metal dials had almost entirely supplanted the traditional enamel dial, and experimentation was rife. Not only could metal dials be made faster and in larger numbers, but the range of potential decorative finishes was limitless. Numerals and indexes could be applied, painted or punched outwards; tracks could be added in a variety of finishes, sizes and thicknesses; subsidiary dials could be decoratively engine-turned. The surface of the dial could be lacquered, painted, or sectored and 'shaded' by varying the satin finishes across the surface. While many techniques had been employed before, it was the experimentation of design in the 1930s that transformed the dial's appearance. Such variation meant that watch houses could offer a greater range of designs, yet without the need for a large quantity of watch models: the same model could be fitted with several different dial options, from classic and traditional to modern or avant-garde.

There is no doubt that it was the wristwatch that primarily drove the creativity of the 1930s. The innovation and foresight of watch manufacturers in the dark days following the Wall Street Crash was already proven by the mid-1930s; in 1934, almost twice as many wristwatches as pocket watches were being exported from Switzerland.[2] Yet pocket and purse watches still played an important part, and forms and styles continued to be shared and modified between the different genres. In addition to the creative and experimental watch cases of the period, also emerging were what we now consider to be the classic forms of the circular and rectangular watch. By the end of the decade, an entirely new structure and pattern book existed for the watch; indeed, such variety of form and style had been developed that the influence of the 1930s can still be found in watchmaking today.

PROTECTIVE SHUTTERS AND SLIDES

Jaeger-LeCoultre's Reverso is one of the icons of twentieth-century watchmaking. The case was developed by the designer René-Alfred Chauvot, who filed his patent in France on 4 March 1931 (no. 712.868). The patent application was described as being for: '[Une] montre susceptible de coulisser dans son support et pouvant se retourner complètement sur elle-même' – that is, a watch that could slide within a holder and turn completely upon itself.

The French patent was granted on 14 October 1931, and the rights were purchased before its publication by the Swiss businessman César de Trey. In November the same year, de Trey formed a marketing company with Jacques-David LeCoultre called Spécialités Horlogères in order to market the Reverso. During the early years of the Reverso's production, a small number of Reverso cases were sold to other companies, including Cartier, Favre-Leuba, Hamilton, Patek Philippe and Vacheron Constantin. However, in 1934 Spécialités Horlogères was renamed the Société de Vente des Produits Jaeger-LeCoultre, and it was this firm that acquired the Reverso patent.

The Reverso's primary aim was to protect the glass of the watch, and from the outset the model was aimed at the sportsman. It is said that César de Trey had originally approached René-Alfred Chauvot to design a watch that could withstand the rough and tumble of a game of polo – de Trey had apparently seen a gap in the market when challenged to produce a shock-proof watch by a polo player whose watch glass had just been broken during a match. With its elegant, clean lines and rectangular shape, the watch's design was perfectly suited to the Art Deco period. Reversing to a plain back, the watch also offered the tempting possibility for the buyer to personalise their watch with their own initials, their family crest or a unique decorative motif. Early advertisements for the model already showed examples with monochrome, enamel-decorated initials and monograms.

During the 1930s, other solutions for protecting the watch's glass continued to appear. One of the most eye-catching models was named the Montre à Volets (shutter watch) and created by the Parisian jeweller

RIGHT LeCoultre Reverso, patented in
1931, this example c. 1935.
A steel reversible rectangular-shaped
wristwatch with black dial and centre
seconds
Length 33 mm, width 23 mm

OPPOSITE Advertisement for the
Jaeger–LeCoultre Reverso from
December 1932

REVERSO

Montre suisse de haute précision, produit des Spécialités Horlogères S.A. à Lausanne (Suisse). Distributeurs pour le monde entier des produits d'Horlogerie fine : JAEGER LeCoulTre

SE PORTE COMME TOUTE AUTRE MONTRE MAIS PEUT SE PROTÉGER A VOLONTÉ

Il est d'un très grand intérêt de pouvoir protéger sa montre de tous les accidents qui la menacent, la montre-bracelet en particulier, au cours de notre activité normale et surtout sportive. La REVERSO, que l'on retourne sur elle-même d'un simple geste (de façon qu'elle offre aux chocs éventuels son dos robuste et non son cadran), constitue donc un remarquable progrès. Son mouvement extraordinairement précis, la robustesse et l'élégance de sa boîte, la durée que lui vaut sa résistance aux heurts, permettent de placer la REVERSO au tout premier rang des montres de confiance.

Avant de faire l'achat d'une montre-bracelet, demandez à voir la REVERSO, faites-en faire devant vous la démonstration ; c'est, vous le verrez, la montre qu'il vous faut.

La montre REVERSO se fait en un seul modèle, mais en deux grandeurs, pour l'homme et pour la femme. Boîte en or ou en acier nu inoxydable Staybrite, ou combinaison des deux métaux.

REVERSO STANDARD à partir de 575 fr.

CLERC

4, PLACE DE L'OPÉRA - PARIS

Catalogue franco sur demande

Création TRIO. Pub. André Hirsch.

Verger Frères. These watches, with shutters over the dial, were designed to open and close rather like a Venetian blind. Made in wrist, pocket and pendant form, they are wonderfully redolent of the Art Deco period. The cases were designed with two crowns, one at three o'clock and another at nine, creating a perfectly symmetrical shape to the watches. While the crown at three o'clock acted as a standard button for winding and hand-setting, the opposing crown at nine o'clock opened and closed the shutters, in turn revealing or concealing the watch's dial and creating a protective barrier for the crystal. Watch cases made by Verger Frères were extraordinarily creative, and during this period the company had an especially close working relationship with the watchmaker Vacheron Constantin. The images below illustrate a Vacheron Constantin Montre à Volets wristwatch with a case made by Verger Frères in 1930. The case is composed in two colours of gold, with a white gold body and flat, yellow gold bezel engraved with stylised Art Deco and triangular hour indexes that have been filled with enamel paint. The shutters themselves are formed of banded yellow and white gold.

Movado continued to develop and market their Ermeto range, with a whole variety of different styles appearing

during the 1930s, while Rolex released a pocket watch version of their rectangular Prince with a spring-released cover over the dial – this was marketed to both men and women and named the Sporting Prince or Sporting Princess accordingly. Vesta cases seem to have provided the inspiration for many purse watches of the period. One such watch, signed by Texina (a sub-brand of the Swiss watchmaker Georges Dimier SA), is shown opposite (bottom). Instead of the vesta case's hinged lid, the user slid the front cover backwards to reveal the time on the dial within. This example has a sprung closure so that, when the cover is released, the cover automatically closes on concealed runners. Made in 1931, this form of purse watch remained particularly popular during the first half of the decade, with examples often made in sterling silver with decorative, engine-turned covers, frequently with a blank cartouche to allow the owner's initials to be engraved. One advantage of the design lay in the fact that it could be operated with one hand, and for those examples with a sprung closure, checking the time was particularly quick and easy.

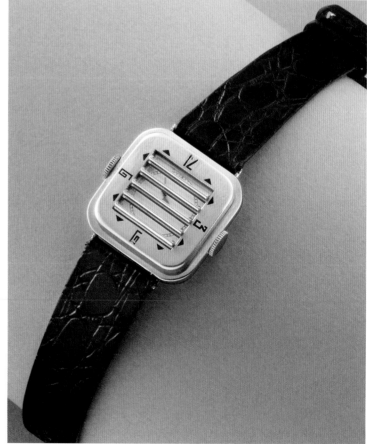

AUTOMATIC WATCHES AND THE ROLEX PERPETUAL

During the early years of the 1930s, a host of automatic movements were developed by a variety of different watch manufacturers. Some, such as the Glycine and Autorist automatics, were based around John Harwood's 'hammer' automatic movement. Skirting around the Harwood patent was doubtless made easier by the watchmaker's bankruptcy, which perhaps meant a challenge to the patent was less likely. Other makers approached the automatic movement in rather unusual and novel ways. The Rolls automatic (designed by Léon Hatot SA of Paris), for example, incorporated a movement that, with its dial, slid up and down within the watch case, the motion of which activated a lever mounted on the frame to wind the watch. As it reached either end of the case, the movement and dial buffered off springs. Although intriguing to see in action, the constant swinging back and forth of the dial may easily have proved an irritation to the user, and this model was produced for only a short period – about 1930 to 1934.

Rolex were ultimately the winners of the early battle for dominance of the automatic field. In 1931 a self-winding 'perpetual' movement was designed and patented by Émile Borer of Aegler (Aegler being Rolex's primary movement supplier). Research suggests that the first Rolex Perpetual watches were released two or three years later, towards the end of 1933 or early in 1934.[3] The highly competitive environment meant that Rolex would have been keen to secure a patented, winning design, but in light of the complaints over the inefficiency of early automatic models by some of their rivals, Rolex would have been particularly focused on ensuring that, upon release, their automatic watch was heralded as a success. Rolex's early automatic movements were to be fitted into the firm's Oyster case; in so doing, Rolex's founder's dream of a perpetual watch that would not require daily winding and need not be taken off when in water was to be realised.

Part of the success of Rolex's automatic movement was in not attempting to reinvent the entire mechanics of the calibre. These early Perpetuals used a standard, manually wound calibre movement, onto which the automatic

BELOW Rolls, c. 1930–34.
A silver rectangular-shaped automatic wristwatch, the movement and dial sliding within the case to wind the watch (cal. 5½‴)
Length 37 mm, width 17 mm

BELOW, LEFT Rolex Oyster Perpetual,
c. 1935.
A steel automatic wristwatch with
luminous numerals and hands (cal. 11¾′′′)
Diameter 32 mm

BELOW, RIGHT The rotor module from
the Rolex Oyster Perpetual

rotor mechanism was mounted. This had the advantage of using a tried-and-tested base movement, rather than integrating an automatic system, from scratch, into an entirely new movement. Although requiring a thicker watch case to accommodate the automatic module, the system meant that a full rotor, moving freely and continuously in a 360-degree arc, could be used. Such a system resulted in a quieter movement, which contrasted with the 'hammering' action from a semi-rotor buffering off springs, as in the Harwood, or the sound of a movement sliding on runners as in the Rolls automatic. Crucially, this watch also allowed the watch to be manually wound if required, something that had not been possible in other early automatic watches. The Rolex Perpetual had a 35-hour power reserve that could be obtained by, on average, less than half a day's wear. Illustrated below is a particularly early example of the Rolex Oyster Perpetual that dates to about 1935. The back of the movement is shown below right, with the semi-circular rotor mounted uppermost. One can see instructions in both English and

French engraved to assist the watchmaker in dismantling the rotor work in order to access the main body of the movement beneath – perhaps a nod to watchmakers who had been quick to criticise the complexity and difficulty of servicing other early automatic watches.

By sealing the watch successfully in the Oyster case and ensuring the watch stayed running automatically, Rolex had in fact created a sensational timepiece. The enemies of the mechanical movement – dirt, dust and water – could be kept at bay even more successfully with the Perpetual, since manual adjustment of the time would be required perhaps no more than once per week, even by the most punctilious. This meant the crown was hardly ever unscrewed, ensuring that a tight seal was maintained at almost all times. With such brilliance of design, it is little wonder that the Oyster Perpetual remains the basis for Rolex's success today.

EIGHT–DAY WRISTWATCHES

With convenience in mind, and given the perceived lack of reliability of early automatic watches, another solution was offered in the form of the 'eight-day' wristwatch. As its name suggests, such a watch required winding only once a week; however, although eight-day movements were not uncommon in small desk timepieces, this genre's miniaturisation and application to a wristwatch was both a tricky and costly exercise. In 1931 LeCoultre introduced their calibre 124, one of the first shaped calibres for wristwatches that offered an eight-day power reserve. The great challenge in producing a long-duration movement is ensuring the even distribution of power throughout the watch's running period – when a movement's spring barrel is fully wound, its power is at its greatest, but as the spring uncoils, this power is reduced. Unless the release of energy from the spring is evenly controlled by a precision-gear train and escapement, the varying strength of a mainspring can play havoc with a watch's timekeeping. For a watch wound daily, with a power reserve of 35 hours or so, such variances can be easily adjusted for; however, a movement with a duration of eight days presents a far greater degree of complexity. Part of LeCoultre's solution was in utilising two mainspring barrels instead of a standard single barrel. In order to accommodate both barrels, the LeCoultre movement was a broad rectangle in shape, with the two large barrels fitted at either end of the movement. The movement's shape and size (28 mm × 19.73 mm) meant that it was ideally suited for use in the fashionable rectangular wristwatch cases of the 1930s.

Vintage eight-day wristwatches are extremely rare. For instance, research suggests that only four examples were made by Patek Philippe in the 1930s using ébauches by LeCoultre. The example shown here was made in 1931 with an 18 ct yellow gold rectangular case. Cartier also produced a small number of eight-day wristwatches during this period, introducing their version of the model in 1931 using the same LeCoultre ébauche discussed above. The movements were fitted to Cartier's elongated, rectangular Tank Allongée cases. In addition to the maker's signature, the dials of these watches were invariably marked 'eight days'.

It seems strange that eight-day wristwatches did not prove more popular. Despite the exceptional quality of the LeCoultre movements, perhaps there was a reluctance among the public to put their trust in a watch that would be wound only once a week, or maybe their original cost simply proved too prohibitive compared to aesthetically similar watches with standard, daily-wound movements.

BELOW AND OPPOSITE Patek Philippe 8 Days, made in 1931. An 18 ct yellow gold manually wound wristwatch with eight–day–duration movement (cal. 9‴ LeCoultre ébauche) Length 38.5 mm, width 22 mm

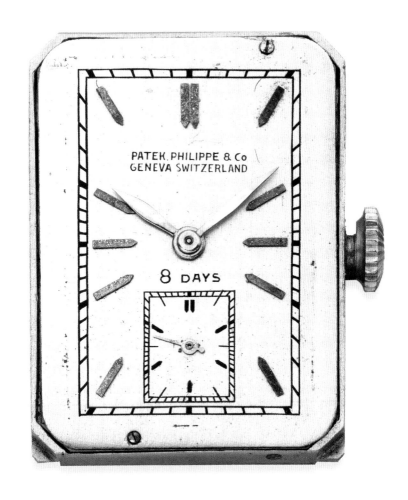

LINDBERGH AND WEEMS

Longines were quick to associate themselves with the pioneers of flight. The watchmaker's chronographs and chronometers were supplied to many early air expeditions as aids to navigation. In May 1927 Charles Lindbergh, a 25-year-old American pilot, flew from Roosevelt airport on Long Island, New York, to Le Bourget airport just outside Paris, thereby becoming the first person to fly non-stop and solo across the Atlantic. At the time, Longines was the official timekeeper for the World Air Sports Federation and was responsible for timing Lindbergh's flight. Following this flight, Lindbergh and Longines worked together to develop a pilot's watch. The result was an 'hour angle' watch, appropriately known as the Longines Lindbergh.

With a massive case measuring 47 mm in diameter, the Longines Lindbergh was designed for visual clarity and ease of use while in the air. Acting as a tool to find longitude, by calculating the time difference between the pilot's current location and Greenwich, the difference could be turned into degrees of longitude. The watch was in fact just one part of the navigational calculation, since the pilot/navigator would also need to be able to determine the solar time of their current position, as well as the equation of time. As the earth makes one rotation of 360

degrees every day, each hour may represent 15 degrees. Consequently, each 15-degree increment was printed beneath the hour numerals displayed on the Longines Lindbergh dial, to aid the positional calculations. Bordering the case, a rotating bezel was calibrated to allow correction for the equation of time. At the dial centre, a rotating seconds disc could be synchronised to the central seconds hand and was designed to be set to a time signal transmitted to the aircraft. The user rotated the disc (via the crown) while receiving an audible radio time signal, aligning the seconds disc's '60' marker to the centre seconds hand at the instant of the last 'beep' of the time signal. This displayed the time difference between the aviator's current position and the location of the time signal's transmission, thereby assisting with the calculation of the plane's current position. Seconds synchronisation was important since an inaccuracy of a few seconds could lead to several miles of navigational error. This seconds-setting feature was in fact originally developed in conjunction with Longines by the naval Captain Philip van Horn Weems and patented in 1929. Although initially intended for naval navigation, its application to air navigation was quickly recognised by Lindbergh and others.

BELOW Longines Weems, Ref. 5350, made in 1937.
A large silver wristwatch with seconds-setting facility (cal. 18.69Z)
Diameter 47 mm

OPPOSITE Longines Lindbergh, Ref. 3210, made in 1938.
A large silver hour-angle wristwatch with seconds-setting facility (cal. 18.69N)
Diameter 47 mm

CHRONOGRAPHS

OPPOSITE Audemars Piguet no. 43792, sold in 1938 to the Geneva retailer Bader Nel Maxima.
An 18 ct yellow gold chronograph wristwatch with three-tone dial, outer telemeter and inner spiral tachymeter scales, subsidiary dials for constant seconds and 30-minute register, and luminous hour indexes and hands (cal. 13 CHRO CPT)
Diameter 33 mm

BELOW Universal Genève Compur, c. 1936.
A steel medical chronograph wristwatch with black lacquered dial and outer pulsometer scale, subsidiary dials for constant seconds and 45-minute register (cal. 281)
Diameter 30 mm

Throughout the 1930s, the chronograph wristwatch became increasingly common. Multiple scales, including tachymeters, telemeters and pulsometers, were added to dials to allow the watch to perform a variety of functions. While many owners may have used their chronographs for little more than timing a boiled egg, these were edgy, modern timepieces that were perfect for watchmakers to market to a public whose attitudes to the wristwatch were just beginning to turn in the latter's favour. Modern, complex and with swirling calibrations that were often banded in multiple colours, these watches had a sense of purpose beyond simple time telling. The intricacy of their dial calibrations also had the advantage of suggesting that the watch was of superior precision.

While not all this gadgetry may have been used for its intended purpose, there were genuine and important uses for the chronograph. Timing motor cars during races was of course essential for the organisers, yet the wrist chronograph also allowed the amateur enthusiast to keep their own records. Dials that were calibrated with tachymeters would, for example, enable the user to easily compute the speed of a car when travelling over a set distance. For the doctor, the pulsometer chronograph was an extremely helpful tool. Such medical dials were calibrated and marked for a specific number of pulses – for example, if graduated for 30 pulsations, the doctor would start their chronograph as they began counting their patient's pulse and stop it again after feeling the subject's thirtieth pulse; the now static seconds hand would display the patient's pulse rate per minute against the scale printed at the edge of the dial. Chronographs also had their uses for photographers as a tool to time exposures; within industry, meanwhile, a dial calibrated for production counting could be used, for example, by a factory manager to time how long a component took to make and, by using the corresponding scale, calculate hourly production rates.

Prior to the 1930s, the single-button chronograph had largely dominated this genre, often with all functions activated via the crown. In such watches, the crown was

multifunctional, allowing the watch to be wound and set in addition to starting, stopping and resetting the chronograph. An alternative format separated the pusher from its crown, placing the former to the case side, usually just above the crown. As the 1930s advanced, however, the use of two buttons became increasingly common. Such an arrangement had the advantage of lending the watch a more balanced, symmetrical design, with a pusher placed above and below the crown. The upper pusher would usually be equipped to start and stop the chronograph, while the lower pusher would reset to zero, although variations of function were common – some chronographs, for example, started solely via the upper pusher and then were stopped and reset via the lower pusher. In design terms, the harmonious placement of twin chronograph pushers was dominant by the end of the 1930s. Universal Genève was one of the leading developers of chronographs and among the first to introduce the two-button chronograph in 1934; the watchmaker was also the first to introduce an hour register in addition to minute register to the dial of a chronograph wristwatch.

Towards the end of the decade, Rolex launched a very small series of fly-back centre seconds wristwatches under the reference number 3346. Although not strictly speaking chronographs, these watches were nevertheless intended for timing. Known by either the model name Centregraph or Zerograph, the watches had a continuous centre seconds hand and a single pusher which, when depressed, would reset the centre seconds to zero, upon which it would immediately restart running. The fly-back function was especially useful to aviators and those who needed to time repeated events in succession. However, the most significant feature of the watch was its rotating bezel, which was calibrated to 60 seconds/minutes. By aligning the 0/60 marker of the bezel with either the second or minute hand, the user could read off either seconds or minutes elapsed against the bezel. This was the first time that Rolex had added a rotating bezel to its Oyster model, and it was a feature that would play an important part in the formation of a new range of sports watches more than a decade later, in the 1950s.

BELOW Tissot, c. 1938.
A steel single-button chronograph wristwatch with two-tone dial, outer telemeter and inner spiral tachymeter scales, subsidiary dials for constant seconds and 30-minute register (cal. Lemania CHT15)
Diameter 37 mm

OPPOSITE Rolex Oyster Centregraph, Ref. 3346, c. 1937.
A steel wristwatch with fly-back centre seconds and rotating calibrated bezel (cal. 10½‴)
Diameter 32 mm

PERPETUAL CALENDARS

Perpetual calendar watches are among the most mechanically sophisticated timepieces in horology. Displaying the days of the week, months of the year and date, they will also self-adjust for the varying lengths of the months and even the extra day of 29 February in a leap year. In other words, as long as a perpetual calendar watch is kept running, it will continually show the correct date without any need for adjustment by its owner.

Although by 1930 examples of the perpetual calendar pocket watch had been made for around 170 years – quite possibly the earliest was made by the English watchmaker Thomas Mudge in about 1762[4] – the application of this form of calendar mechanism to a wristwatch was extremely rare. At a time when the majority of circular men's wristwatches were between 28 and 32 mm in diameter, the physical display area available on the watch's dial was very restricted. Traditionally, perpetual calendar pocket watches had commonly (though not always) displayed their calendar indications separately, in subsidiary dials for days of the week, months of the year and date, often with an additional counter displaying the leap year cycle itself. Cramming all these registers onto a wristwatch's dial while ensuring they were still useful and legible was certainly challenging. Part of the solution to this issue was dispensing with the dial indicating the leap year cycle and incorporating apertures in place of dials for the display of the days of the week and months of the year; this meant that only one additional scale was then required for the date indication. While not an entirely new concept, as calendar apertures had previously been used in pocket watches, their use in the calendar wristwatch became more prevalent from this period on.

Illustrated here is an early perpetual calendar wristwatch created by Breguet in 1935.[5] This wristwatch has a silver dial with traditional Breguet styling: a variety of decorative, engine-turned finishes and classic Roman numerals on a satin-finished chapter ring. The movement's ébauche was manufactured by Victorin Piguet & Cie, a family firm of Swiss watchmakers specialising in mechanical complications, especially calendars, chronographs and repeaters. Between them, the Piguet family executed a dazzling array of mechanical masterpieces, often incorporating unusual features such as, in this instance, a retrograde date: rather than showing the date as a full, circular display, the movement of this watch is geared to show the date in a wide arc. This required an additional mechanism to ensure that the gold sword-shaped date hand would jump across the dial to the 1st as each month ended – having already adjusted to the length of the month. Quite apart from the pleasing action of the retrograde hand, calibrating the date in an arc greatly enhanced the clarity of the dial's display by not interfering with or overlapping the other indications. Indeed, the only major obstruction to the display is the broad, sword-shaped date hand, which rather obscures from view the aperture for the day of the week on the 5th of each month and the aperture for the month of the year on the 27th day of each month. A remarkable watch, this Breguet cost 10,000 francs when it was sold on 24 December 1935.

WORLD TIME WATCHES

Watches that indicated different time zones around the world were not new, and the most common way to show these zones was via a series of subsidiary dials (see p. 27). Unifying the display on a single dial to allow local time to be read in a convenient manner, while also indicating the hour in a variety of locations around the world, required some clever mechanical engineering, and the dominant figure of this genre was the Swiss watchmaker Louis Cottier.

Louis-Vincent Cottier, a watchmaking genius from Carouge, just outside Geneva, was the son of Emmanuel Cottier, the latter a maker of watches and automata. Louis was obsessed with how a watch displayed time, inventing ingenious 'complications' for watches that displayed time without hands, such as jumping digital-hour watches and even a linear, dashboard-inspired time display. He also created specialist aviator watches and, like his father, automata. In 1931 Louis invented the Heure Universelle mechanism, which would allow the hour in each time zone to be displayed simultaneously.

Cottier produced this complication for a variety of watch firms, including Agassiz, Patek Philippe, Rolex and Vacheron Constantin.

Made in 1933, the watch illustrated below left is one of the earliest examples of a world time watch to incorporate Louis Cottier's Heure Universelle mechanism (Vacheron Constantin's archives show that Cottier completed his first world time module for them in 1932). Elegantly designed and intuitive to use, with the owner's time zone displayed at the twelve o'clock position and the hands set to the current time zone, the recessed 24-hour ring will rotate as time advances, so that one can view the current hour in all major time zones. These zones are marked with triangular indexes, and a variety of cities and locations are displayed on the bezel, some in multiple, so that a total of 31 named positions are shown. Since the case, dial and movement are all integral to the technical function of the watch, Cottier would have supervised the production of each element. Interestingly, the dial of the present watch shows London and Paris indicated in the

BELOW, LEFT Vacheron Constantin Ref. 3372, made in 1933.
An 18 ct white and pink gold open-faced lever watch with world time indication displayed on a three-tone dial, the world time mechanism made by Louis Cottier (cal. RA 17‴ 15/12)
Diameter 45 mm

BELOW, RIGHT Cover of the 1938 *Journal Suisse d'Horlogerie et de Bijouterie*, illustrating another of Vacheron Constantin's world time models using the Cottier system

ABOVE Patek Philippe Ref. 1416, made in 1939.
An 18 ct yellow gold world time wristwatch, the world time mechanism made by Louis Cottier (cal. 12‴ HU) Diameter 31 mm

same zone: Greenwich Mean Time. It was not until 15 June 1940 – during and because of the Second World War – that Paris converted to Central European Time. Cased in two-colour gold, the watch has an 18 ct white gold bezel and case back, while the band, pendant and bow arc all made from 18 ct pink gold.

As international communication and travel continued to develop, the world time watch would become an increasingly useful gadget. Wrist versions of the world time watch began to appear before the end of the decade. In 1939 Patek Philippe introduced two such models, the Ref. 1415 and Ref. 1416. These wristwatches had a rotating bezel engraved with a variety of world locations, representing the different time zones. The user simply rotated the bezel so that their current location/zone was indicated at the twelve o'clock position, and when the hands on the watch were then set to their local time, the dial's outer 24-hour ring would indicate the hour in each zone around the world. Throughout the 1940s and '50s the major watch houses continued to offer models with world time mechanisms by Louis Cottier, both in pocket and wristwatch form.

THE HENRY GRAVES SUPERCOMPLICATION

In 1925 one of Patek Philippe's greatest patrons, Henry Graves Jr, commissioned the watchmaker to create the most complex watch ever made. During the previous two decades, Patek Philippe had increasingly received special requests from the rich businessmen and industrialists of the United States. Henry Graves was himself a wealthy man, born into a prominent banking family; his father, Henry Graves Sr, was a partner in the New York bank Maxwell & Graves. Another major patron of Patek Philippe during this period was the automobile manufacturer James Ward Packard. Between them, Graves and Packard appeared to vie with one another to obtain watches of ever greater precision and complexity from the major watchmakers, especially those made by Patek Philippe. For the watchmakers, the revenue that these commissions brought was of course very welcome; however, the attempts to create ever more complex and ingenious functions and displays also pushed the makers to the very limits of horological possibilities. This process enabled the development of new systems of display and, crucially, improvements in the miniaturisation of parts, which in turn would allow further innovation in the smaller scale of the wristwatch.

Henry Graves's commission would become known as the Supercomplication and included an astonishing 24 functions/complications. Such was the complexity of the watch that it would take almost eight years to complete, requiring years of planning, study and experimentation before construction could begin in earnest. Patek Philippe engaged the services of many of the finest Swiss watchmakers, astronomers, mathematicians and dial and case makers of the day. Finally, in December 1932, Patek Philippe was able to ship the completed watch from Geneva to New York, accompanied by a rather nervous letter directed to the customs officials, pleading with them not to wind the watch or test its functions.[6] The Supercomplication was delivered to Henry Graves on 19 January 1933.

In order to incorporate all the visual forms of its complications, the watch was double-dialled. To the front or 'mean time' dial, standard time was displayed together with: a perpetual calendar showing days of the week, months of the year, date, and phases and ages of the moon; a split-seconds chronograph with registers for 60 minutes and 12 hours; a subsidiary seconds dial; further dials for indicating the state of wind (the power remaining in the spring barrels) of the striking and going trains; and an additional gold central hand for alarm time indication. To the back or 'sidereal' dial, sidereal time was displayed together with: times of sunrise and sunset; the equation of time; subsidiary seconds; and a large

aperture displaying the star chart for the night sky over New York City. In addition to the alarm function, the watch also included *grande* and *petite sonnerie* (striking time in passing, like a clock), and minute repetition for chiming time on demand. The watch weighed 535 g and had a traditional case design of bassine form, yet of course the watch's complexity meant that it had unusually large proportions: a diameter of 74 mm and a depth of 36 mm (including the glasses). Thirteen functions were operated from the case, via the crown and a series of slides, switches and buttons. There were a total of 900 components, including 110 wheels, 50 bridges, 430 screws, 90 springs, 120 mechanical elements, 70 jewels, 2 dials and 19 hands.[7] The dials were made by the specialists Stern Frères – at the time, the Stern family were in fact poised to take over Patek Philippe, and by the time the watch was delivered to Henry Graves, Charles and Jean Stern were managing Patek Philippe as the firm's new owners. Both dials were made specially for the watch and were traditional in style, despite the immense complexity of their displays. The sidereal dial was made from a plate of gold that was given a silvered finish, the three subsidiary dials were slightly recessed into the surface, and the disc for the sky chart was made from gold and overlaid with blue champlevé enamel; the hands were made from blued steel. The mean time dial was white enamel and had to accommodate seven layers of hands – the two split-seconds hands, hour hand, minute hand and alarm hand, and double hands within each of the subsidiary dials – all of which had to glide seamlessly over one another. To help achieve this, the subsidiary dials were 'double sunk' to provide extra depth. All hands to this dial were of blued steel except for the gold alarm hand; the disc for moon phases was gold, heightened with blue enamel.

For Patek Philippe and the other watchmakers involved in the watch's construction, the huge US$15,000 cost of the watch must have provided a welcome lifeline – its construction continued through the Wall Street Crash of 1929 and its immediate aftermath. Henry Graves's Supercomplication is the most complicated watch ever made without the assistance of computer technology, and it would remain the most complicated watch made with or without computer assistance for 56 years, until the advent of another Patek Philippe watch, the Calibre 89, in 1989 (see pp. 284–85).

OPPOSITE Patek Philippe, Henry Graves Supercomplication, commissioned in 1925, completed in 1932 and delivered on 19 January 1933.
A gold double-dialled and double open-faced minute-repeating clock-watch with Westminster chimes, *grande* and *petite sonnerie*, split-seconds chronograph, registers for 60 minutes and 12 hours, perpetual calendar accurate to the year 2100, moon phases, equation of time, dual power reserve for striking and going trains, mean and sidereal time, central alarm, indications for times of sunrise and sunset, and celestial chart for the night-time sky of New York City at latitude 40° 47', longitude 73° 58' (cal. 25‴) Diameter 74 mm

OPPOSITE, TOP LEFT Beneath the mean time dial, showing the calendar mechanism and moon phases mounted on a separate steel plate

OPPOSITE, TOP RIGHT Beneath the sidereal time dial, showing the train and mechanism to drive the star chart, displays of sunrise and sunset and equation of time mounted on a separate plate

OPPOSITE, BOTTOM LEFT Beneath the mean time dial with calendar mechanism removed, displaying gearing for power reserve indicators, mechanism for repeaters, and winding mechanism for alarm

OPPOSITE, BOTTOM RIGHT Beneath the sidereal time dial with sidereal time train removed, displaying time and chronograph mechanisms

TOP Mean time dial with perpetual calendar, moon phases, split seconds chronograph with registers, state of wind and alarm indication

BELOW LEFT Sidereal time dial with star chart, times of sunrise and sunset, and equation of time

BELOW RIGHT Case side with switches/ slides for *petite sonnerie* (LS), *grande sonnerie* (GS) and alarm winding

RECTANGULAR WATCHES

Advertisements from the 1930s are filled with a dazzling array of rectangular and barrel-shaped wristwatches. Rectangular watches had, of course, increased in popularity during the 1920s, with Cartier releasing their Tank Cintrée (see p. 56) at the beginning of the decade and Rolex introducing the Prince at its end.

During the 1930s the Rolex Prince was available in several different models. The watch's movement took advantage of its rectangular housing by placing the balance and mainspring at opposing ends of the movement. This allowed both elements to be larger and resulted in improved timekeeping and a longer running reserve. Indeed, almost all Prince watches sold during the decade were chronometer rated, and Rolex advertised the model as running for 58 hours on a single wind. Such accuracy and efficiency was combined with elegant styling, the model being available in a variety of styles and a choice of metals. The consumer could pick from silver, steel, gold or platinum, with further options including combinations of white and yellow gold or steel with gold caps or mounts. The image on the right illustrates a classic flared-sided example of the Prince in a steel case. Interestingly, the steel Prince, which was introduced in 1934, was priced slightly higher than models in silver, no doubt in large part due to the greater labour involved in producing the case in this harder metal.[8] In addition to the choice of case style, metal and dial finishes, Rolex also released a version with jumping hours: an aperture to the dial in place of the twelve o'clock numeral displayed the hour in digital format, while a single hand displayed the minute on the upper dial, with seconds beneath.

RIGHT Rolex Prince Ref. 1490, c. 1935.
A steel duo-dial wristwatch with flared sides and two-tone pink dial (cal. 7.5 × 14.5‴)
Length 42 mm

OPPOSITE Patek Philippe Ref. 508, made in 1937.
An 18 ct yellow and white gold rectangular wristwatch with cylindrical hooded lugs (cal. 8‴85)
Length 34 mm

Rectangular and tonneau-form watches lent themselves to highly detailed finishes, and case makers produced some exceptionally elaborate examples during the 1930s, including multifaceted, stepped cases that could be further enhanced with contrasting satin or brushed surfaces and polished chamfers. The Vacheron Constantin wristwatch illustrated above left shows an especially elaborate and beautiful example of this genre from the first half of the 1930s. Combining white and yellow gold, the case is hexagonal with multiple facets that incorporate a variety of finishes. The image opposite displays a watch by Patek Philippe that has an equally sophisticated case design. Made in 1939, this example has been treated with several contrasting satin finishes to enhance the watch's unusual shape. Such exuberant experimentation was rife in the 1930s, and even rectangular watches of classic design could be given a new twist. Cartier, who had continued to introduce new and elegant rectangular models during the 1930s, released an avant-garde take on their traditional Tank model. Launched in 1936 and known as the Tank Asymétrique,[9] this was a truly modernist wristwatch, seemingly years ahead of its time.

As the 1930s gave way to the 1940s, the rectangular watch would become a little less experimental. While watchmakers would continue to release an impressive range of shaped watches, the designer's hand was somewhat less free – the Second World War ensured production was in large part focused on satisfying the military on both sides of the conflict, while in many countries the restrictions on the import of watches for civilian use suppressed the ability of watch brands to offer the wider ranges of the pre-war period.

ABOVE, LEFT Vacheron Constantin, c. 1935.
A two-colour gold multifaceted hexagonal wristwatch (cal. 7½‴)
Length 38 mm

ABOVE, RIGHT Cartier Tank Asymétrique, made in 1937.
An 18 ct yellow gold asymmetrical wristwatch with movement by LeCoultre
Length 36 mm

OPPOSITE Patek Philippe Ref. 510, made in 1939 and retailed by Walser Wald in Buenos Aires.
An 18 ct pink gold multifaceted rectangular wristwatch (cal. 9‴90)
Length 42 mm

WATERPROOFING THE SHAPED WATCH

In 1931 Cartier released their Tank Étanche model, a wristwatch based on their already classic rectangular Tank design. Waterproofing a rectangular or 'shaped' wristwatch is considerably more challenging than sealing a circular-cased watch. In order to achieve the necessary resistance, the movement of the Tank Étanche, together with its dial, was first screwed into an inner gold case back; this was then surrounded by a rectangular-shaped seal made of caoutchouc that held the crystal and integrated the stem of the winding crown; the outer gold case top and back were then fitted to the watch and the case was clamped tightly together with gold screws. The images below show an early example of the Tank Étanche, the case of which was made for Cartier by Edmond Jaeger. The model appears to have been made in very small numbers, no doubt due to the complexity of producing the specially sealed case. Interestingly, Cartier would retail another form of rectangular wristwatch in the 1930s, one that was manufactured by Omega, a model known as the Marine.

The Marine, introduced in 1932, was the first wristwatch to be officially tested and certified for diving.[10] In 1936 the Omega Marine was tested by immersion in Lake Geneva to a depth of 73 metres, returning to the surface unharmed and in working order. A year later, in 1937, the Marine was officially tested to withstand pressure of 13.5 atmospheres, the equivalent of immersion to 135 metres, at the Swiss Laboratory for Horology in Neuchâtel.[11] The Marine's case, which was adapted from designs by Louis Alix registered under Swiss patent 146310 in 1931, was composed of two main parts. The watch was effectively in two halves that were clamped together by means of a clip to the back of the case. The main body of the watch, which housed the dial and movement, slid into the upper case and, by means of internal gaskets, a watertight seal was achieved. Glasses that were not shaped in the round were especially difficult to waterproof, and in order to achieve a strong and tight seal around the dial aperture of the Marine's

BELOW Cartier Tank Étanche, with London import hallmarks for 1932. An 18 ct yellow gold rectangular-shaped water-resistant wristwatch with gold bracelet, movement by the European Watch & Clock Co. Length 37 mm

OPPOSITE Omega Marine, Ref. OT 680, made in 1932. An 18 ct yellow gold rectangular-shaped water-resistant wristwatch with associated gold bracelet (cal. 19.4T1) Length 36 mm, width 24 mm

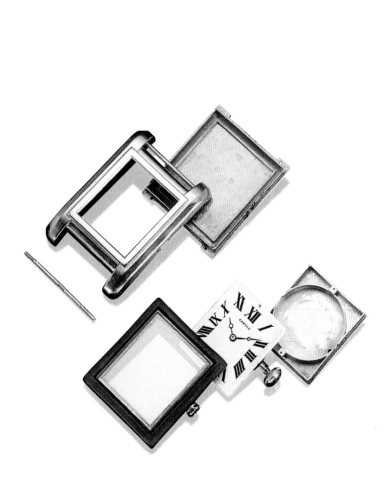

outer case, a sapphire crystal was used – this was one of the first applications of this type of glazing in a wristwatch and at the time was advertised as being nine times as strong as glass. Steel versions of the watch were fitted with waterproof straps made of seal skin and had a special folding clasp.

Rather like the hermetic watches of the 1920s (see pp. 72–73), the disadvantage of the Omega Marine was the necessity of removing the inner case daily for winding. Although the unclipping of the case to access the winder was undoubtedly a much quicker operation than unscrewing the bezel of the earlier Hermetic watches, it was still somewhat fiddly. Perhaps more significantly, the constant uncoupling and sliding would have risked wear not only to the seals but to the metal of the case itself, both of which would have potentially compromised the long-term integrity of the watch's water-resistance. Nevertheless, one may assume that most purchasers were not keen divers, and the general resistance the case

afforded against the ingress of both dirt and moisture, as well as the added protection the double casing would have given to the crown, its stem and the movement itself, should have ensured an especially robust and reliable model. Indeed, the Marine was clearly popular, with production continuing throughout the 1930s.

The Omega Marine illustrated below is one of the earliest examples of the model to have been made and was sold by Omega to the US market on 26 May 1932 (the gold bracelet is a later addition). The inside of the outer case is stamped: 'U.S. Patent Appl 520.818'; this application, which was filed in March 1931 and later granted under US patent 1907700 on 9 May 1933, followed Louis Alix's original Swiss patent of 1931.

VAN CLEEF'S CADENAS AND A CARTIER RING WATCH

With the advent of the wristwatch, wearing time on one's wrist was not always considered politic, and dress watches for ladies often went to considerable lengths to masquerade, first and foremost, as items of jewellery. In 1935, Van Cleef & Arpels introduced their Cadenas or 'Lock' watch. Designed to look like a bejewelled bracelet, it had an asymmetrically shaped case with inset dial facing the wearer. This almost wholly disguised the bracelet's watch element, allowing the owner to view the time privately and at a glance. The image at opposite top illustrates an early example of the Cadenas that dates to the late 1930s. The platinum case is set with single-, circular- and brilliant-cut and baguette diamonds. Two lengths of snake-form linking allow the bracelet to be attached to the wrist, while the clasp clips on to a semi-circular, diamond-set hoop that sits in front of the watch's dial and 'locks' the bracelet in place. Wallis Simpson, the Duchess of Windsor, owned an example of this model, and it is rumoured that it was the Duke

(the former King Edward VIII) and Duchess themselves who originally suggested the design concept.

Other timekeeping solutions for ladies included ring watches; a platinum and diamond example made by Cartier is shown opposite (bottom). Made in 1937, the watch is housed in a geometrically designed platinum case that is set with single-cut and baguette diamonds. While it might seem rather obvious that the ring is set with a watch to its centre, the dial is only just over 4 mm in width, giving the time element itself a subtlety that, considering its setting, is rather surprising. The ring's watch movement is LeCoultre's calibre 101. This movement, which was the smallest in the world, had been introduced by LeCoultre in 1929; it was a mere 14 mm in length, just 4.8 mm wide and 3.4 mm thick. Comprising 74 parts, the calibre 101 weighed in at just about 1 gram. The winding crown is set to the movement's reverse, meaning that, in this instance, it is concealed from the front of the ring.

BELOW Retail card for the platinum and diamond Cadenas watch formerly in the collection of Wallis Simpson, Duchess of Windsor, from the Van Cleef & Arpels Archives

RIGHT Van Cleef & Arpels Cadenas, made
in the late 1930s.
A platinum, white gold and diamond-set
bracelet watch (cal. Cyma 354)
Length 170 mm

BOTTOM Cartier, made in 1937.
A platinum and diamond-set ring watch
with LeCoultre movement (cal. 101)
Width 17.5 mm, thickness 5.5 mm

THE MOST ACCURATE WRIST-WATCH OF 1945
AT THE GENEVA OBSERVATORY

Chronometer

A 30 ᴹ/ᴍ OMEGA CHRONOMETER

OBTAINED THE BEST RESULT EVER ACHIEVED IN THE WRIST WATCH
CLASS—770,4 POINTS—AT THE 1945 TRIAL OF THE GENEVA OBSERVATORY

OMEGA

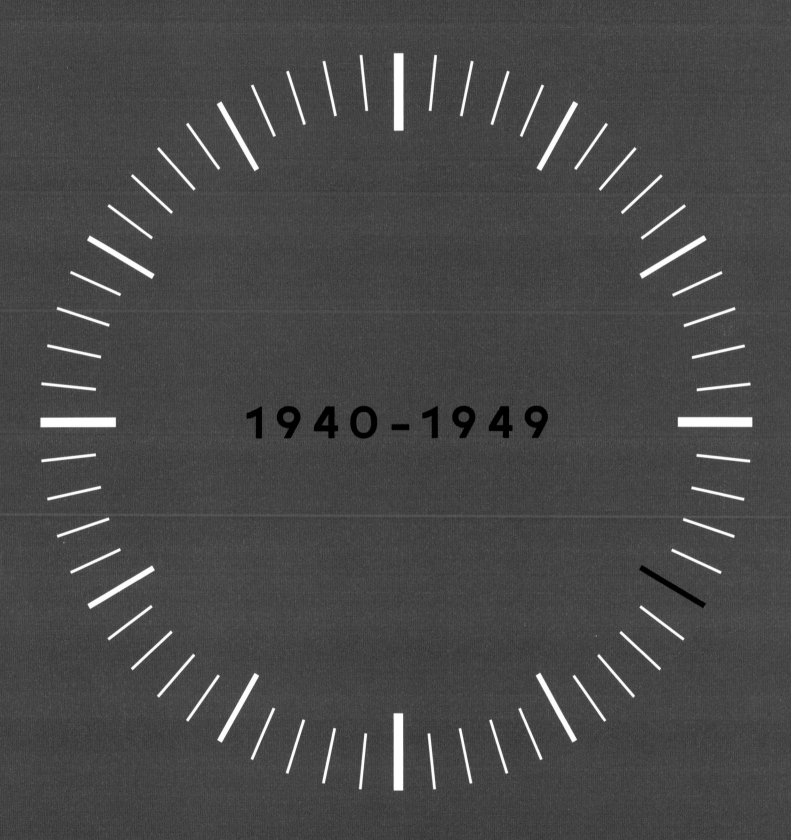

1940-1949

THE 1940s

The 1940s marked the beginning of the golden age of vintage mechanical watch production. The threat of the electronic watch was still far in the future, and the wristwatch, by now the dominant personal timekeeper, had matured in design and form. The result was the increasing visibility of brand identity as firms established their house styles. Inevitably, however, the Second World War had a dramatic impact on the production of watches in the first half of the decade, with a significant proportion of output concentrated on supplying the armed forces on both sides of the conflict. Meanwhile, wartime restrictions placed by many countries on the import of watches limited their supply for civilian use. Total exports of Swiss watches and watch movements, which had reached record highs after the world economy emerged from the depression of the 1930s, were suddenly subjected to renewed shock. Exports shrank from a pre-war high of nearly 24 million pieces in 1937 to reach a low of just under 12 million in 1944, the lowest figure since 1933.[1] Nevertheless, creativity was by no means stifled, and this era would witness continued development, especially in the areas of calendar and chronograph wristwatches.

As watch brands began to refine their house styles, defining individual models became increasingly important to them. Rolex had very much led the charge in this direction. Early on, the company's founder, Hans Wilsdorf, had recognised the marketing appeal of labelling models with specific names. During the 1930s Rolex were already using a reference numbering system, and by the end of the decade model lines such as the Oyster and Prince were well established. As Rolex continued to launch new watches in the 1940s, some of the firm's other iconic model names began to emerge, including the Air-King, which first appeared in the middle of the decade. Other watchmakers followed suit, and in 1948 Omega launched their Seamaster range. Inspired by the robust, water-resistant military watches that the firm had been making for the British during the war, the Seamaster would become Omega's most

BELOW, LEFT Patek Philippe Ref. 1526, introduced in 1941, this example made in 1945.
An 18 ct yellow gold perpetual calendar wristwatch with moon phases (cal. 12‴120Q)
Diameter 34 mm

BELOW, RIGHT Rolex Oyster Air-King Ref. 4499, c. 1946.
A steel centre seconds wristwatch (cal. 10.5‴)
Diameter 34 mm

OPPOSITE Patek Philippe Calatrava Ref. 96, made in 1941.
A steel wristwatch with black dial and radial Arabic numerals (cal. 12‴120)
Diameter 31 mm

enduring model line, with multiple variations produced in the succeeding decades.

The use of multi-tone dials became more prevalent in the 1940s. Already employed in the 1930s, electroplating techniques were used to deposit a layer of precious metal onto the dial's surface, usually in tones of yellow or pink gold or silver. This surface would then be meticulously worked with fine powder pastes and wire brushes to create contrasting, grained satin bands with varying depths of tone. Two-toning was often used to complement the calibrations of the watch's dial. The main dial body would frequently be finished in a single tone or colour, while the minute or hour ring was rendered in a contrasting colour or an opposing satin finish. This was particularly effective on the dial of a chronograph, where multiple scales could be separated from one another through the use of tonal variation.

Watches with water-resistant cases continued to be introduced. Several brands turned to Taubert & Fils, a specialist case-making company that was still

manufacturing hermetically sealed cases under the name Frères Borgel. During this period, Borgel's cases were usually made in two parts, with a solid upper body into which a separate case back was screwed. These robust cases were also used for calendar and chronograph models, with their pushers specially constructed to resist the ingress of water.

During the decade, protective devices were increasingly incorporated into movements to help guard the balance from shocks. Anti-magnetic parts were also commonly used within the watch's workings – a magnetised watch will play havoc with its timekeeping. Such features were often mentioned on watch dials to emphasise the model's attributes.

Although watches with hooded lugs were already in use in the 1930s, their range and incorporation grew greatly during the 1940s. This style of lug produced a deliberate blurring between the watch case and its leather strap or metal bracelet. By placing hoods over the tops of the lugs, the join between band and case could be

BELOW, LEFT Rolex Oyster Ref. 3358, c. 1942.

A steel and pink gold tonneau-form wristwatch with two-tone dial (cal. 10½‴)
Length 38 mm

BELOW, RIGHT Patek Philippe Ref. 1463, made in 1949.

A pink gold chronograph wristwatch with two-tone dial and subsidiary dials for constant seconds and 30-minute register (cal. 13‴ CH)
Diameter 34 mm

OPPOSITE Rolex Oyster Perpetual Ref. 3065, c. 1946.

A yellow gold and steel automatic wristwatch with hooded lugs and steel-and-gold-link bracelet (cal. 9¾‴)
Diameter 31 mm

31 VICTOIRES
DE HAUTE PRECISION
ROLEX
GENEVE
SUISSE
OROLOGERIA ASTRUA
TORINO
ROLEX
OYSTER PERPETUAL
CHRONOMÈTRE
SWISS MADE

OPPOSITE Vacheron Constantin, made in
1945, presented in 1947.
An aluminium open-faced lever watch
(cal. 17‴-439/7)
Diameter 45 mm

ABOVE Tissot, c. 1942.
A steel open-faced lever watch with
three-tone dial
Diameter 46.5 mm (cal. 38.2)

RIGHT Vacheron Constantin, made in
1949.
An 18 ct yellow gold 'mystery' wristwatch
with black dial (cal. 9‴)
Diameter 30 mm

concealed. This allowed case designers the opportunity to create a housing that was not wholly bound by the need to incorporate protruding lugs, and they could instead create shapes that appeared to sit on top of the strap or bracelet, rather than within it. Rolex introduced hooded versions of their Oyster Perpetual model; the image on page 123 shows one of these, in which a curved strip of metal is soldered between the lugs, under which the strap or, as in this instance, the bracelet passes. Interestingly, this style of lug fixture would influence the later Rolex bracelets whose end pieces would mimic the curved pieces of these hooded lugs, yet be separate and detachable from the watch's case.

One of the most novel and surprising watches from this period was made by Vacheron Constantin for the Aluminium Company Canada Ltd (ALCAN), a firm that boomed during the war years, supplying aluminium to the Allies. ALCAN commissioned the specially made watches as gifts for their employees to recognise long service, and the case backs were engraved with an appropriate commemorative dedication. These watches had their cases, dials and much of their high-grade, precision-regulated movements made in aluminium, with the result that the model weighed just 19.61 grams – less than half that of an equivalent watch in a gold or silver case. Styled as an open-faced dress watch, at first glance the model appears to be almost identical to many other watches of the period. Yet closer inspection reveals an unusual tone of grey to the dial, while picking the watch up is the most curious sensation, for it feels so light to the touch that one's immediate reaction is that the casing must be empty. Produced between 1938 and 1952, the watches are among the lightest ever made.

As the decade ended, exports of Swiss watches had begun a dramatic recovery. The relaxation of import restrictions imposed by many countries during the war had seen demand soar. In 1945, total exports of complete Swiss watches and finished movements rose by nearly 59 per cent compared with the year before. By 1947, Swiss exports were more than double the 1944 level of 11.8 million pieces, averaging just under 24 million pieces per year between 1947 and 1949.[2] The range and diversity of models was rapidly increasing to meet demand, innovation was once again a driving force and, as the 1950s opened, the future of the mechanical watch would seem assured.

SHAPED WATCHES

One of the most noticeable features of this period was a continuing improvement in the construction of cases. The popularity of the rectangular watch in the 1930s had brought with it some inherent design issues. Circular watches were considerably easier to construct with case backs and glasses or crystals that were tight-fitting and able to withstand a certain degree of dirt and moisture ingress, even without additional waterproofing features. By contrast, guarding the movement of an oblong or square-cased watch was extremely difficult. The angles and edges of the 'shaped' watch did not naturally lend themselves to tight closures and seals, their crystals were more susceptible to chipping at their edges, and both these and the case backs were more prone to warping with wear, all of which risked allowing dirt and moisture to enter the watch with consequential damage to both the movement and dial. This problem was exacerbated by the fact that most square and oblong watches of the 1920s and '30s were constructed with thin metal cases, making them even more prone to wear.

Improvements in both the quality and handling of steel in case construction helped lead to more robust case construction. In 1936 Schmitz Frères & Cie, under Swiss patent 189190, had designed a new water-resistant case system for both circular and shaped watches. The method was licensed to a small number of manufacturers, including Gallet, who used it to produce their Clamshell circular chronograph, and also Cyma, who released a rectangular Watersport model in the 1940s. Cyma's watch had a relatively thick two-part casing and the synthetic crystal had a broad, flat lip that sat comfortably under the bezel of the upper case. The two halves of the case were clamped together and tightened via four screws drilled through the underside of the lugs. Together with a water-resistant crown, the design was robust and offered a good level of protection to both movement and dial.

Makers of the finest watches were increasingly generous with the amount of gold and platinum used in the production of their precious metal cases. This resulted in not only a flurry of new shapes but also

BELOW Cyma Watersport Ref. 25310 5550, c. 1940.
A steel rectangular–shaped wristwatch with case made according to Swiss patent 189190 (cal. 364k)
Length 38.5 mm, width 22.5 mm

BELOW, LEFT Patek Philippe Ref. 1450
'Top Hat', introduced in 1940, this
example retailed by Beyer, Zurich,
in 1947.
An 18 ct pink gold rectangular wristwatch
with hooded lugs (cal. 9'''90)
Length 37 mm

BELOW, RIGHT Patek Philippe Ref. 1593,
introduced in 1944, this example retailed
by Freccero, Montevideo, in 1947.
An 18 ct pink gold rectangular wristwatch
with flared sides (cal. 9'''90)
Length 42 mm

a range of more robust designs. Patek Philippe released an elegant array of rectangular watches during the 1940s. Compared to the shaped watches of the 1920s and '30s, these tended to be relatively substantial in proportion, with heavier cases that had a dramatically different feel to the standard models of the previous generation. In 1940 the firm launched their Ref. 1450 wristwatch, with hooded lugs. Popularly known as the 'Top Hat', this rectangular model had a gently curved case, yet the lugs were bold and stepped and, with the fixtures for the strap concealed, the shape of the case was clean and sharp. A few years later, in 1944, Patek Philippe's Ref. 1593 was released. With a deep curvature to the case sides, the model was shaped like an hourglass and, in a striking departure from the traditional rectangular watch, the back was no longer curved, but flat. This more defined and bold shaping of rectangular models was to become increasingly visible in the watches of Patek Philippe, Vacheron Constantin and Audemars Piguet throughout the 1940s and into the 1950s.

Straight-sided rectangular and square models continued to be made alongside the more shapely, oblong models. The bezels of the former were often broader than those of earlier periods, in some instances significantly so. One particularly remarkable model from the 1940s is a skeletonised rectangular wristwatch made by Audemars Piguet, illustrated on page 129. Skeletonised watches – which have the bridgework of their movements hollowed out and decoratively finished or engraved – are extremely rare in the first half of the twentieth century. It is believed that only around ten examples of this particular Audemars Piguet model were made. Each one is unique, since the *horloger squeletteur* was given free rein to cut and engrave the movement to their own design. As there is no dial, the hour indications are engraved and filled with black enamel to the bezel. Skeletonised watches would continue to appear only infrequently in the decades to come, before becoming more widely available towards the end of the century.

OPPOSITE Patek Philippe Ref. 439,
made in 1942 and sold by Cartier in 1943.
An 18 ct gold square-shaped wristwatch
with flat bezel (cal. 10'''110)
Length 32 mm

RIGHT Audemars Piguet Ref. 5036, sold
in 1948.
An 18 ct yellow gold rectangular-shaped
skeletonised wristwatch (cal. 10'''TS)
Length 34 mm, width 24 mm

LADIES' WATCHES

Wristwatches for ladies remained relatively small, yet, in common with the developments seen in other watches of the period, models aimed at women were beginning to transform into more recognisably 'modern' styles. Watches that concealed the dial from view continued to be popular. The rectangular wristwatch illustrated opposite was made by Jaeger-LeCoultre for Cartier. This example, manufactured in 1943, has an inner case that slides on runners within the main body of the case. A finger may be used to move the inner case from right to left, thereby revealing the dial; upon release, the two halves spring back together, once again hiding the dial from view. This design had the advantage of providing the watch with a greater level of protection, ensuring the crystal was guarded against accidental knocks while simultaneously protecting the movement with its double casing. In this model, as with many others of the period, LeCoultre used their small Duoplan movements. These were wound through the back rather than the side of the watch – such positioning meant that the crown was hidden from view and the clean lines of the case were therefore uninterrupted.

Although the small, 'cocktail' wristwatch was a popular theme during the decade, a new trend also developed for bracelet watches that were formed of bolder, thicker links of sinuous, flowing forms. Many of these bracelets were ordered from the specialist firm Gay Frères, one of Geneva's finest bracelet makers. Often the models were produced with a concealed dial, the face revealed by opening a hinged cover or, occasionally, as in the example pictured on page 133 (right), with the watch's case and dial sliding out from the bracelet. Watches with these substantial gold bracelets were also frequently heightened with precious stones. The left-hand image on page 133 shows a wristwatch where the watch case and lugs are based on the classic cocktail watch design, yet the lugs have been enlarged and are set with substantial round-cut diamonds. A ruby-set connecting link joins the heavy-gauge bracelet to the watch's head and, in so doing, transforms the lugs into an integral part of the bracelet. Such was the popularity of these styles that the fashion for thick-link bracelet watches would continue well into the following decade.

BELOW Movado Ref. 14177, c. 1940. A steel curved, rectangular-shaped ladies' wristwatch with black dial (cal. 65) Length (including lugs) 23.5 mm, width 13 mm

OPPOSITE Cartier/Jaeger-LeCoultre Baguette Coulissante, made in 1943. An 18 ct yellow gold rectangular-shaped ladies' wristwatch, the inner case sliding to reveal the concealed dial (cal. Duoplan) Width (closed) 22 mm

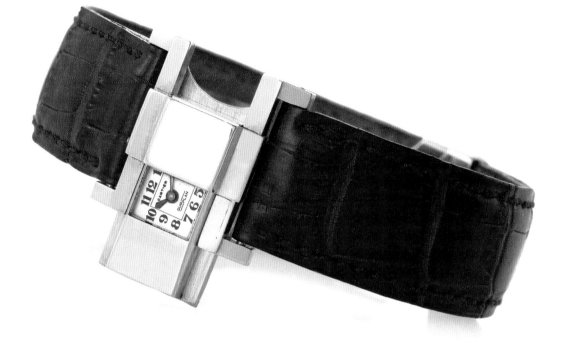

OPPOSITE Patek Philippe, made in 1942.
A ladies' platinum and yellow gold
diamond- and ruby-set wristwatch
with bracelet
Diameter 17 mm

RIGHT Jaeger-LeCoultre Ref. 1776,
c. 1945.
A ladies' 18 ct pink gold wristwatch with
concealed dial and bracelet by Gay Frères
(cal. 426)
Diameter 19 mm, overall length 160 mm

BELOW Patek Philippe Ref. 2164, sold in
1947.
A ladies' 18 ct pink gold, diamond-
and ruby-set wristwatch with bracelet
by Gay Frères (cal. 7'''70)
Diameter 20 mm, overall length 165 mm

MILITARY WATCHES

Watches for aviators took many forms during the Second World War. Longines continued to produce watches for pilots and navigators based on the Lindbergh and Weems models (see pp. 96–97); however, they also made a range of other watches to aid navigation. These included a patented fly-back system with central minute register, which, although first introduced in the 1930s, began to appear more frequently in the 1940s. A typical example of this type of watch is illustrated on the right. The black dial has Arabic numerals and luminous hands for hours and minutes. Two slim additional hands are positioned to the centre, one with a chromed finish, the other painted red, which indicate seconds to the dial's outermost scale and minutes elapsed to the innermost scale, respectively. Unlike a standard chronograph, these two hands are constantly in motion – the pusher above the crown merely resets them with one depression, upon which they immediately restart. The small counter to the base of the dial is a standard constant/subsidiary seconds dial.

In Germany, A. Lange & Söhne were one of a handful of companies to supply the German Luftwaffe with aviation watches – a typical example is shown opposite (top). Made by the firm in about 1940, this aviator's watch has a 55 mm diameter case and correspondingly large dial. The dial surface is black with highly visible luminescent Arabic numerals and tracking for minutes/seconds at the dial's edge, while the centre of the dial is calibrated in a separate ring for hours. All hands, including the seconds, are luminescent; the hour hand is deliberately shortened to follow its inner hour ring. Designed first and foremost for utility, the large size and luminous dial allowed readings to be easily taken both during the day and at night. A 'hack' feature designed by the German watchmaker Junghans stopped the balance (and therefore the movement) when the crown was pulled into the hand-setting position, thereby allowing the user to easily synchronise the seconds hand to a time signal. These were precision timekeepers that were designed to be accurate to within one second per day – a specific requirement of the Wehrmacht.[3] The watches also had oversized crowns, enabling them to be wound and adjusted even with gloved hands, and were fitted with extra-long wrist straps designed to fit over the wearer's flight suit.

In the mid-1930s, the Italian Royal Navy commissioned Panerai to produce a specialist diving watch for the navy's frogmen. Designed both to be highly legible and to fit over a diving suit, these watches were oversized. Panerai's first model was named the Radiomir, a name derived from the luminous varnish used for the hour

OPPOSITE Longines Ref. 23646,
c. 1948.
A steel single-button fly-back
chronograph wristwatch with centrally
set minute-recording hand (cal. 12.68z)
Diameter 37 mm

RIGHT A. Lange & Söhne, c. 1940.
A steel oversized aviator's wristwatch
with centre seconds, made for the
Wehrmacht (cal. 48.1)
Diameter 55 mm

BELOW Panerai Radiomir Ref. 3646,
c. 1940.
A steel oversized diver's wristwatch,
designed for the Italian Navy (cal. 618)
Width 47 mm

indexes, which was made of zinc sulphide, mesothorium and radium bromide – a formula patented by Guido Pancrai in 1915. With a case measuring 47 mm in diameter, the dial was consequently large and the luminous numerals were visible even deep underwater. The dial was layered with the numerals incised into the top portion of the dial, and these hollows were then filled with the luminous material. Having established a reputation for producing reliable waterproof wristwatches, it was to Rolex that Panerai turned for assistance in casing the watches. The steel cases followed the Oyster principle, with a screw-down crown and screw-down bezel and case back. Rather than milling to the edge of the case back as found on Rolex's standard Oyster watches, the oversized case backs of the Panerais had multifaceted edges, and the lugs at each end of the case were joined by solid bars onto which the strap could be stitched. Bearing the reference number 3646, these first-generation Radiomir watches were made, with a few alterations, between 1938 and the early 1950s.

During the Second World War, the Air Ministry in Britain ordered watches from a number of different manufacturers. These included the Ref. 2292 from Omega; the dial and hands were specially made by Omega for this model and were designed for use by pilots and navigators in the RAF. The case backs of these watches were made of steel; however, the upper cases were formed from a less expensive alloy known as Duralumin, which consisted of aluminium, copper, magnesium and manganese. Duralumin also had the advantage of having a more matt, silvery white appearance than steel and was less reflective, therefore helping to prevent distracting glare from the upper case while the watch was in use. The 2292's case has distinctive elongated lugs and, in the traditional military fashion, solid bars between the lugs to ensure the wrist strap cannot become accidentally detached. To the outside case back, these watches are usually engraved with the Air Ministry's military coding/serial number.

Towards the end of the war, in 1945, the British War Department placed orders with several different watchmakers to produce a new type of robust, waterproof model for the army. These watches were to have a black, luminous dial; a 15-jewel, high-precision movement; a shatterproof 'crystal'; a water-resistant steel case with waterproof winding crown; and solid, fixed-bar lugs. The cases were engraved 'W.W.W.' for 'Watch, Wrist, Waterproof' and were further engraved with the manufacturer's serial number as well as the military store number. A total of twelve manufacturers are known to have delivered versions to the British Army; all were of very similar styling to that of the Omega wristwatch illustrated opposite right.

Deck watches, in the form of pocket watches, were used by navies on both sides of the conflict during the Second World War. These high-grade timepieces were deployed on ships as well as submarines. A. Lange & Söhne produced large deck watches which, in common with the firm's aviator watches, the Wehrmacht specified must have a daily deviation of less than one second.[4] The image at top left illustrates a standard version of one of these observation watches, with two subsidiary dials – constant/subsidiary seconds to the right, and, to the left, the power reserve; this latter dial served to show how much power was left in the mainspring, thereby helping to ensure those in charge of the watch did not allow it to run out of power. These watches were made with plain silvered dials or, occasionally, with the entire dial surface coated in luminous paint – the latter type being used on German U-boats. Plain, utilitarian-dial deck watches with centre seconds were also in use both during and after the war. The image at bottom left shows a Longines deck watch made just after the end of the war. With a nickel-chrome case, the dial is of white enamel with black Arabic numerals and tracking for the minutes and seconds. Both the bezel and case back screw down to the body, thereby ensuring a tight seal and providing some protection from the ingress of moisture. In common with many other military Longines watches, the minute hand has a distinctively shaped tip to increase legibility.

Military watch designs would prove highly influential in the development of new watch models immediately after the war and in the decades that followed. Their clear, utilitarian styling and robust designs, together with the advances they incorporated in terms of anti-magnetism and water-resistance, saw many of their features adapted for civilian use.

CHRONOGRAPHS

A proliferation of chronographs permeated the 1940s. By this time, the chronograph was invariably a two-button model, with pushers placed symmetrically at either side of the winding crown. While the majority of chronographs displayed two subsidiary dials – one for the constant or subsidiary seconds and one for recording minutes while the chronograph was running – a third dial for registering hours elapsed was increasingly available.

Having been the first company to introduce a chronograph wristwatch with hour register during the 1930s, Universal introduced a new Aero-Compax model in 1940, which featured four subsidiary dials, creating a perfectly symmetrical appearance. Three subsidiary dials displayed constant seconds and registers to record 30-minute and 12-hour intervals while the chronograph was running. The fourth subsidiary dial was placed beneath the twelve o'clock position; this dial was not connected to the going or chronograph trains of the movement and was set independently via a crown to the case at nine o'clock. Known as a 'memento' dial,

this allowed the user to set, to the minute, a time of departure or the commencement of an event, with the indication serving as a static reminder.

As the decade opened, Rolex launched a new Oyster cased chronograph, the Ref. 3525. In addition to the standard Oyster features of screw-down crown and screw-down case back, the model featured round, water-resistant chronograph pushers. The round-button chronograph had begun to appear towards the end of the 1930s, and during the 1940s watch brands increasingly released models with this style of pusher, while continuing to offer the more traditional rectangular pusher designs. Chronographs were rarely made in square or rectangular cases, the circular dial lending itself much more readily to the display of multiple scales and subsidiary counters. However, Rolex, who had previously offered a square chronograph, released a new model with a cushion-form case in 1949. This had a broad, scooped bezel that was stepped at its inner edge to hold the watch's crystal.

Split-seconds chronographs, which allowed the timing of two events via two central chronograph hands, were more readily available during the 1940s. However, the complexity and consequent expense of this form of chronograph meant that production numbers were low. Patek Philippe launched a split-seconds chronograph model in 1939 under reference number 1436. While Patek Philippe had previously offered the complication, this was the first time a dedicated model with a specific reference number had been in production by the firm. To illustrate the rarity of this model, when Patek Philippe ceased production of the Ref. 1436 just over 40 years later, in 1971, it is thought that a total of just 165 pieces had been made, equating to an average of fewer than five pieces per year.

BELOW Rolex Gabus Ref. 8206, c. 1949. An 18 ct gold square-shaped chronograph wristwatch with subsidiary dials for constant seconds and 30-minute register, inner spiral tachymeter scale (cal. 69)
Width 29 mm

OPPOSITE Patek Philippe Ref. 1436, first introduced in 1939, this example made in 1947.
An 18 ct yellow gold split-seconds chronograph wristwatch with subsidiary dials for constant seconds and 30-minute register, outer tachymeter scale (cal. 13′′′ CHR)
Diameter 33 mm

CALENDAR WATCHES

OPPOSITE **Patek Philippe Ref. 1518,** first released in 1941, this example dated 1946.
A yellow gold perpetual calendar chronograph wristwatch with moon phases and subsidiary dials for constant seconds and 30-minute register, outer tachymeter scale (cal. 13‴130 Q)
Diameter 35 mm

BELOW, LEFT Universal Genève Tri-Compax Ref. 22279, c. 1944.
A steel triple-calendar chronograph wristwatch with moon phases, subsidiary dials for constant seconds, 30-minute and 12-hour registers, outer telemeter scale (cal. 481)
Diameter 34 mm

BELOW, RIGHT Movado Calendograf Ref. 14776, c. 1945.
A steel triple-calendar wristwatch (cal. 475)
Diameter 32 mm

The 1940s witnessed a surge in the production of calendar wristwatches, from simple apertures displaying only the date to watches displaying the day, date, month and moon phases. In 1941 Patek Philippe launched their Ref. 1518, a perpetual calendar wristwatch with additional chronograph function. A highly significant watch, this was the first perpetual calendar wristwatch to be produced in series; prior to this date, perpetual calendar wristwatches had been manufactured either on an ad hoc basis or to special order. Yet what really makes this model stand out is its styling – a design so harmonious and classic that it has formed the template for many complication wristwatches right up to the present day. From 1941 to 1954 Patek Philippe produced 281 examples of the model – a tiny production run by today's standards, but this represented a substantial investment for the period in such a complex wristwatch. The model was quickly followed by the Ref. 1526, which also featured perpetual calendar and moon phases but without the addition of a chronograph. Patek Philippe's continuing development of perpetual calendar wristwatches ensured that they remained the dominant manufacturer of this complication for the next 40 years.

Universal Genève were heavily involved in the development of calendar and calendar/chronograph watches during this period. To mark the fiftieth anniversary of the watchmaker, in 1944, Universal released what has since become one of the most recognised vintage wristwatches, the Tri-Compax. This triple-calendar wristwatch, while not a perpetual calendar, displayed the days, months and moon phases in apertures, with four subsidiary dials indicating the date, constant seconds, and chronograph registers for 30 minutes and 12 hours. An enormously popular model, its success was undoubtedly assisted by an important breakthrough in the US market. In 1942 the Henri Stern Watch Agency – Patek Philippe's US distributor – became the official importer of Universal watches to the United States. This was a coup for both companies, as restrictions covering watch imports were severe during the war;

however, the US military's requirement for chronograph watches had enabled the Herni Stern Watch Agency to obtain a licence to import Universal watches.[5]

A plethora of alternative date displays were marketed by other watchmakers during the decade. Movado's Calendograf models were produced with apertures for day and month indication, while the date was shown at the edge of the dial. This layout had the advantage of allowing the date to be displayed in a larger format than that permitted by a more traditional subsidiary date dial. Date indication was via a central hand, often long and slim with a coloured triangular or circular tip to clearly delineate it from the hour and minute hands. Placement of the date at the extremity of the dial was favoured by many manufacturers, including Omega for their triple-calendar Cosmic model and Rolex for their triple-calendar chronograph models.

In 1945 Rolex announced the launch of a new model to coincide with the company's ruby jubilee celebrations. Initially launched under reference number 4467, with milled bezel, further models, including the Ref. 5030 (with smooth bezel), were introduced before the end of the decade. Although wristwatches with date apertures

had been produced previously, the significance of the Rolex design lay in the simplicity of its layout, and the watch helped establish the default three o'clock placement of the date window that to this day remains the most common placement of this feature. For Rolex, these models, which would later be designated under a new Datejust line, represented another updating of the Oyster design and added a further feature that would help to develop the company's reputation. Although the Datejust has undergone many modifications over the years, the basic principles of its design remain little changed.

ABOVE Rolex Dato-Compax Ref. 4768, c. 1948.
A steel and pink gold triple-calendar chronograph wristwatch with subsidiary dials for constant seconds, 30-minute and 12-hour registers, outer tachymeter scale (cal. 13‴)
Diameter 35 mm

OPPOSITE Rolex Oyster Perpetual Ref. 5030, c. 1948.
An 18 ct yellow gold automatic wristwatch with date indication (cal. 10½‴)
Diameter 36 mm

AUTOMATIC WRISTWATCHES

A renewed attempt by the watch industry to market the automatic wristwatch led to the introduction of a range of new calibres during the 1940s. Although it may seem surprising that so few of the major brands had previously released automatic movements, their reticence to invest in this area should be viewed against the backdrop of the public's continuing mistrust of a watch that wound itself, largely a result of the perceived unreliability that had dogged many of the first generation of automatic models.

Most of the automatic movements that were launched in the 1940s were based upon the 'bumper' system, first exploited in a wristwatch by Harwood (see p. 79). Eterna had begun marketing an automatic wristwatch at the close of the 1930s with their new calibre 834 and, in 1944, introduced an updated version of this movement named the calibre 1076H. Like the Harwood, the Eterna had a semi-rotor that buffered off springs as it reached the beginning and end of its arc of motion. A similar system was used by several other manufacturers, including Omega, who introduced their own automatic

calibres, the 30.10RA PC and 28.10RA PC, in 1942 and 1943 respectively. Despite the seemingly strange 'hammer' action of these bumper automatics, the system was efficient and relatively robust, and, crucially, its design allowed for a slimmer watch – this was achieved by the swinging 'weight' being partially integrated into the body of the movement. Part of the criticism of early rotor automatics was the thickness of their cases and the fact that their case backs had a pronounced, domed surface – necessitated by the way in which the rotors were mounted above the back plate of the movement. In this area, therefore, the 'bumper' movement had a clear design advantage. To illustrate the point, the first Rolex Perpetual rotor movement (cal. 620NA), from the early 1930s, had a height of 7.5 mm. By contrast, the slimmest of the first two Omega bumper calibres mentioned above was just 4.5 mm in height; remarkably, this was just 0.5 mm thicker than Omega's regular-production, manually wound wristwatch calibres of the period. This is significant since it meant that the shape and style of the wristwatch's case

BELOW Eterna, c. 1946.
A steel 'bumper' automatic wristwatch with two-tone dial (cal. 1076H)
Diameter 34.5 mm

was not unduly influenced by the size of its movement, allowing the watch a sleeker profile. Nevertheless, the rotor design would eventually win the battle for supremacy, and a few new, slimmer 'rotor' movements did appear in the 1940s. These included the Bidynator, released by Felsa in 1942 (5.2 mm high), and Longines' calibre 22A (5.5 mm high), introduced in 1945. It was also significant that both the Felsa and Longines calibres had the advantage of winding the watch while the rotor moved in either direction – most early bumper automatics wound in one direction only.

Despite the growing efficiency of the automatic movements, complaints were still common from owners whose watches ran out of power – one wonders how much of this was down to a lack of activity, the automatic system relying on the motion of the owner during the day. In 1948, Jaeger-LeCoultre introduced their Powermatic model (calibre 481), a 'bumper' automatic wristwatch that had the addition of a power reserve indication. Located beneath the twelve o'clock position, an aperture displayed the amount of power left in the mainspring in hours, turning red when almost fully unwound. By this period, automatic watches could also be manually wound, and the wearer was therefore able to top up the power of their watch with a few turns of the crown/ winder, making the power reserve warning indicator a particularly useful feature.

COIN AND ENVELOPE WATCHES

The heyday of the purse watch had passed, and while production of Movado's famous Ermeto model continued, the range and diversity of this genre among other makers was greatly depleted. However, one unusual form of watch that continued to make an appearance was the gold coin watch. Examples of coin watches had already been marketed in the 1920s and they were a novelty that would reappear throughout the remainder of the century. Almost invariably made using $10 or $20 gold coins (other denominations and currencies were occasionally used), these remarkable timepieces were formed by hollowing out the inside of a coin and integrating a hinged inner case that contained the watch's dial and an extra flat movement. The example illustrated opposite was sold by Patek Philippe in 1941. In common with the finest examples of these coin watches, a push-piece to open the front of the coin is flush with, and almost entirely concealed by, the milling to the coin's sides. Remarkable objects, these watches have a pleasing weight and their quality is quite exceptional.

One of the most charming types of purse watch was a model made in the form of an envelope. Intended to be purchased as gifts, the fronts of these watches were engraved with the recipient's name and address, while the 'franking' to the envelope could be dated with a special occasion such as a birthday or anniversary. One of these envelope watches, made in silver and retailed by Cartier in 1940, is shown here (top). The watch is engraved with the name and address of the recipient, and close inspection shows that the envelope is 'franked' with the date of Christmas Day – 25 December 1940. To the reverse of this watch, a simple engraved motif imitates the flap to the back of an envelope. A gold version of this model is shown on the right; this example is 'franked' with the date 20 June 1943, the birthday of James Ortiz, whose name and address appears to the front. The back is further engraved 'From Mr and Mrs Ortiz / New York City' in the manner in which one might inscribe a return address. These watches open by sliding apart the two halves of the cover, in a similar fashion to the Ermeto design by Movado.

TOP Cartier, c. 1940.
A silver purse watch in the form
of an envelope
Length (closed) 38 mm

BOTTOM Cartier, c. 1943.
A pink gold purse watch in the form
of an envelope
Length (closed) 36 mm

RIGHT AND BELOW Patek Philippe retailed
by Astrua, Turin, sold in 1941.
A $20 gold coin watch (cal. 9‴)
Diameter 34 mm

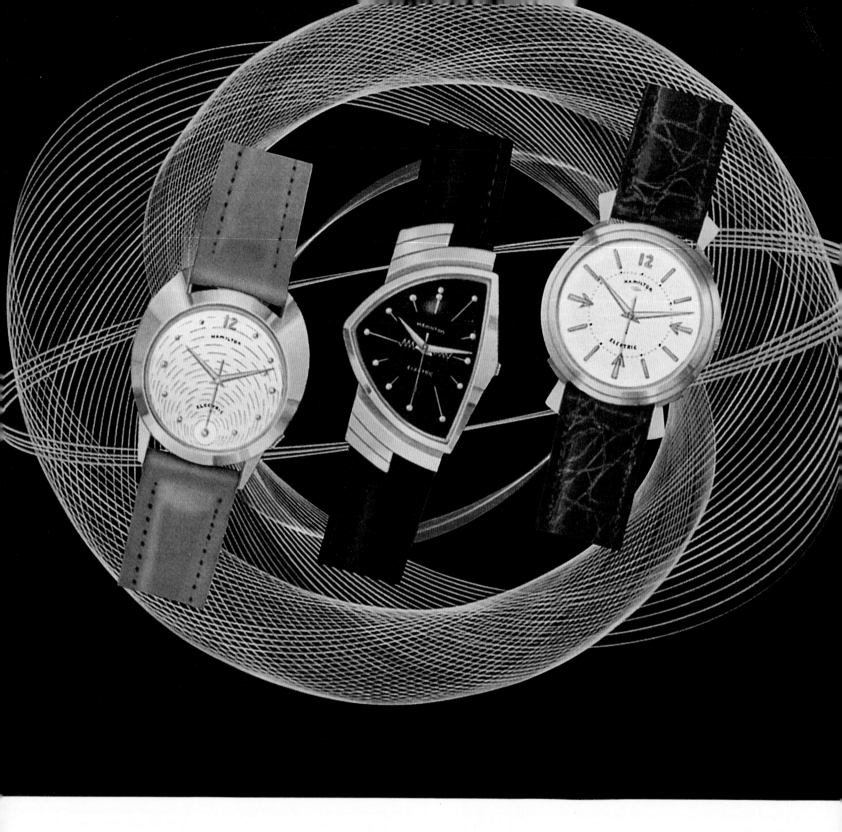

Hamilton—the world's first electric watch!

It's no secret that electricity is the best way to run a wrist watch. Greater accuracy. Fewer parts. Less care. But it was real news early this year when Hamilton was *first* to produce the electric watch. Your Hamilton jeweler will tell you more about this, the biggest watch news in 477 years. *(Left to right)* Spectra, $150; Ventura I, $200; Van Horn, $175. Hamilton Watch Company, Lancaster, Pennsylvania.

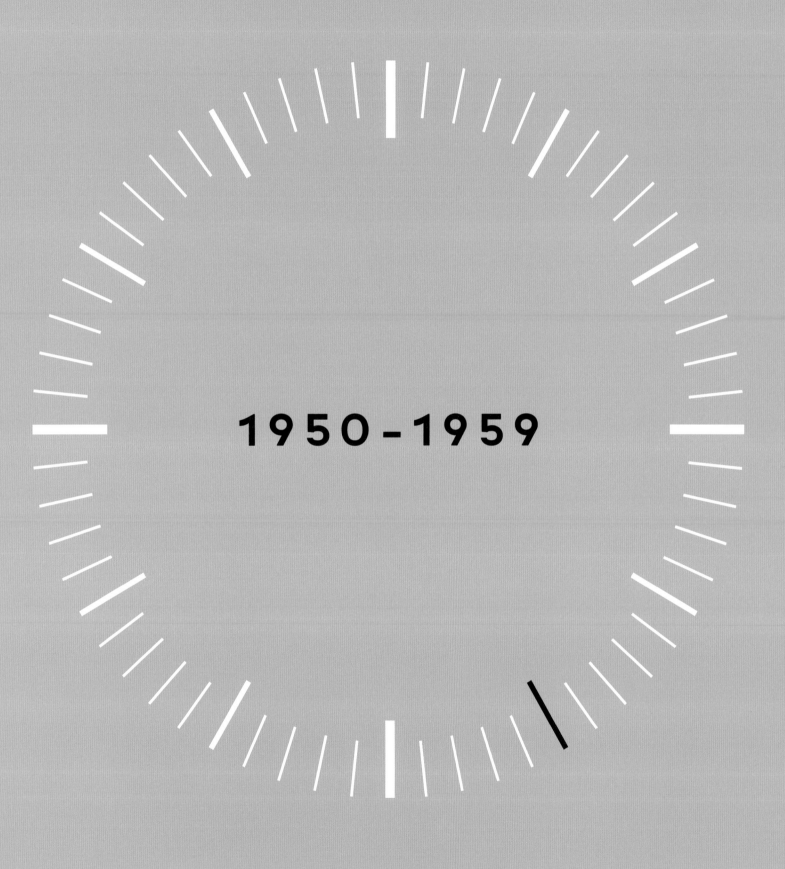

1950-1959

THE 1950s

As the US and much of western Europe entered a period of strong economic growth, the 1950s witnessed a period of positive expansion for the Swiss watch industry, with exports increasing by almost 54 per cent over the decade. Indeed, the decade had a jump start with a 38 per cent increase in the export of watches and watch movements between 1950 and 1951 alone.[1] Although by now many classic watch styles had firmly taken root, there was a renewed sense of innovation within the industry, somewhat akin to the enterprising spirit of the 1930s. Boosted by the increasing demand for fine watches, the 1950s would see the rapid development and release of a new range of models fit for a changing world.

The war had heavily influenced watch design, and the bold styles established in the 1940s would be further developed during the new decade. The soft iron 'cages' used during the Second World War to protect the movements of pilots' watches from the effects of magnetism would find new markets within the growing ranks of scientists, technicians, engineers and civilian pilots. Meanwhile, the advent of intercontinental air travel would create new avenues for watchmakers to pursue, leading to a range of watch models offering indications to help manage changes in time zone.

A sense of exploration and adventure permeated the post-war world. In 1943 Jacques Cousteau and Émile Gagnan had developed their Aqua-Lung system, thereby opening up the world's oceans to a new obsession: scuba diving. Fascination with life under the surface of the sea reached fever pitch in 1956 with the release of the French documentary *Le Monde du silence*, one of the first films to show the depths of the ocean in colour. Co-directed by Jacques Cousteau and Louis Malle, the film was based on Cousteau's book *The Silent World: A Story of Undersea Discovery and Adventure* (1953). Watchmakers seized on the public's appetite for this new underwater world by releasing a variety of diving watches throughout the decade.

While discoveries were being made in the depths of the seas there was, simultaneously, a battle to conquer the world's highest peaks. Rolex had supplied their Oyster

BELOW Tudor Oyster Elegante Ref. 7960,
dated 1958.
A stainless steel manually wound centre
seconds wristwatch (cal. 2402)
Diameter 34.5 mm

watches to several Himalayan mountaineering expeditions during the 1930s and '40s. For Rolex, these expeditions provided an excellent testing ground for their Oyster watches, exposing them to some of the most extreme conditions on earth. However, they also provided the watchmaker with a brilliant form of marketing alliance, and to celebrate Edmund Hillary and Tenzing Norgay's successful ascent of Mount Everest in 1953 (for which Rolex also supplied watches), Rolex launched their Oyster Explorer model. Designed to be both robust and highly visible, the dial was black with bold luminescent numerals – the configuration of a triangular-shaped twelve o'clock and Arabic numerals at three, six and nine o'clock was a style similar to that which had been used earlier in the 1940s; however, this configuration, combined with the black dial, would become an iconic Rolex dial design that would be applied to the company's Explorer models for decades to come.

No doubt encouraged by the gathering growth in post-war economic activity, Hans Wilsdorf, the governing director of Rolex, staged a relaunch of his Tudor brand in 1952, the highlight of which was the new Tudor Oyster Prince. Though the Oyster case was not a new addition to the Tudor line, an emphasis was placed on the new Prince model as a watch of extreme durability. Following a similar pattern to the Rolex Explorer's marketing, Wilsdorf supplied each of the 30 members of the British North Greenland expedition of 1952–54 with a Tudor Oyster Prince, providing yet another useful testing ground and publicity opportunity for his watches. Wilsdorf had always intended the Tudor to be a less expensive alternative to his Rolex brand, and the Tudor Oyster models in particular would undergo a transformation during the 1950s. While sharing much of the Rolex DNA through the release of watches such as the Tudor Submariner in the same year (1954) as the Rolex Submariner, the Tudor brand was also given its own identity with an extraordinary variety of dials and some novel models such as the Tudor Advisor, an alarm wristwatch.

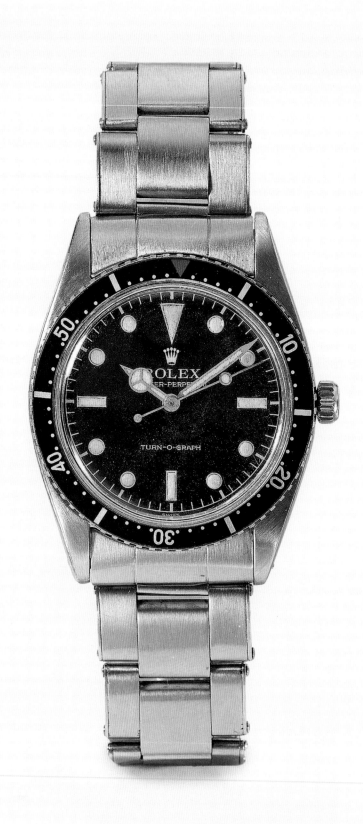

Rotating bezels very much defined the era of the 1950s for sports-style watches. In 1953 Rolex launched their Turn-O-Graph model, and although it was by no means the first wristwatch to have a rotating bezel, its design became a blueprint for an array of future models. By aligning the bezel's triangular marker at the 0/60 position with the centre seconds hand, the watch could be used as a simple chronograph by reading off the time elapsed from the bezel's markings; by instead aligning the bezel with the minute hand, longer periods could be recorded. The Turn-O-Graph was marketed as a multi-use watch, one that could, for example, be used by a businessman to time the duration of a long-distance phone call; a doctor to help calculate a patient's pulse rate; a photographer to time development of a film, and so on. Standard versions of the model were styled with black dials and bold luminous numerals, showing the influence of military watches of the 1940s. Using Rolex's Oyster case, the watch was also waterproof, further boosting its appeal to a broad audience. This 'tool' watch

concept (meaning a watch designed for specific uses) would lead to a succession of releases in the decade, including the Rolex models of Submariner, GMT-Master and Milgauss.

As the 1950s opened, Omega were rapidly developing their new Seamaster range. These modern, robust models had notably thicker bezels and lugs compared with civilian models of the previous generation. Based on one of the military models Omega had supplied to the British Army during the war, the watches were designed to be waterproof and resistant to climatic and atmospheric changes. Throughout the decade, Omega released a range of Seamasters, from manually wound to automatic watches and from date models to chronographs. In 1954 Longines released a similarly robust model named the Conquest; this watch had a screw-down case back that was centred with a gold plaque bearing a fish logo heightened in green enamel, representing the manufacturer's guarantee of water-resistance. In a similar way to Omega's Seamaster, the

Conquest would be developed by Longines as a 'line' of models, all under the banner of the Conquest name. One of the first additions to this family of watches was a calendar version, introduced in 1956. Omega's Seamaster line was soon joined, in 1952, by a new deluxe wristwatch model named the Constellation. The Constellation would be produced in a broad range of styles, all of which would have observatory-certified chronometer movements, and their case backs would bear an embossed logo featuring an observatory building under a constellation of stars. Among the most opulent of these models was the Constellation Grand Luxe, which was released in the middle of the decade. The model was available in pink, yellow or white gold as well as platinum; however, they were monochromatic in appearance – regardless of the case metal, the dials would match the colouring of their cases. The Grand Luxe's dial would also feature a so-called 'pie-pan' edge – a multifaceted, downward chamfer.

Watches with flared or teardrop-shaped lugs continued to appear during the 1950s. Some square and rectangular watches were given curvaceous, flowing sides, but in general there was an increasing angularity to elements of watch design as the 1950s progressed. The softer shapes of the 1930s and '40s gave way to more facets and chamfers. Traditional *feuille* (leaf-shaped) hands became much less prevalent, with angular styles such as the alpha, dauphine and straight baton hands beginning to dominate. Hour indexes and numerals were also becoming increasingly bold in appearance. Raised and applied hour markers were frequently multifaceted, allowing light to play across their surfaces, thereby producing added depth and contrast. Diving watches followed the military precedents of black dials with thick luminous hour indexes and hands. Two-tone finished dials continued to be available but their use was often restricted to chronograph and calendar watches, where secondary tones would be used primarily for utilitarian reasons, highlighting specific scales for example, rather than being used for their decorative merits alone. Silvered, pink and champagne coloured dials tended to

BELOW Longines Conquest Calendar Ref. 9007-6, c. 1957.
A pink-gold-capped and steel automatic centre seconds wristwatch with date (cal. 19ASD)
Diameter 35 mm

OPPOSITE Omega Constellation Grand Luxe Ref. 2930, c. 1959.
An 18 ct pink gold automatic centre seconds wristwatch with pink pie-pan dial and 18 ct pink gold bracelet (cal. 505)
Diameter 35 mm

OPPOSITE, TOP Patek Philippe Ref. 2540
sold in 1958.
An 18ct yellow gold automatic wristwatch
with cushion-form case and diamond-set
hour indexes (cal. 12‴600 AT)
Width 32mm

OPPOSITE, BOTTOM Cartier, c. 1955.
An 18 ct yellow gold woven belt-form
bracelet watch with concealed dial
and diamond-set buckle (cal. 49C)
Width 19 mm, overall length 220mm

BELOW Vacheron Constantin, c. 1952.
An 18 ct pink gold wristwatch with
two-tone guilloché dial (cal. P453/3B)
Diameter 35 mm

have a 'silk' matt finish to their surface, while black dials could be either matt or gloss in finish. Just before the middle of the decade, textured dials with stippled surfaces, often referred to as 'honeycomb' or 'waffle' dials, began to appear; such dials remained an option for much of the remainder of the decade. The technique of guilloché was used to create highly decorative, engine-turned finishes: using a hand-turned lathe known as a rose engine, multiple contrasting finishes could be built up and engraved onto the dial's surface. Vacheron Constantin were particularly experimental in this area, creating a range of sophisticated patterns for dress-style watches during the 1950s. Colourful enamel dials were also offered by several manufacturers. Although many wristwatches for women continued to follow established patterns during the 1950s, one of the most striking developments was a trend for watchmakers to release models in men's and ladies' versions, with similar styling given to each version both in terms of case and dial design. Nevertheless, dress-style watches with small dials, as well as concealed dials, remained popular. The thick and often bulbous bracelets of the 1940s continued to be found throughout the 1950s, and these were joined by wider, woven bracelets. Asymmetrical designs were also increasingly prevalent as the decade wore on.

A feature that was becoming somewhat more visible was the enhancement of designs for men through the incorporation of diamonds or other precious stones. While a few watches for men had featured diamonds in the previous two decades, their application to some of the larger-sized watches of the 1950s was notable. Makers such as Patek Philippe and Audemars Piguet offered diamond-set dials as an option for a small number of their models: these would see the replacement of printed or applied indexes with diamonds, usually a combination of round and baguette cuts. Some models would push the boundaries further, with cases also enhanced with gem settings. Such watches showed just how far the wristwatch had come since the first timid wristlets of the early twentieth century.

In 1954, Universal, in partnership with Scandinavian Airlines (SAS), developed an anti-magnetic wristwatch that would be suitable for use by the latter's flight crew. SAS had recently launched a new route from Copenhagen to New York which flew over the North Pole. This new route exposed the planes to strong magnetic fields that could adversely affect the timekeeping of a mechanical wristwatch. The Polerouter was designed to counter these effects and provide precision timekeeping for the airline. Originally named the Polarouter, the case had a bold design with flowing, so-called *bombé* lugs. The watch's bezel was broad and flat, enhancing the model's perceived solidity. An inner steel bezel was calibrated at the hours, with fine milling between each marker. The dials were invariably centred with a cross-hair motif, itself a design element that would recur on models by a variety of different makers.

Calendar and chronograph wristwatches remained extremely popular, and while the finest makers, such as Audemars Piguet, Patek Philippe and Vacheron Constantin, dominated the luxury end of the market, the availability of good-quality affordable alternatives was growing. At the start of the 1950s, Record were one of the few independent watch manufacturers to have developed their own in-house movement calibre with the combined complications of day, date, month and moon indication. Their Datofix model, first introduced in the 1940s, was once again on the company's exhibition stand at the 1950 Basel Watch Fair. Available in a variety of case designs, the majority of Record's calendar watches were housed in chrome- or gold-plated cases with steel backs. Well designed and highly legible, the Datofix was a stylish and aspirational-looking model, ideally suited to the post-war era. In 1953, to celebrate the company's fiftieth anniversary and capitalise on the popularity of the calendar watch, Record launched a Datofix model for women, which they billed at the time as the smallest wristwatch to have been made with moon phases.

BELOW, LEFT Audemars Piguet, made in 1956.
An 18 ct yellow and white gold wristwatch, the bezel set with baguette sapphire hour indexes (cal. 2002)
Diameter 29 mm

BELOW, RIGHT Universal Polerouter Ref. 20217-5, c. 1955.
A stainless steel automatic centre seconds wristwatch (cal. 138SS)
Diameter 36 mm

OPPOSITE, TOP Record Datofix, c. 1950.
A chromed and steel triple-calendar wristwatch with moon phases (cal. 107C)
Diameter 33 mm

OPPOSITE, BOTTOM Vacheron Constantin Ref. 6087, made in 1955.
An 18 ct yellow gold chronograph wristwatch with subsidiary dials for constant seconds and 30-minute register (cal. 13‴)
Diameter 35 mm

At the Savoy Plaza Hotel in New York on Thursday, 3 January 1957, a press conference was held by the Hamilton Watch Company to announce the release of the first series-produced electric wristwatch. Using battery power, these early electric watches incorporated both a traditional gear train and balance but were modified for electrical impulse. Hamilton commissioned the industrial designer Richard Arbib to create one of the launch models. Arbib's design, which was called the Ventura, was a futuristic-looking wristwatch that had an asymmetrically shaped case that boldly represented the beginning of a new era. The idea of an electric watch was by no means new, and although Hamilton's first electric watch would be beset with issues, the fact that an electric watch had been developed for series production at all must have been enough to furrow the brows of many traditional watch manufacturers. The question was where this would lead; for the time being, many traditional techniques were employed alongside the electrical power source of the new Hamilton watch, yet clearly technology would not stand still. During the next two decades the rise of the electronic wristwatch would pose a threat to the very survival of the mechanical watch industry.

RIGHT Hamilton calibre 505, an updated version of the firm's first electro-mechanical calibre 500

OPPOSITE, LEFT Hamilton Ventura, c. 1957. A 14 ct yellow gold asymmetrically shaped electrically/battery-powered mechanical wristwatch (cal. 500) Length (including lugs) 49 mm

OPPOSITE, RIGHT Hamilton Pacer, c. 1958. A 10 ct gold-filled asymmetrically shaped electrically/battery-powered mechanical wristwatch (cal. 500) Length (including lugs) 49 mm

DIVING WATCHES

At the beginning of the 1950s, the increasing interest in scuba diving, both for civilian and military purposes, led to the development of specialist diving watches. These were rugged, waterproof watches that had utilitarian designs and were clearly influenced by the military watches of the previous decade. In 1953 Blancpain introduced their Fifty Fathoms model, the first modern diving wristwatch. The model was developed by Blancpain following a request made by two French naval officers, Captain Maloubier and Lieutenant Riffaud, for a practical watch that could be used by their new elite unit of combat divers. The Fifty Fathoms had a black dial with thickly painted luminescent hour markers and white luminescent hands to ensure maximum visibility at depth under the sea. The model also had a bezel that was calibrated at each five-minute increment with luminescent markers. Rotating the bezel allowed the diver to align the triangular marker of the bezel with the minute hand of the watch, at the start of their dive. As the minute hand continued to advance, the time elapsed since the start of the dive could be read against the bezel's calibrations. Such a system allowed the user to quickly calculate the length of the dive and keep track of the amount of air left in their breathing apparatus. For safety reasons, the bezel rotated in a counter-clockwise direction only, ensuring that if it was accidentally knocked, the bezel would only turn in the direction that indicated

a longer dive duration than had actually taken place. The Fifty Fathoms quickly gained a successful reputation and orders were placed by a number of navies around the world. In 1956 the model was used by Jacques Cousteau during filming for his Oscar-winning sea exploration film *Le Monde du silence*.

Almost simultaneously with the launch of the Fifty Fathoms in 1953, Rolex began producing their first Submariner models, which they exhibited at the Basel Watch Fair of 1954. In common with the Fifty Fathoms, the Submariner also had a black dial with bold luminescent hour numerals and a rotating bezel calibrated at each five-minute increment. Rather than luminescent numerals to the bezel, however, the Submariner had a luminescent dot within a triangular marker at the bezel's 0/60-minute marker. These earliest Submariners included models with depth ratings of 100 or 200 metres.

Both the Fifty Fathoms and the Submariner had a tremendous influence on future diving watches, the bold luminescent dials and rotating bezels proving to be highly practical features that ensured the raw DNA of these early models was passed on through the generations. For the watch manufacturers, the diving watch was a great commercial success, as, far from being restricted to the diving fraternity, their sporty, robust designs and high performance ensured that they had wide-ranging appeal.

BELOW Blancpain Fifty Fathoms, introduced in 1953, this example c. 1954. A stainless steel automatic centre seconds diver's wristwatch with luminescent hour indexes and hands, rotating bezel with luminescent calibrations (cal. AS 1361) Diameter 41 mm

OPPOSITE Rolex Oyster Perpetual Submariner 'Big Crown' Ref. 6538, dated 1959. A stainless steel automatic centre seconds diver's wristwatch with luminescent hour indexes and hands, rotating bezel with luminescent accented red triangle (cal. 1030) Diameter 37 mm

WATCHES WITH TIME ZONES

With demand increasing for watches that indicated the time in multiple zones, Tissot entered the world time market in 1951 with their Navigator wristwatch. This model used a central rotating disc to display, simultaneously, the current time in 24 locations around the world. To do this, Tissot introduced a new movement calibre, the cal. 28.5-N21, which incorporated a pusher set to the case side that allowed the uncoupling of the central world time disc to allow local time to be set. The time was read in the usual twelve-hour format against an outer black track to the dial's edge, with corresponding hour numerals engraved and filled in black to the bezel. The inner revolving disc was for the 24 world locations, with the time in each location indicated against applied Arabic and triangular numerals that were divided into 24 hours. To select the local time, the crown would be pulled out into the hand-set position and the inner disc rotated until the current city/location was lined up beneath the 24-hour numeral/twelve o'clock position. When this had been set, the pusher above the crown would be pressed

inwards, thereby disengaging the central disc; the hands could then be moved to the 24-hour numeral/twelve o'clock position. Pressing the crown inwards reactivated the central world time disc, and the actual local time could then be set; when this had been done, the time in all zones would be correctly displayed.

The year 1952 saw the introduction of a new world time wristwatch by Patek Philippe. The model, known by the reference number 2523, used a world time mechanism devised by Louis Cottier (see p. 104) and was an updating of the earlier, smaller world time wristwatches that Patek Philippe had offered from the late 1930s onwards. The watch featured a central time dial that was bordered with a 24-hour ring, the latter indicating the hour in a series of world locations listed on a bezel to the dial's edge. A crown to the left case side rotated the disc with the world locations, and the user would ensure that their current zone was indicated at the twelve o'clock position. The hands could then be set using the crown at the right-hand side of the case; this

BELOW Tissot Navigator Ref. 4002-2, c. 1952.
A gold-capped and steel automatic world time wristwatch (cal. 28.5-N21)
Diameter 36 mm

BELOW, LEFT Patek Philippe Ref. 2523, made in 1954.
An 18 ct yellow gold dual crown world time wristwatch with cloisonné enamel map of Europe (cal. 12‴120 HU)
Diameter 35 mm

BELOW, RIGHT Rolex Oyster Perpetual Date GMT–Master Ref. 6542, retailed by Serpico y Laino, Caracas, dated 1957.
A stainless steel automatic centre seconds wristwatch with 24–hour or second time zone indication, with luminescent hour indexes and hands, rotating bezel with Bakelite insert and luminescent calibrations for 24 hours (cal. 1030)
Diameter 38 mm

simultaneously rotated the 24-hour ring, and if the user ensured that the appropriate day or night hour was pointing at their current location, which they had previously set at the twelve o'clock position, the correct hour would then be displayed for all time zones.

In 1955 Rolex released the GMT-Master. The watch used the company's Oyster case and had a rotating bezel that was calibrated for 24 hours. In addition to standard hour, minute and seconds hands, a slim central red hand with triangular tip acted as a secondary hour hand. Revolving once every 24 hours, this additional hand indicated hours to the watch's bezel. The watch could therefore be used to show time in the current time zone, simultaneously in both 12 and 24 hours, or, alternatively, the bezel could be rotated and the hour of a second time zone could be aligned to the secondary hour hand, thereby creating a dual-time wristwatch. Initial versions of the model included a stainless-steel version with a Bakelite bezel graduated in red and blue for day and night hours, and an 18 ct gold version with maroon

Bakelite bezel. These early versions of the models had their hour indexes both to the dial and bezel rendered in luminous paint. The GMT was the official watch of Pan American Airways, the leading intercontinental airline of the period, and was used by its pilots to assist in calculating time zone differences, enabling them to continue, as advised, to observe home time to minimise jet lag, while also allowing the time at their destination to be easily read.

CHRONOGRAPHS

For much of the 1950s, the classic chronograph styles established in the 1930s and '40s continued to dominate. Patek Philippe, for example, kept in production chronograph models that had initially been introduced in the 1930s, including the references 130, 530, 533 and 1436, together with further models from the 1940s, such as the Ref. 1463 and Ref. 1579. Quite simply, these established chronographs had been so well styled and designed that there was little reason for them to be substantially altered, and therefore changes, when they were made, tended to be modest stylistic updates to dial finishes, numerals and tracks.

Rolex continued to release new chronograph models, largely concentrating on their Oyster cases but again following patterns that had been formed during the previous decade. The image opposite illustrates a pink gold chronograph that was introduced around 1950. Although this particular chronograph is a rare model, its aesthetics are similar to other models introduced by Rolex during the decade, especially in the style of its case

and the configuration of printed scales and tracks on the dial. During the 1950s, Rolex chronographs were available with two subsidiary dials showing constant seconds and 30-minute register or with an additional third subsidiary dial for hour recording.

In 1952 Breitling introduced their Navitimer – a conflation of the words 'navigation' and 'timer'. This chronograph wristwatch had a rotating bezel that was calibrated with a flight-specific slide rule to enable the user to perform navigational calculations. The model was quickly taken up by flight enthusiasts, and by the middle of the decade Breitling was producing Navitimer models for the US-based Aircraft Owners and Pilots Association (AOPA). An early example of the model that already displays the Navitimer's distinctive styling is shown on page 170 (left). The dial is black with bold luminescent Arabic numerals and hands, while the slide rule is calibrated in white to the edge of the dial. The watch has three subsidiary dials, including chronograph registers that allow up to twelve hours of time to be

BELOW Patek Philippe Ref. 1579, made in 1955.
An 18 ct pink gold chronograph wristwatch with subsidiary dials for constant seconds and 30-minute register, outer tachymeter scale (cal. 13‴ CH)
Diameter 36 mm

OPPOSITE Rolex Oyster Ref. 6032, c. 1950.
An 18 ct pink gold chronograph wristwatch with subsidiary dials for constant seconds and 30-minute register, outer scales for tachymeter and telemeter (cal. 13‴)
Diameter 36 mm

recorded. Around 1954, Breguet began producing their Type XX pilot's wristwatch for the naval air arm of the French Navy. The model had a black dial with luminous numerals and incorporated a special fly-back mechanism that, when the chronograph seconds hand was reset, immediately restarted, allowing the pilot or navigator to make multiple calculations quickly and easily. The bezel rotated and was calibrated with a triangular index; this could be aligned to the minute or seconds hand as a further means of measuring elapsed time. A second generation of the model was produced for civilian use, and the model would make repeated appearances in the decades ahead.

Undoubtedly one of the most significant chronographs introduced during the decade was the Speedmaster, which Omega launched in 1957, initially under reference number 2915. Produced in a waterproof case and marketed alongside their Seamaster line of watches, this model was also heavily influenced by the styling of military watches. The dial was black with luminescent

baton indexes and was first released with a broad, arrow-tipped hour hand. There were three subsidiary dials, which consisted of a constant/subsidiary seconds dial and two registers for the chronograph, one recording minutes and the other, hours. Although the model would undergo a series of updates over the years, the styling of the original Speedmaster would provide the blueprint for its successors and ensure the model's place as one of the most influential wristwatches of all time.

BELOW, LEFT Breitling Navitimer for Aircraft Owners and Pilots Association, c. 1955.
A stainless steel chronograph wristwatch with subsidiary dials for constant seconds, 30-minute and 12-hour registers, outer scales for flight-specific slide rule with rotating bezel (cal. Valjoux 72) Diameter 40 mm

BELOW, RIGHT Breguet Type XX, made for the French Air Force, c. 1955.
A stainless steel fly-back chronograph wristwatch with rotating bezel and subsidiary dials for constant seconds and 30-minute register (cal. Valjoux 222) Diameter 38 mm

OPPOSITE Omega Speedmaster Ref. 2915, made in 1958.
A stainless steel chronograph wristwatch with subsidiary dials for constant seconds, 30-minute and 12-hour registers, bezel calibrated for tachymeter (cal. 321) Diameter 39 mm

CALENDAR WATCHES

OPPOSITE Rolex Oyster Perpetual Ref. 6062, c. 1952.
An 18 ct yellow gold automatic triple-calendar wristwatch with moon phases (cal. 9¾''')
Diameter 36 mm

BELOW Rolex Oyster Ref. 6036 Dato-Compax, c. 1950.
An 18 ct pink gold triple-calendar chronograph wristwatch with subsidiary dials for constant seconds, 30-minute and 12-hour registers (cal. 72C)
Diameter 36 mm

OVERLEAF, LEFT Patek Philippe Ref. 2497, made in 1952.
An 18 ct yellow gold perpetual calendar wristwatch with centre seconds and moon phases (cal. 27SC Q)
Diameter 37 mm

OVERLEAF, RIGHT Patek Philippe Ref. 2499, made in 1951.
An 18 ct pink gold perpetual calendar chronograph wristwatch with moon phases and subsidiary dials for date, constant seconds and 30-minute register, outer tachymeter scale (cal. 13''' CH Q)
Diameter 37 mm

With the increasing popularity of calendar watches, the year 1950 saw Rolex release a new Oyster model that displayed the day, date, month and moon phases. Registered under reference number 6062, this watch had a chronometer-rated movement and was one of the first automatically wound triple-calendar wristwatches. The dial had a clear display with apertures for day and month beneath the twelve o'clock position, while the date was shown to the edge of the dial and indicated via an additional central hand. Above the six o'clock position, a subsidiary seconds dial was combined with an aperture for moon phases. Some early examples of the model were fitted with star-shaped hour indexes. This model was one of the few to be fitted with Rolex's new Super Oyster crown. Unlike the standard Oyster crown, the Super Oyster did not screw down to the case and instead operated like a standard crown, using three gaskets to maintain water-resistance. However, the Super Oyster crown itself was not a success, and its production ceased within five years.

Rolex also contiuned to market a chronograph with triple calendar, the so-called Dato-Compax, which had first been introduced towards the end of the 1940s. The image below illustrates an example of the model that was made in around 1950. The dial has a silvered, two-tone finish, the date showing within the secondary tone at the dial's edge and indicated via a central date indicator hand; apertures for the day and month appear beneath twelve o'clock. There are three subsidiary dials, two of which are dedicated to the chronograph, one recording minutes elapsed and the other hours, while the third sub-dial is calibrated for constant/subsidiary seconds.

Towards the end of 1950, Patek Philippe were assembling the first example of a new perpetual calendar wristwatch. Given the reference number 2497, the model was released the following year. With a 37 mm diameter case that had a broad, scooped bezel and stepped lugs, this was a considerably bigger and bolder watch than its predecessor of the 1940s, the Ref. 1526 (see p. 120). One of the most

significant features of this new model was the incorporation of a centre seconds hand. The use of a centre seconds hand required the case to be deeper, including a raising of the bezel to ensure clearance between crystal and hands; however, the larger case perfectly absorbed the model's new proportions. Early versions of the Ref. 2497, such as that shown on page 174, were still heavily influenced by the designs of the 1940s, with combination Arabic and dot numerals and *feuille* (leaf-shaped) hands. By the mid-1950s, the model was also available with dauphine hands and faceted baton indexes, together with a sister model, the Ref. 2438, which was released with a waterproof version of the 2497's case. In 1950 Patek Philippe also began production of a new perpetual calendar chronograph wristwatch, the Ref. 2499 (see p. 175). Similarly styled to the 2497, the supplementary chronograph function saw the addition of subsidiary dials for constant seconds and minute recording. This would become one of the defining models of the twentieth century – indeed,

although the design underwent modifications through the years, the basic layout of its dial and shape of its case remained little changed until 1985, when production of the model ceased. Even then, its replacement would share many of the characteristics of its predecessor.

Halfway through the decade, in 1955, Audemars Piguet manufactured the first perpetual calendar wristwatch to display the full leap year cycle on its dial. Added to its Ref. 5516 model, this was a feature that had previously appeared only on pocket watch dials. However, the smaller size of the wristwatch meant that a display of this type would make the individual months extremely difficult to read. Nevertheless, the practicality of showing the leap year cycle had an obvious advantage: for the owner of a watch without such a display, there was no way to be sure that their watch was set up and running in the correct cycle until 29 February in a leap year was reached – and imagine the disappointment if on that date your watch failed to advance correctly because it was set to the wrong year. In order to circumvent the conundrum of how to

BELOW Vacheron Constantin Ref. 4764, c. 1953.
An 18 ct yellow gold cushion-form triple-calendar wristwatch with moon phases (cal. 12½‴)
Length 43 mm, width 34.5 mm

display leap years and months clearly on the diminutive wristwatch dial, Audemars Piguet used two separate month displays – a standard twelve-month display was shown in its own subsidiary dial at three o'clock, while a further dial was shown at six o'clock. This additional subsidiary dial was sectioned and clearly marked for the four years of the leap year cycle, with smaller divisions for each of its 48 months. The dial, which was made in gold with a silver-plated finish, was brilliantly designed: the main body had a silk-matt surface, while all the calendar indications were displayed within rings of a higher-sheen, circular satin finish. The date was calibrated to the edge of the dial, and the days of the week were held in their own subsidiary dial. The day, date, month and leap years were all indicated via blued steel hands, which contrasted with the yellow gold hands for the hours, minutes and seconds – the latter being displayed in combination with the leap year cycle at the base of the dial. Finally, the ages and phases of the moon were shown via a gold and blue enamel disc in an aperture at twelve

LEFT Audemars Piguet Ref. 5516, made in 1955.
An 18 ct yellow gold perpetual calendar wristwatch with leap year display and moon phases (cal. 13VZSSQP)
Diameter 36 mm

o'clock. Only three examples of this model were made by Audemars Piguet in 1955, with a further six leap-year display perpetual calendar wristwatches going into production in 1957.[2] Despite the advantages of showing the full cycle, the practice of displaying the leap year on the dial of perpetual calendar wristwatches would not become common until the 1980s.

The decade also saw the introduction of increasing numbers of date-only calendar watches. In 1950 Movado launched their Calendoplan model, a watch that displayed the date within an aperture to the dial. Especially significant was the fact that this watch had a date corrector button placed at the side of the case below the crown. Although corrector buttons were commonly used for triple-calendar watches, they were extremely unusual in date-only watches; most models relied on the user to manually advance the hands through 24 hours until the correct date was reached. In 1952 Omega launched their Seamaster Calendar wristwatch, Ref. 2627. This was Omega's first model to display the date within an aperture (rather than via a date ring with a separate hand for indication). The date aperture was placed at the six o'clock position, and the model was automatically wound via Omega's

bumper-automatic calibre 353 movement. The Ref. 2627 had a bold case with relatively long lugs that were gently flared and had chamfers to their upper outer edges. Measuring 35 mm in diameter, the case had rounded sides and a screw-down back. Depth-rated to 30 metres, this was a practical everyday wristwatch that was described in Omega's contemporary marketing materials as being designed 'for the man of action'.

In 1956 Rolex made a move towards a new type of calendar wristwatch, releasing a model that fell between the triple calendars and date-only models. This new model would become one of the watchmaker's most emblematic models and was named the Day-Date. A bold and self-assertive model with its heavy gold bracelet, the Day-Date brazenly and unashamedly spoke of its owner's success. With an aperture for date at two o'clock, the distinguishing feature of the Day-Date was its long, arched aperture, which stood proudly at the twelve o'clock position displaying the days of the week in full. Rolex described the watch in their marketing materials as 'the crowning achievement of Rolex'.

ABOVE, LEFT Movado Calendoplan, hallmarked 1953.
A 9 ct yellow gold manually wound wristwatch, the date aperture with dedicated pusher for quick adjustment (cal. 120)
Diameter 33.5 mm

ABOVE, RIGHT Omega Seamaster Calendar Ref. 2627, c. 1952.
A stainless steel automatic centre seconds wristwatch with date aperture (cal. 353)
Diameter 35 mm

OPPOSITE, TOP Rolex Oyster Perpetual Day-Date Ref. 6611, c. 1958.
An 18 ct yellow gold automatic centre seconds wristwatch with day and date indication (cal. 1055)
Diameter 36 mm

OPPOSITE, BOTTOM Detail from a Rolex catalogue showing an early Day-Date

ALARM WATCHES

The history of the alarm watch stretches back to the sixteenth century, but it was not until the middle of the twentieth century that successful commercial production was achieved within the confined space of the wristwatch case. At the end of the 1940s the Swiss firm Vulcain introduced their Cricket wristwatch, a model with two separate barrels, one for winding the mainspring of the watch's going train, the other to power the alarm function. While the technology itself was not new, what Vulcain achieved was the production of a standard-sized movement calibre that was able to emit a sound loud enough to alert its owner. The watch had a cover over the movement that acted as a form of bell, against which a 'hammer' within the movement would vibrate when the alarm was activated. This produced a chirping, cricket-like sound, from which the model earned its name. A further cover was placed over the 'bell' for added protection, and this was pierced in order to allow the sound to escape more easily. Ingeniously, the springs for the going and alarm trains were both wound using the single crown at three o'clock; turning the crown in one direction wound the going train (for time), while in the other direction, the alarm's spring barrel was charged. The pusher above the crown acted as a 'switch' to engage the alarm setting mechanism and could also be depressed to silence the alarm when it sounded.

TOP Jaeger-LeCoultre Memovox,
c. 1951.
An 18 ct gold centre seconds wristwatch with alarm (cal. P489/1)
Diameter 34.5 mm

RIGHT LeCoultre Memovox Parking,
c. 1958.
A gold-capped and steel centre seconds wristwatch with parking meter alarm (cal. 814)
Diameter 34 mm

Early alarm wristwatches appear to have been largely aimed at the businessperson, to act as a reminder for a meeting or other event; however, many such watches were remarkably loud – and often more so when placed flat on a table, thus ensuring they were suitable as a morning alarm. Jaeger-LeCoultre, who would become the leading maker of alarm watches, named their first alarm model, launched in 1950, the Memovox – literally, the 'Voice of Memory'. Initially a manually wound model, LeCoultre released several further versions during the decade. These included their first automatic alarm watch in 1956, and in 1958, to celebrate the firm's 125th anniversary, a Memovox World Time and Memovox Parking model were added to the collection; the latter ensured you did not forget the expiration of your parking meter payment. The Memovox was fitted with two crowns: the lower wound and set the time, while the upper crown charged the alarm barrel and turned a central disc; the disc had a triangular pointer which the user aligned to the time they desired the alarm to sound.

In 1955 Movado launched their Ermetophon, an alarm version of their sliding-cover purse watch. Like LeCoultre's Memovox, the Ermetophon had two crowns, one for the going train and a second for the alarm. Like earlier versions of the Ermeto, this model was case-wound, and the action of opening and closing the covers wound, in tandem, both the going train and alarm barrels. Each opening and closing of the case was designed to provide three and a half hours of running time, meaning the user was only required to open their watch seven times a day to power it for 24 hours. The Ermetophon had a stand integrated into the case back which, when the covers were opened, could be hinged outwards to stand the purse watch on a bedside table. With the dials invariably bearing luminescent accents to the numerals and hands, the Ermetophon acted as the perfect travelling alarm clock.

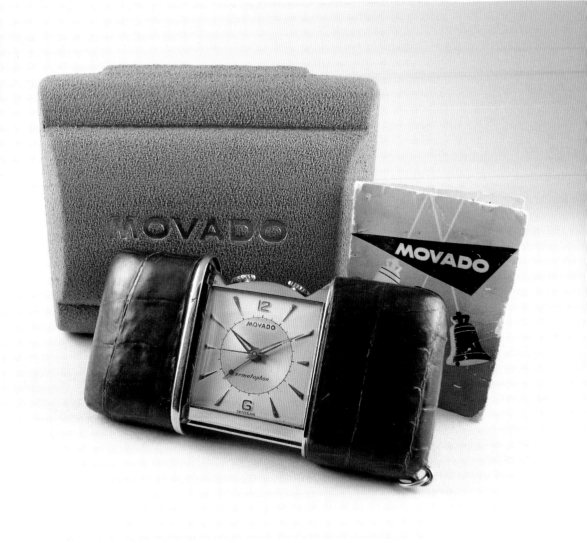

ANTI-MAGNETIC WATCHES

The effects of magnetism on the movement of a watch had long been understood. Steel parts within a movement can become magnetised and thus greatly impact a watch's timekeeping. A magnetised balance spring, for example, may see the coils of the spring 'stick' together, leading to a much faster balance swing, which of course results in highly inaccurate timekeeping. Part of the solution to avoiding such effects was in manufacturing the watch's parts, where possible, from metal alloys that were less susceptible to, or even resistant to, magnetism. The introduction of components such as the Nivarox balance spring during the 1930s had already reduced, but not eliminated, the susceptibility of a watch to the effects of magnetism. During the Second World War, air forces had required protection for the watches of their pilots and navigators – flight instruments could be highly magnetic and consequently injurious to the performance of airborne watches. One particularly successful solution involved the construction of a 'cage' of soft iron, which took the form of an inner casing that surrounded the watch movement, absorbing any magnetism the watch might encounter. These cages had been used in some military-issue watches by the International Watch Company (IWC) and others during the war. In 1948 IWC began supplying the British military with a new model that would become commonly known as the Mark XI; as well as incorporating the soft iron anti-magnetic cage, this model had a crystal that was specially secured to prevent the risk of detachment during sudden drops in pressure. The benefit of these developments was by no means restricted to the military, and demand for highly anti-magnetic watches for a range of civilian uses was growing by the middle of the twentieth century.

BELOW International Watch Co. Mark XI,
c. 1951.
A stainless steel manually wound anti-magnetic centre seconds wristwatch made for the British military (cal. 89)
Diameter 36 mm

Accurate timekeepers had long been essential tools for engineers and scientists, and the requirement of a wristwatch that could be used in laboratories, where exposure to strong magnetic fields was often unavoidable, had become increasingly important by the 1950s. The International Watch Company was one of the first firms to introduce a civilian version of their anti-magnetic wristwatch. This new watch, launched in 1955 and named the Ingenieur, was designed to withstand magnetism of 1,000 gauss (gauss being a measurement for magnetic induction). Although originally created for engineers, technicians, chemists, pilots and doctors, the watch had a number of other features that ensured its appeal to a much wider public. The first version of this watch contained IWC's calibre 85 movement, which incorporated a highly efficient bi-directional rotor that automatically wound the movement in both directions of travel. This system had been developed by Albert Pellaton, the head of IWC's engineering division. Also significant was the fact that the watch was designed to be water resistant up to 10 atmospheres (100 metres). The Ingenieur was a classic example of 1950s watch styling, having a robust stainless steel case with thick lugs and a clean, chamfered bezel. The dial was invariably silvered and calibrated with applied, pointed, faceted baton indexes and matching dauphine hands, and a 'flash' symbol travelled through the Ingenieur model name to the lower half of the dial.

Soon after the Ingenieur's introduction, Rolex released their own specialist anti-magnetic watch, the Milgauss. Like the Ingenieur, the Milgauss used a soft iron cage to surround the movement and protect the watch from magnetism. The model was also guaranteed to resist magnetic fields up to 1,000 gauss, and this claim was confirmed by scientists at the CERN laboratory in

OPPOSITE Rolex Oyster Perpetual
Milgauss Ref. 6541, c. 1958.
A stainless steel automatic anti-magnetic
centre seconds wristwatch with rotating
bezel calibrated for minutes (cal. 1066M)
Diameter 37 mm

BELOW, LEFT Omega Railmaster Ref.
2914, c. 1957.
A stainless steel manually wound
anti-magnetic centre seconds wristwatch
(cal. 284)
Diameter 38 mm

BELOW, RIGHT Jaeger-LeCoultre
Chronomètre Geophysic Ref. E168,
made in 1958.
A stainless steel manually wound
anti-magnetic centre seconds wristwatch
(cal. P478/BWSbr)
Diameter 35 mm

Switzerland, where the Milgauss was later tested.
Rolex used their Oyster case for the Milgauss to ensure
water-resistance, and the first versions of the model
were automatically wound via a modified version of the
watchmaker's calibre 1065, which was marked 1065M
(this was later replaced by the 1066M). The watch was
fitted with a rotating bezel that was divided into 60 minutes,
allowing it to be used to measure time elapsed. A few
design changes were made to the model during the first
years of production; however, the black 'webbed' dial
and 'lightning bolt' centre seconds hand of the mid-
to late 1950s is the most instantly recognisable version
of the model.

In 1957 Omega launched their own specifically
anti-magnetic wristwatch, the Railmaster. Designed to
more of a military theme than the Ingenieur or Milgauss,
the Railmaster was a manually wound watch that, like
Rolex's and IWC's models, used a soft iron 'cage' for
the movement. The dial was matt black with luminescent
triangles at the hours and Arabic numbers at the quarters,
and early versions of the model also had distinctive
luminescent hands, with a broad arrow tip to the hour
hand. The stainless steel case was robust and again
reminiscent of military wristwatches, with a substantial
screw-down case back, broad lugs, and a thick bezel
that was faceted with a chamfered side and flat top.

Jaeger-LeCoultre marked their 125th anniversary in
1958 with the release of a new watch named the Geophysic.
Manufactured for only one year, the launch of the model
was also timed to coincide with the International
Geophysical Year (IGY), which ran from July 1957
until December 1958. The IGY involved the participation
of 67 countries in the mutual pursuit of advances in
a variety of scientific endeavours. The anti-magnetic
Geophysic wristwatch had a movement surrounded
by a Faraday cage that was resistant to magnetic fields
up to 600 gauss. In design, the watch had a precision-
graduated dial, the outer track with elongated batons
to mark the seconds and minutes.

AUTOMATIC WATCHES

Patek Philippe introduced their first automatic wristwatch in 1953. Although relatively late to the market with this technology, by choosing to focus purely on manually wound watches in the previous decades, the firm had arguably managed to avoid the negativity that surrounded some of the early entrants to this field. The watch chosen to receive the new automatic movement was the model reference 2526. Often viewed as one of the first 'modern' Patek Philippe models, this watch had a bold case with thick, downturned lugs and a substantial screw-down case back. Made solely in gold or platinum, this watch was a clear symbol of the owner's status, the more so when paired with one of the fine, precious metal bracelets that were available as an option with the model. The automatic movement (calibre 12-600 AT) utilised a solid 18 ct gold rotor, the weight of which ensured smooth and efficient winding. These rotors were beautifully finished with engine-turned decoration – all the more remarkable when one considers that, in the days before display case backs, the owner would never have the pleasure to see it.

Jaeger-LeCoultre continued with the use of a power reserve indication for some of their automatic models to ensure a wearer could easily see how much wind remained in the watch's movement. In the early 1950s LeCoultre introduced a new model which they named the Futurematic. Especially unusual was the fact that this model entirely dispensed with a manual winding function. This was a bold move, for part of the criticism of early automatic watch models of the 1920s and '30s was the inability for most to be manually 'topped up' with power if required. LeCoultre were so confident in their new model that they deemed the manual function surplus to requirement, and certainly the addition of a power reserve function to the watch's dial must have done much to allay users' concerns that the watch might stop without warning. By placing a crown to the case back of the model that merely served to adjust the hands, the circular shape of the watch was interrupted only by the lugs that held the watch strap in place.

TOP Patek Philippe Ref. 2526, made in 1953.
An 18 ct pink gold automatic wristwatch with enamel dial and gold bracelet (cal. 12‴600 AT)
Diameter 35 mm

RIGHT Patek Philippe calibre 12–600 AT, introduced in 1953.
Automatic calibre with lever escapement, 30 jewels, Gyromax balance, precision regulation and 18 ct gold rotor

Although the majority of automatic wristwatch models during this period were circular in shape, square and cushion-form watches were also available. Vacheron Constantin, for example, produced a relatively large square model known to collectors as the 'Cioccolatone'. This model had curvaceous, stepped case sides and was fitted with a rotor automatic movement.

In the battle to reduce the depth of the automatic watch's case, the bumper automatic movement was still in widespread use during the 1950s. However, the use of rotors became increasingly prevalent as the decade advanced. In 1954, another important development for the automatic watch occurred with Buren's patent for a movement (cal. 1000 series) that incorporated a micro-rotor. Released commercially in 1957, this invention allowed the rotor, the automatic drive and the movement train to be placed on the same plane as each other, rather than stacking the components. Almost simultaneously with Buren's introduction, Universal released their own micro-rotor (cal. 215), leading to a legal battle between the two firms. While the incorporation of the micro-rotor within these two calibres enabled the two watchmakers to reduce the depth of their movements (the slimmest being Universal's, with a height of 4.1 mm), it was another firm that more fully realised the potential of this system. In 1959 Piaget took the watch world completely by surprise, launching a new super-slim calibre, the 12P. Using a 24 ct gold micro-rotor, the weight of which ensured efficient winding, the movement had a depth of just 2.33 mm, almost 2 mm thinner than the slimmest of the Buren and Universal calibres. This was a dramatic development that would pave the way to the extra-slim automatic watches of the following decade and place Piaget at the forefront of the dress-style wristwatch market.

DECORATIVE ENAMEL DIALS

During the 1950s, specialist Swiss manufacturers such as Stern Frères and Huguenin & Cie produced a dazzling array of enamel dials for a range of different watchmakers. These dials ranged from plain, translucent enamels in single colours to detailed scenes with multiple colours using the cloisonné technique. Rolex were among those to offer enamel dial options for some of their models; the image below illustrates an example from the early 1950s. The dial of this watch has an amber-coloured translucent enamel finish that covers almost the entire dial surface, leaving a silvered, 'pearled' minute track to the edge. The gold, multifaceted hour indexes are applied to the surface, as is the print for the Rolex signature and model text.

Cloisonné enamel dials had been produced in very small numbers during the 1940s, yet their heyday was undoubtedly the 1950s. Although never produced in great quantity, this dial genre was available in a range of subject matters, the most popular of which depicted sailing ships, stylised floral motifs, animals and maps – the last occasionally used, appropriately enough, by Patek Philippe to enhance the dials of their world time watches. The manufacturing of these dials involved complex procedures. The surface of the dial, usually gold, silver or copper, would first be prepared; this included counter-enamelling the surface to ensure a base layer of enamel was applied to both sides, thereby preventing the metal from distorting and damaging the enamel decoration during firing. Wire, often in gold, was then fixed to the dial to create the desired pattern, and the furrows these created were filled with powdered enamels before being fired in a specialist kiln. Several applications and firings would be made. The production of a rich and tonally varied design relied as much on the artist's ability to successfully mix different enamels as it did on their knowledge of how the colours would change during firing.

BELOW Rolex Oyster Perpetual Ref. 6101/6085, c. 1951.
An 18 ct yellow gold automatic centre seconds wristwatch with amber-coloured translucent enamel dial (cal. 9¾''')
Diameter 33 mm

OPPOSITE, LEFT Vacheron Constantin, made in 1950.
An 18 ct yellow gold centre seconds wristwatch with cloisonné enamel dial made by Stern Frères depicting a sailing ship (cal. 9'''–466/2B)
Diameter 31.5 mm

OPPOSITE, RIGHT Patek Philippe Ref. 2494, made in 1954.
An 18 ct pink gold wristwatch with cloisonné enamel dial made by Stern Frères depicting stylised flowers (cal. 12'''400)
Diameter 33 mm

Corbeille
10/179
10/192
10/183
10/16
10/20 — Feuillage — fond violet —
Motif abstrait — sur fond beige
St. Georges & le Dragon
Bateau 3 mâts
Oie sur fond violet
10/22
10/17
10/14
10/18
Poisson sur fond rouge
10/196
10/185
10/182
10/187
10/195
10/186
10/188
10/198
Fond vert avec étoi
Email blanc avec p
Croix sur fond bl
10/189

LEFT Huguenin Frères & Cie, dated 1956.
A group of dials with examples of
translucent enamels, cloisonné enamels
and polychrome enamel-painted scenes.
Diameter of dials 16.5 mm–43 mm

A further form of enamel dial (although more rarely
seen during this period) consisted of miniature scenes
painted in polychrome enamel. In this process, the dial
plate was first coated with a layer of enamel in a single
colour. Coloured enamels were then mixed with an oil
binder and painted onto the surface. Several firings
in the kiln followed, often after the application of each
individual colour. This again required a detailed knowledge
of the properties of each enamel to ensure the most
resilient enamels were applied first.

PIAGET

présente

en première mondiale

LA SEULE MONTRE
AUTOMATIQUE
ULTRA-PLATE

Epaisseur du mouvement :

2,3 mm

Cette réalisation technique

quasi incroyable est l'œuvre

du spécialiste des montres

les plus minces du monde.

CHEZ LES PLUS GRANDS JOAILLIERS DU MONDE

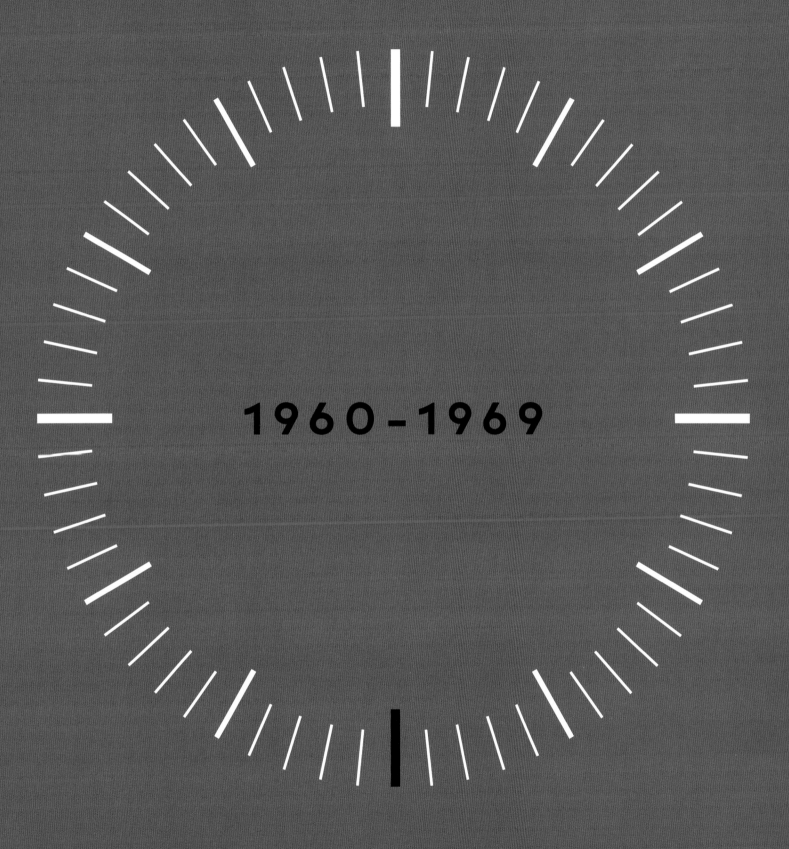

1960-1969

THE 1960s

Although the classic watch styles established in the preceding two decades would continue to be found throughout the 1960s, there was an increasing focus on clean, pared-down designs in which the emphasis was on utility and clarity of display. However, the 1960s was also a period of significant cultural and social change, the influence of which the watch world was by no means immune to. While traditionally styled watches continued to be widely available, the rejection by some designers of established forms led to some radical reinterpretations of watch designs. This resulted in the appearance of a diverse range of asymmetrical and abstracted case designs where much was also made of variation in surface texture.

Slim watches were especially well matched to the simplified designs of the 1960s. Extra-slim manually wound watches were readily available from a variety of manufacturers; however, the growing popularity and demand for automatic watches led to the development of ever thinner automatic movement calibres, allowing watch manufacturers the opportunity to broaden their

offerings within this genre. The introduction of the micro-rotor during the second half of the 1950s had already led to the production of some slimmer automatic models, but it was Piaget's introduction of a super-slim automatic movement, the calibre 12P in 1959, that would prove especially significant to the development of the dress-style wristwatch during the 1960s. With a height of just 2.3 mm, Piaget's movement incorporated a micro-rotor made from 24 ct gold, the weight of which ensured efficient winding of the watch, despite the fact that the rotor was necessarily both small and slim. A remarkable movement, its development, together with the company's super-slim manually wound calibres, transformed Piaget's production. Armed with these movements, Piaget's designers successfully captured the mood of the period, releasing a range of stylish models that would help the company dominate the dress watch market for the next two decades.

Variations of the silvered dial increased greatly as the decade progressed. With the rising popularity of satin

BELOW Piaget ultra-thin 12′′′ calibre 12P. Automatic movement, the 24 ct gold micro-rotor visible to the lower right Diameter 27 mm, height 2.3 mm

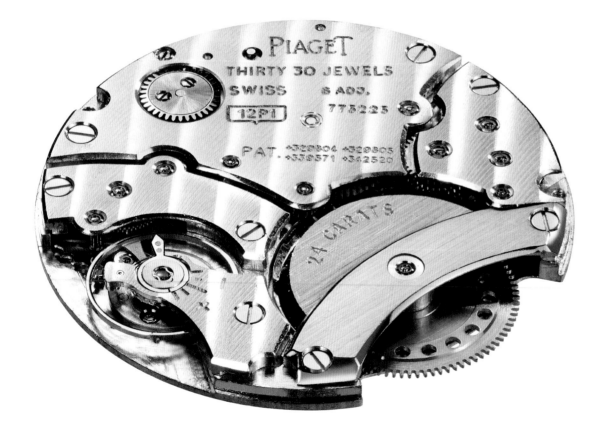

RIGHT Audemars Piguet Ref. 5129, sold
in 1961.
A platinum and diamond-set wristwatch
with concealed lugs (cal. 2001)
Diameter 35 mm

BELOW Piaget, c. 1960.
An 18 ct yellow gold ultra-thin automatic
wristwatch (cal. 12P)
Diameter 34 mm

sunburst finishes, a whole variety of other styles emerged, including dials with vertical, diagonal or multi-directional grained surfaces. Straight, baton-shaped hour and minute hands began to dominate as the shaped styles of earlier decades began to fade from view. The use of minute tracks was deemed less essential, and many models appeared without such calibrations to their dials. Omega's Seamaster models became noticeably slimmer, and a new De Ville line was launched to concentrate on the dress watch side of the market. Meanwhile, Longines released their new Flagship line. Largely classically styled, the Flagships were also decidedly less chunky than the watchmaker's Conquest models of the previous decade.

Rolex made a number of updates to their models during the 1960s. Now with a signature line of established models, many Rolex designs, such as the Submariner, GMT, Datejust and Day-Date, received relatively subtle stylistic updates, ensuring they retained their essential DNA. Adjustments were more obvious to the Milgauss and Turn-O-Graph models – in the 1950s,

these had been similarly styled to the Submariner, and so, with the experimental period over, both were given a new identity. The Turn-O-Graph retained its signature rotating bezel but was transformed into a dress-style model that was marketed under Rolex's Datejust range. Meanwhile, the Milgauss was given a dramatically different look, with a simplified and more utilitarian design; the watch had an outer track calibrated to fifths of a second, implying heightened precision. The design was focused on extreme clarity, a look ideally suited to the scientific community to whom the watch was most closely associated and marketed.

In keeping with the period's move towards clean design, Patek Philippe's Travel Time (Ref. 2597), patented in 1959, offered an alternative solution to the world time or two-time-zone wristwatch. With a classic and clear dial layout, the complexities of the world time calibrations were entirely removed. To the left case side of the watch, two recessed pushers allowed the hour hand to be advanced or retarded quickly and easily, jumping

BELOW, LEFT Omega Seamaster De Ville Ref. 165.020, c. 1966.
A stainless steel automatic centre seconds wristwatch with bracelet (cal. 552)
Diameter 34.5 mm

BELOW, RIGHT Longines Flagship Ref. 3104-1, sold in 1962.
A stainless steel automatic centre seconds wristwatch (cal. 340)
Diameter 35 mm

LEFT Rolex Oyster Perpetual Datejust
Turn-O-Graph Ref. 1625, introduced
in the early 1960s, this example c. 1967.
A stainless steel automatic centre
seconds wristwatch with date and
bracelet (cal. 1570)
Diameter 36 mm

BELOW Rolex Oyster Perpetual Milgauss
Ref. 1019, introduced in the early 1960s,
this example c. 1968.
A stainless steel automatic, anti-
magnetic centre seconds wristwatch
with bracelet (cal. 1580)
Diameter 37 mm

in hour increments. By not requiring the crown to be pulled out and the hands manually adjusted for time zone change, this system also did not interfere with the watch's timekeeping. When the hands of a mechanical watch are adjusted, a few seconds of timekeeping can be gained or lost, and Patek Philippe used this fact as part of the model's marketing appeal. Soon after production began, the firm introduced a secondary hour hand to the model. This meant that two time zones could be shown simultaneously, allowing the user to display both home time and local time; when the user was not travelling, the two hour hands could be overlapped to create a standard display. Chronographs and calendar watches also followed the move towards simplified displays, with the use of day and/or date apertures increasingly favoured over the earlier triple-calendar formats.

Towards the end of the decade, one of the most defining models of the second half of the twentieth century was introduced. Known as the Golden Ellipse and launched by Patek Philippe in 1968, the model's

design was based on the golden section, an ancient mathematical ratio that was used by some to determine the 'perfect' proportions for a building or object. The elegant, simple form of the model's elliptically shaped case, combined with a striking blue, satin-finished dial that was devoid of calibrations – save for the slim, straight baton indexes and hands – seemed to encapsulate the very design ethos of the 1960s.

The rise of the electronic watch could no longer be ignored, and the release in the US of the Bulova Accutron model in 1960 must have sounded the alarm at many watch manufacturers. Unlike earlier battery-powered watches that had sought to electrify the mechanical watch movement, the Accutron almost entirely dispensed with the traditional watchmaker's art. Indeed, the model was advertised so as to encourage the public to wear an 'Accutron' rather than a 'watch', making clear the company's belief that they had invented an entirely new time-telling medium. This threat from the electronic watch caused a scramble among the traditional Swiss

BELOW Patek Philippe Ref. 2597, made in 1960.
An 18 ct yellow gold dual time zone wristwatch (cal. 12‴400 HS)
Diameter 35 mm

BELOW, LEFT Patek Philippe Ellipse
Ref. 3548-1, introduced in 1968.
An 18 ct yellow gold elliptically shaped
wristwatch with integrated 18 ct gold
bracelet (cal. 23-300)
Length 32 mm, width 27 mm

BELOW, RIGHT Seiko Astron made
in 1969.
A gold quartz centre seconds
wristwatch (cal. 35A)
Width 41 mm

watch manufacturers to produce a quartz rival, and in 1962 a consortium of Swiss watchmakers set up the Centre Electronique Horloger (CEH) in Neuchâtel. Pooling their resources, the group – which included, among others, Ebauches SA, IWC, Omega, Piaget, Rolex and Patek Philippe – set out to build a quartz calibre that could be put into series production. By 1966 the first prototype, known as the Beta 1, was ready, and in 1967 a second, the Beta 2, had been completed. Examples of these calibres were tested at the Neuchâtel Observatory, where they won first prize and far exceeded the accuracy of the best mechanical chronometers, with an average daily variation of just 0.0003 seconds during the test period. In 1969 a calibre suitable for series production was created; named the Beta 21, it would be released at the Basel Watch Fair of 1970. The Swiss-made Beta 21 was a big and bulky movement – a far cry from the increasingly slim mechanical movements of the period – and the calibre's size was to have a dramatic impact on case designs of the early 1970s. Meanwhile, on

25 December 1969 the Japanese watchmaker Seiko had successfully released the first commercially available quartz wristwatch, the Astron. The 1960s had seen the export of watches from the US and Japan grow dramatically, and this trend would continue throughout the 1970s and would be formed increasingly of electronic watches. The dawn had arrived of what would become known as the Quartz Crisis, a period that would threaten the very survival of the mechanical watch industry.

ASYMMETRICS

During the late 1950s and into the 1960s, there was
a reaction among some designers against the classical
watch shapes that had been established during the previous
two decades. One of the most influential figures in this
area was a young jewellery designer named Gilbert
Albert. In 1955, at the age of 24, Albert was spotted
by Henri Stern, the president of Patek Philippe. Albert
designed a range of asymmetrically shaped watches that
began to appear at the very end of the 1950s, before being
more widely available throughout much of the 1960s.
These watches would defy convention, and through them
Albert offered a fresh approach to watch design, one that
was inspired by his love of modern sculpture, especially
works by Constantin Brancusi and Piet Mondrian.
The asymmetric watches that Albert produced included
both pocket and wrist versions. The dials of the watches
were kept simple, usually with slim baton indexes,
often crossing the dials in a spider's web design.

TOP Patek Philippe Ref. 3270, designed
by Gilbert Albert, retailed by Serpico
y Laino, Caracas, made in 1962.
A ladies' 18 ct yellow gold asymmetrical
wristwatch (cal. 13.5-320)
Length 20 mm

RIGHT Patek Philippe Ref. 3424,
designed by Gilbert Albert, made in 1961.
An 18 ct yellow gold asymmetrical
wristwatch (cal. 8‴85)
Length 37 mm

OPPOSITE Patek Philippe Ricochet Ref.
788/1, designed by Gilbert Albert, made
in 1964.
An 18 ct yellow gold asymmetrical pocket
watch (cal. 23-300)
Length 44 mm

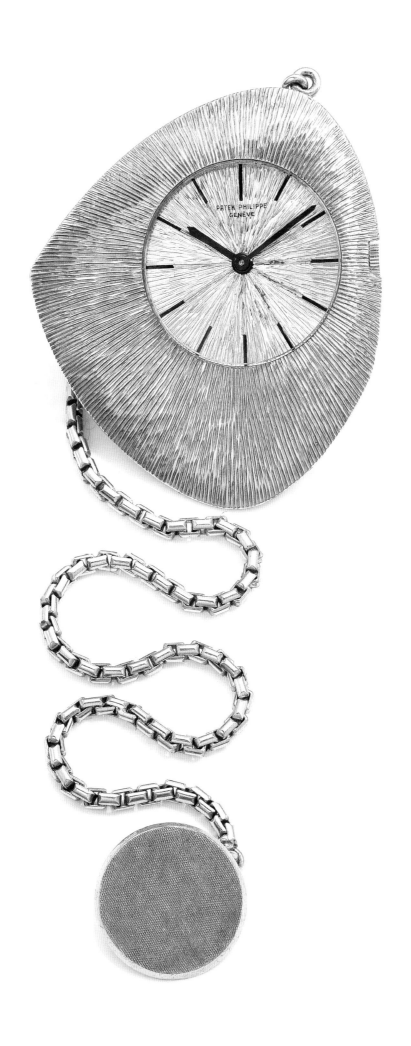

Although unusually shaped, the clean lines of the asymmetric forms that Albert created fitted perfectly with the 1960s aesthetic for clear, uncluttered design. In 1962 this aesthetic was taken a step further by Rolex with the introduction of a new model named the Midas. Also asymmetrically shaped, this model was designed by another jewellery designer, Gérald Genta, as a homage to the mythological figure of King Midas. Genta's inspiration came from the architecture of ancient Greece and, specifically, the temple of the Parthenon. Genta took the sharp lines of a square form, adding a peak to the left side, where the winder was partly concealed from view. An integrated bracelet was fitted to match the asymmetry of the watch's case – the bracelet had a straight side to the right and tapering side to the left, the left side following the line to the case's peak. The dial was almost entirely plain, with no numerals or calibrations.

Released in 1967, the Cartier Crash wristwatch went further into abstraction with an asymmetric case of surrealist appearance. Popular legend dictates that the model was influenced by a badly distorted Cartier wristwatch that had been damaged during an accident and which had been taken to Cartier in London for repair. Although the firm had played with asymmetry remarkably early in their production of wristwatches, notably with their parallelogram Tank Asymétrique of the 1930s, the Crash took design abstraction to a whole new level with its bold and daring look. An inspired and highly unusual wristwatch, its popularity among collectors led to its rerelease several times during the succeeding decades.

It is interesting that, despite the highly accurate and refined movements incorporated in all these watches, the ability to use them to tell the exact time was seemingly of secondary importance. With a lack of calibrations for minutes and in some instances without hour indexes, the precise reading of time was by no means easy. Design had been given the ultimate precedence, for, with these watches, function was forced to follow form.

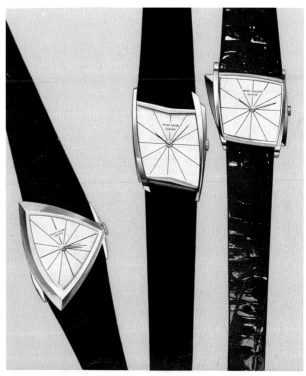

From left to right : Ref. 3412 (cal. 23-300), 3424 and 3422 - 18 K yellow gold.

Once again, at the Geneva Observatory,
THE MOST ACCURATE WRIST WATCH
is
A PATEK PHILIPPE

Printed in Switzerland   PERP 150

LADIES' WATCHES

OPPOSITE Piaget Ref. 9826 A6, sold in 1966.
A ladies' white gold and diamond-set oval bracelet watch (cal. 9P)
Width 24 mm

BELOW Bulgari Serpenti, c. 1965.
A ladies' gold, enamel and diamond-set snake-form bracelet watch, the dial concealed beneath the serpent's hinged head, with movement by Piaget
Width of serpent's head approx. 16 mm

Piaget were extremely influential in the development of a new style of watch for women. With the ultra-thin, manually wound and automatic calibres that the firm had developed in the late 1950s, Piaget set about introducing elegant, slim watches for women that were no longer constrained by the traditional, diminutive size of the cocktail watch. This new style sat well with the growing trend in the 1960s for simplified designs and saw dials often calibrated with straight hour indexes and matching baton hands. The cases could be embellished by bezels set with diamonds or other precious stones, all the while with an emphasis on slim refinement. Integrated mesh, woven and fine-link watch bracelets, often with textured surfaces, were becoming increasingly fashionable during the 1960s, and these bracelets were ideally suited to Piaget's new style of dress watch. Such bracelets could be seamlessly soldered to the watch's case. Usually of one fixed size, without the possibility to adjust their length, the bracelets could be uniquely tailored for the purchaser, lending them a feeling of the bespoke. The dress watch

with integrated textured bracelet would remain a popular offering for the next 30 years.

Despite the growing trend for simplified watch designs, the 1960s also witnessed the development of a number of highly unusual and innovative models for women that challenged the role of the watch as primarily an object of utility. As in previous decades, the concealed dial wristwatch remained a popular design concept, especially for the most elaborately decorated ladies' wristwatches. During the 1960s Bulgari developed their Tubogas flexible bracelets into a range of snake-form watches. These extraordinary creations were produced with a variety of decorative schemes. The watch itself was concealed within the serpent's head, the top of which would hinge open to reveal the time dial. While the tip of the tail was invariably styled to match the head, the flexible sprung bracelet would often be left undecorated, the design naturally imitating stylised scales. However, in their most elaborate form, the entire length of the bracelet was decorated with coloured enamelled scales.

Several other manufacturers produced remarkable bracelet watches with concealed dials, the most imposing of which were often unique and occasionally made for exhibition purposes. Gilbert Albert, the Swiss jewellery designer, produced some extraordinary bracelet watches, winning the prestigious 'Oscar' prize at the Diamonds International Awards ten times, twice for Omega, three times for Patek Philippe and five times under his own name. His creative talent led to a daring reinterpretation of the watch's form and to the production of many avant-garde designs. The image at opposite top illustrates an 18 ct gold bracelet watch Albert made for Omega in about 1966. The bracelet has a bow-like shape and the undulating surface has the appearance of conjoined gold nuggets.

In 1969 Omega commissioned the British jeweller Andrew Grima to produce a collection of watches for a special exhibition titled, appropriately enough, *About Time*. Incorporating a range of daring, modernist designs, the models blurred the lines between watch and jewel.

One of the most innovative elements used throughout the range was the replacement of the traditional watch crystal with a coloured semi-precious stone. The image at opposite bottom illustrates a watch by Grima that seems to echo the Brutalist architecture of the period in rich, golden form. The watch's crystal is formed from a step-cut green tourmaline. Hallmarked for 1969, the model is similar to a watch named Utopia that Grima made for the *About Time* exhibition.

CHRONOGRAPHS

In the early 1960s Rolex introduced a new chronograph model under reference number 6238. Initially produced with dials stylistically similar to those of the previous decade, the model was soon modified to have a silvered, satin-finished dial with applied angular baton indexes. The subsidiary dials were calibrated with block-style Arabic numerals. A cleaner, crisper look, this was a dramatic new image for the Rolex chronograph. In 1963 the firm introduced what would become one of the most famous watches of the twentieth century, the Cosmograph, which would soon be designated the Daytona to celebrate Rolex's sponsorship of the NASCAR Stock Race at Daytona Beach, Florida. Initially introduced under reference number 6239, a range of models would follow. All these Daytona models would feature calibrations to their bezels, usually marked in units per hour, with some references featuring steel bezels, while others had black acrylic inserts. Dials varied, being either matt black with white subsidiary counters or the reverse, with silvered dials and black subsidiaries. An exotic form of the dial,

popularly named the 'Paul Newman' following the picturing of the actor wearing an example, comprised a more colourful option, with the baton hour numerals replaced with small squares at the dial's edge, complemented by distinctive squares within the calibrations of the subsidiary dials.

In 1964, NASA contacted several watch companies to obtain quotations for robust chronograph wristwatches that could be used during their space missions. Of the firms contacted, only four replied, and from these, three watches were selected.[1] The chosen watches underwent extraordinarily rigorous testing during which they were exposed to all manner of shocks and extreme atmospheric changes. Ultimately it was the Omega Speedmaster that impressed above all others – the model's highly legible design, robust construction and ability to perform accurately in extreme conditions had ensured its selection. In fact, the first Omega Speedmaster watches in space pre-dated the official NASA adoption of the model, since the astronauts Walter Schirra and Gordon

BELOW Rolex Pre-Daytona Ref. 6238, c. 1963.
A stainless steel chronograph wristwatch with subsidiary dials for constant seconds, 30-minute and 12-hour registers, outer tachymeter scale, steel bracelet (cal. 72B)
Diameter 36 mm

OPPOSITE Rolex Cosmograph Daytona 'Paul Newman' Ref. 6239, c. 1968.
A stainless steel chronograph wristwatch with subsidiary dials for constant seconds, 30-minute and 12-hour registers, bezel calibrated for units per hour, steel bracelet (cal. 722-1)
Diameter 36.5 mm

Cooper had privately purchased their own Omega Speedmasters, which they wore during space missions in 1962 and 1963.[2] The Speedmaster's use by NASA officially began during the Gemini III mission in 1965. The model was also used during the Apollo missions, and, most famously, on 21 July 1969 the Omega Speedmaster became the first watch to be worn on the Moon; for ever after, the Speedmaster Mark I would be referred to as the 'Moon Watch'. Before the close of the 1960s, Omega launched a new version of their Speedmaster model named the Mark II. The watch had a massive tonneau-form case – a significant departure from the more traditional, circular style of the first Speedmaster models. While the dial closely followed the established Speedmaster design, the tachymeter bezel was affixed to the underside of the crystal rather than being a separate metal bezel with acrylic insert.

The Heuer brand, which had already been involved in automobile racing during the 1950s, supplying dashboard watches, launched a new wristwatch

chronograph named the Autavia in 1962. The Autavia, its name deriving from 'Automobile and Aviation', had originally been introduced as a dashboard chronograph for planes and cars in the 1930s. The new wristwatch Autavia was once again designed for racing drivers and aviators. The Autavia chronographs focused on the legibility of the display and the watch's ease of use. The first models were based on the established styles of military and aviation watches and had the addition of a rotating, calibrated bezel of similar style to 1950s diving watches. In addition to highly visible luminescent hour indexes, these early models had enlarged subsidiary dials for the constant seconds and time-recording dials. In 1963 Jack Heuer, the great-grandson of Heuer's founder, set out to develop a new chronograph model that would be both classic in style and highly legible, in keeping with the new trend for simplified designs. The result was the launch of the Carrera, in tribute to the Carrera Panamericana road race held in Mexico in the 1950s. As the 1960s advanced, Heuer would become

ever more involved in the world of motor racing.
With the rise in popularity of the automatic wristwatch,
Heuer, in collaboration with Breitling and Hamilton,
worked in secret to produce an automatic chronograph.
These chronographs used micro-rotor technology to
ensure that the automatic system could be introduced
without greatly increasing the depth of the movement,
an important consideration for a form of complication
that already required a substantial movement area.
At the time, the Breitling–Heuer–Hamilton joint venture
was in competition with Seiko and Zenith, who were
each working to release their own automatic chronograph
models. On 3 March 1969, Heuer, Breitling and Hamilton
held a joint press conference to announce the release of
their new line of automatic chronographs. The development
of the automatic chronograph movement would result
in the release of a varied assortment of models in the
succeeding decade.

RIGHT Heuer Autavia, c. 1969.
A stainless steel automatic chronograph
wristwatch with date and subsidiary dials
for 30-minute and 12-hour registers,
rotating bezel calibrated for minutes and
hours (cal. 11)
Length of case 47 mm

One of the most famous chronographs of the twentieth century was also released in 1969: the Zenith El Primero. Also an automatic model with date indication, this watch used a full-sized rotor and yet, with a height of just 6.5 mm, manged to be 1.2 mm slimmer than the micro-rotor movements of the Breitling–Heuer–Hamilton enterprise and around 0.7 mm thinner than Seiko's first automatic chronograph calibre. The Zenith movement was a fast-beat calibre with a rate of 36,000 BPH (beats per hour). The fast beat meant that the central chronograph seconds hand could register increments of one-tenth of a second. Zenith's El Primero calibre would become so highly regarded that it would be incorporated into a number of models by other watch brands for decades to come.

LEFT Zenith El Primero Ref. SP 1205, c. 1969.
A stainless steel automatic chronograph wristwatch with date and subsidiary dials for constant seconds, 30-minute and 12-hour registers, tachymeter scale to inner bezel, steel bracelet (cal. 3019 PHC) Diameter 37.5 mm

CALENDAR WATCHES

With the continuing popularity of watches with a date aperture and a general move towards clearer displays, the complex triple-calendar dial became much less visible as the 1960s progressed. Patek Philippe, who remained the leaders in this field, released a new perpetual calendar wristwatch in 1962 under reference number 3448. This was the first series-produced perpetual calendar wristwatch with automatic winding. The dial had a crisp, utilitarian design that focused on the clarity of its display. Notably, the seconds hand, which had moved from a subsidiary dial to the central position in the model's predecessor, was entirely removed from the new model. Aside from simplifying the display, this removal had two further advantages: first, it allowed for a single subsidiary dial dedicated solely to the date; second, it removed the need to incorporate extra wheel- and bridgework for a centre seconds hand, thereby ensuring the watch retained a relatively slim profile – this was an important consideration as the gold automatic rotor was mounted to the backplate of the watch, already increasing the

movement's depth. Patek Philippe also continued to make a perpetual calendar chronograph model, updating but retaining their model from the previous generation (Ref. 2499). Revised once again for clarity of display, the tachymeter scale was removed from the dial's edge, leaving a single scale that acted for both minutes and chronograph seconds. Interestingly, despite regular updates to their perpetual calendar models from the 1940s until the 1960s, Patek Philippe would not significantly alter their perpetual calendar and perpetual calendar chronograph models again until the 1980s.

Although very complex watches were becoming increasingly scarce, a small number of significant complication pocket watch movements from the earlier part of the twentieth century were cased and completed during the 1960s. Examples of watches with perpetual calendar, split-seconds chronograph and minute repetition by Audemars Piguet as well as Patek Philippe are known to have been completed during this period. One such watch, the movement of which was begun in 1907 but

not completed and cased until 1968, is shown opposite. In common with the wristwatches of the period, the design was focused on ensuring a highly legible dial, and this was mixed with a crisply chamfered case.

Rolex introduced their last triple-calendar Oyster model in 1958, and production ceased around 1962. The watchmaker would instead focus on increasing their range of models with a single date aperture, and by the end of the decade these included the Air-King-Date and Submariner Date. Meanwhile, the variety of Rolex Datejust, Date and Day-Date models continued to rise. Although Omega had also offered triple-calendar models during the 1950s, they, like Rolex, also concentrated on more simplified designs with date apertures. In the second half of the decade, Omega introduced a model with an elongated aperture at three o'clock that showed both the day and date; this form of display was used by the watchmaker across a range of different models during the period.

By now, the default place for the date was at three o'clock; however, some models continued to play with the positioning, the date aperture making intermittent appearances at, for example, twelve o'clock or between four and five o'clock. Occasionally the apertures were tapered as they followed their allotted sector of the dial – thinner towards the dial centre and wider towards its edge.

A special Rolex "OYSTER" was fitted to the *outside* of the bathyscaph "Trieste" when it dived to a record depth of 35,798 feet—*nearly 7 miles!* The Rolex was still working perfectly when the "Trieste" returned to the surface after eight hours, having withstood pressures of nearly *seven tons per square inch!* This unique watch is now on permanent display at the Smithsonian Institute in Washington D.C.

Another "first" by Rolex of Geneva — the pace-setting Oyster Perpetual "SUBMARINER" was developed specially for deep-sea and skin divers, but thousands of others have found it the ideal watch for everyday wear. Extra robust, waterproof to 660 feet, it is a favourite with yachtsmen, fishermen, water skiers and all those fond of aquatic sports. Its revolving bezel, which was introduced as a means of measuring time elapsed under water, has commended it to all those who want a simplified stopwatch, as well as an accurate time-piece, on their wrists.

A special Rolex-built gauge, used in the laboratories of Rolex at Geneva for testing the effects on watches of pressures up to 600 atmospheres—the equivalent of *four miles* under the sea!

DIVING WATCHES

OPPOSITE Extract from a Rolex catalogue of the early 1960s showing (top right) the Deep Sea Special, which travelled to the depths of the Mariana Trench in 1960, and (lower left) a so-called 'Explorer' dial Submariner.

BELOW, LEFT Favre-Leuba Bathy 50, c. 1965.
A stainless steel diver's wristwatch with depth gauge and rotating bezel calibrated for 60 minutes (cal. P 320) Diameter 40 mm

BELOW, RIGHT Movado Super Sub Sea, Ref. 206 704 501, c. 1965.
A stainless steel diver's chronograph wristwatch with luminous hour indexes and hands, subsidiary dials for constant seconds, 30-minute and 12-hour registers, outer tachymeter scale, rotating bezel calibrated for 60 minutes (cal. 146HP) Diameter 41 mm

In 1960, Rolex tested an extraordinary diving watch known as the Deep Sea Special by strapping it to the outside of *Trieste*, a bathyscaphe (a type of deep-sea submersible vessel) that was piloted by the Swiss oceanographer Jacques Piccard and US naval lieutenant Don Walsh. *Trieste* reached a depth of 10,916 metres in the deepest-known point of the ocean, the Challenger Deep section of the Mariana Trench, in the Pacific Ocean. Rolex had tested earlier versions of their Deep Sea Special during the 1950s, but the 1960 dive marked a sensational achievement and was, of course, an excellent marketing opportunity with which to further promote the growing success of their commercially available diving watch, the Submariner. The Submariner line had continued to receive subtle updates with the release of each new model within the range. By 1960, one of the most noticeable additions to the new models was the use of the 'crown guard' feature. First introduced to the Submariner in 1959, these guards protruded from the case, sitting either side of the crown to offer protection

from accidental knocks that might otherwise cause harm to the crown and potentially compromise the watch's water-resistance – a dangerous affair if the watch was being used to time a dive. The popularity of Rolex's Explorer model also saw the introduction of a Submariner model with Explorer-style dial.

Further capitalising on the adventures of the bathyscaphes, Favre-Leuba launched their Bathy 50. In common with other diving models, the watch had a rotating bezel calibrated for minutes that could be used to time the length of a dive – the minute hand had an extended, luminescent triangular tip for ease of reading. However, a significant feature of this model was a depth gauge; this sat at the edge of the dial and a central hand indicated to its scale. Capable of measuring depths down to 50 metres, the system operated by allowing water to enter the case and press against a membrane that not only protected the movement but also moved the central indicating hand as the water pressure increased, to provide an approximate depth reading on the dial.

OPPOSITE LeCoultre Polaris Ref. E859,
c. 1967.
A stainless steel diver's alarm wristwatch
with luminous hour indexes and hands,
rotating inner bezel calibrated for 60
minutes, steel link bracelet (cal. K825)
Diameter 42 mm

BELOW Rolex Oyster Perpetual Date
Sea-Dweller Submariner 2000 Ref.
1665, c. 1967.
A stainless steel automatic centre
seconds diver's wristwatch with luminous
hour indexes and hands, rotating bezel
calibrated for 60 minutes, steel link
bracelet (cal. 1570)
Diameter 39 mm

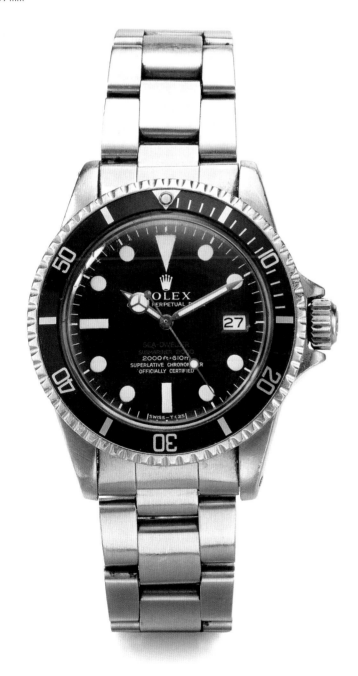

The increasing demand for diving watches led to the
development of diving chronographs and alarm watches.
Movado introduced their Super Sub Sea chronograph,
which followed the traditional diving watch format with
a rotating calibrated bezel and black dial with bold
luminescent numerals. This model had three subsidiary
dials that between them displayed constant seconds as
well as recording minutes and hours elapsed while the
chronograph was running. Jaeger-LeCoultre extended
their alarm watch range to include diving versions of
their Memovox model. In 1961 the firm introduced the
Memovox Deep Sea, an alarm wristwatch with traditional
rotating diver's bezel. In 1968 an updated model called
the Polaris was released; this watch had its rotating bezel
fitted to the underside of the crystal, at the edge of the
dial itself. There were three crowns to the case side,
separately for rotating the inner bezel, controlling the time
function and setting the alarm time. The International
Watch Company adopted a similar inner rotating bezel
for their Aquatimer watch, which was released in 1967.
By using an inner rotating bezel, there was less chance
of the bezel being accidentally moved once it had been
set up for recording a dive's duration.

Following Rolex's deep-sea watch tests, the company
developed a series-produced model suitable for saturation
diving. Launched in 1967, the watch was called the
Sea-Dweller Submariner and was depth-rated to 610
metres. With an even more robust case than the standard
Submariner models, the Sea-Dweller incorporated a
gas escape valve to the case side by nine o'clock. When
resurfacing after deep-sea diving, a watch case may fill
with helium, creating a pressure imbalance that may
force the crystal from the case, thereby ruining the watch;
the gas escape valve allowed the helium to leave the watch
case safely. The helium escape valve was also used in
a special range of Submariner watches developed for
the French industrial deep-sea diving company Comex.

ELECTRONIC AND FAST-BEAT MECHANICAL WATCHES

In 1960, after several years of research and development, the American watch firm Bulova released an electronic watch named the Accutron. The movement was invented by Max Hetzel, a Swiss national who began working at the Bulova Watch Company in 1948. The Accutron's movement was revolutionary, dispensing with the watch's traditional balance and spring. At the heart of the movement was a tuning-fork-shaped oscillator that vibrated 360 times per second. A battery powered the watch's transistorised electronic circuit. These watches were guaranteed to be accurate to within one minute per month, or two seconds per day. Among the Accutron models released was the Spaceview, a watch that dispensed with the dial and allowed the viewer to see directly into the movement. A futuristic-looking watch, its visual impact was dramatic, the watch's circuitry and 'tuning fork' clearly visible. Although the Accutron was available in a range of models with more traditional case and dial designs, the Spaceview was a clear demonstration of the watch's modernity.

Fast-beat mechanical movements were also being developed to improve accuracy. The advantage of a fast-beating movement is in greatly reducing changes in balance amplitude (amplitude being the amount by which the balance rotates in either direction), both as the mainspring unwinds and as the position of the watch changes. A fast-beating balance's oscillations are also less impacted by shocks and the motion of the wearer. In 1959 Longines produced a new calibre that was specially designed for observatory competitions. Known as the calibre 360, the movement's balance oscillated 36,000 times per hour, twice the rate of many other calibres on the market at that time. The movement set new records for accuracy in the wristwatch category at the Neuchâtel Observatory in Switzerland. In 1967 Longines launched a commercially produced fast-beat calibre, the 430, which also beat 36,000 times per hour and which was incorporated into a new collection of models named the Ultra-Chron. Intended as a competitor to the pioneering electronic wristwatches, Longines billed their own watch

BELOW, LEFT Bulova Accutron Spaceview Alpha, made in the early 1960s. A 14 ct yellow gold electronic centre seconds wristwatch (cal. 214) Width 33 mm

BELOW, RIGHT Bulova Accutron, shop display model, c. 1960

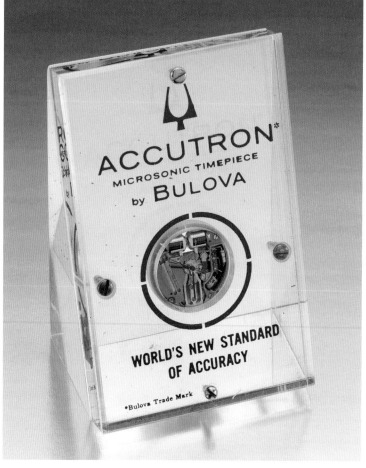

as the most accurate in the world, with timekeeping guaranteed to within a minute per month, or an average deviation of two seconds per day – in other words, exactly the same claim as Bulova had made for their electronic Accutron model. Longines' claim was an extraordinary one for a series-produced mechanical wristwatch. Indeed, Longines' marketing left the public in no doubt that this was a rival to the electronic watch – even the dials of the watches incorporated a symbol shaped like an electric coil. Similar coil symbols were used on the dials of watches by manufacturers of pioneering electronic watches, including models by Hamilton and Lip. The Ultra-Chrons were automatic watches, and it is worth remembering that batteries in early electronic watches did not have long-lasting power and needed replacing at least once per year; a perpetual automatic watch that was of similar accuracy to an electronic watch therefore had much to recommend it. Fast-beat movements were also introduced by Girard-Perregaux, who released their Gyromatic HF model in 1965. This model also had a balance that

oscillated 36,000 times per hour, and, in common with Longines, Girard-Perregaux also won a prize at the Neuchâtel Observatory for their fast beat movement, the latter in 1966. Despite the advances that these new movements brought, however, the fast beat ultimately led to excessive wear of parts, and while examples continued to be made into the 1970s, the 36,000-series calibres would soon be abandoned in favour of rates between the traditional 18,000 and 28,800 beats per hour.

Patek Philippe Hand-crafted.

In 1839, the founding year of Patek Philippe,
finishing a watch entirely by hand was the rule.
Today it is the exception.
Should rare watches made in this way appeal to you,
so will our color brochure
The 7 Crafts of Patek Philippe.
Please write to: Patek Philippe,
Dept. NGN, 41 Rue du Rhône, 1211 Geneva 3, Switzerland.

*Nautilus, the most rugged
of Patek Philippe watches.
Water-resistant to a depth
of 120 meters. Ultra-thin.
Self-winding. Date.
In steel or 18 kt. gold.*

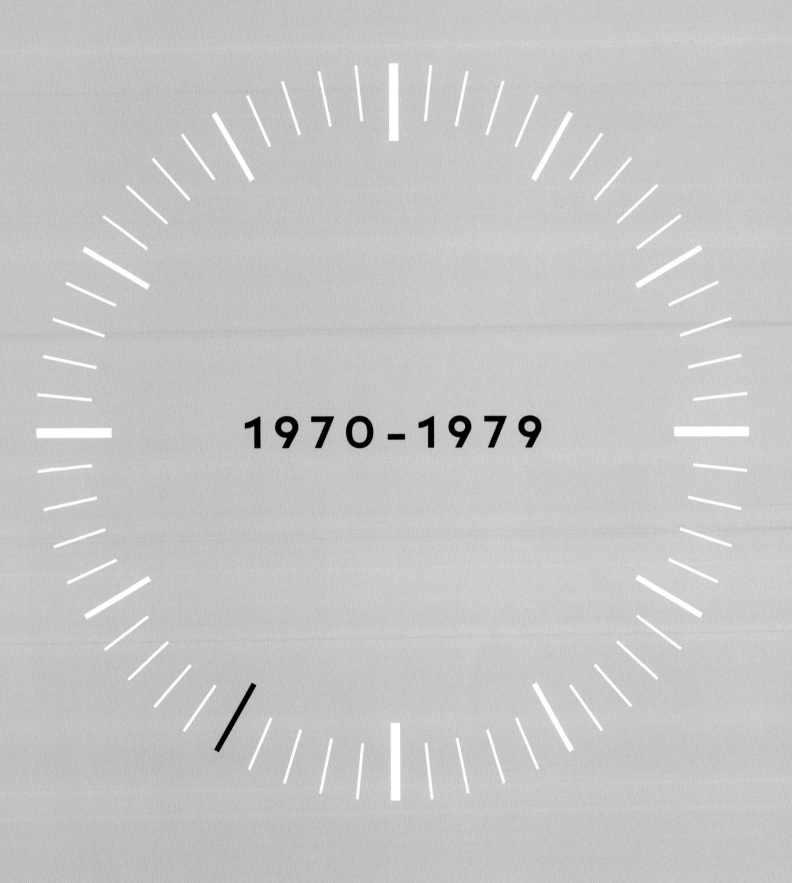

1970-1979

THE 1970s

During the 1960s, Swiss watch exports had continued their seemingly inexorable rise, increasing by some 70 per cent during the decade. However, the Swiss industry was about to face its biggest crisis since the early 1930s. The two major threats came from the US and Japan, where production of low-priced mechanical and – more worryingly for the Swiss – electronic watches had soared. With the oil crisis of 1973 and the world economy entering a period of turbulence, the combination of challenges faced by the traditional watchmakers of Switzerland was verging on the cataclysmic. Over the second half of the decade, exports of Swiss watches and finished movements contracted alarmingly: in 1974, 84 million units had been exported, yet the figure for 1979 would be just under 49 million.[1]

It is easy to forget quite how dramatic, indeed shocking, the arrival of the quartz watch was for the traditional watchmaking industry. For years many had dismissed the very viability of a quartz watch. In an article published in 1970, the horological writer, historian and designer Richard Good FBHI stated: 'When I wrote about the first commercially available electric watch in 1957, I little dreamt that I would be writing about quartz crystal controlled wrist watches in 1970, not just research playthings ... but production items that may be purchased by anyone with sufficient money ... I would imagine that this fact must at the moment be causing many experts to blush in private. According to what they wrote so rashly some years ago the quartz crystal wrist watch was an impossibility and they produced copious scientific arguments to prove it.'[2]

On 6 May 1970, in the same month as Good's article was published, the US watchmaker Hamilton announced to the press the development of a new, electronic quartz watch which they described as a 'wrist computer'. Developed jointly by the Hamilton Watch Company, based in Lancaster, Pennsylvania, and Electro/Data Inc. of Garland, Texas, the prototypes of the model were claimed to have deviated by no more than three seconds per month.[3] What had been developed was a truly

BELOW, LEFT Girard-Perregaux Ref. 9444, early 1970s.
A gold-plated and stainless steel quartz wristwatch with centre seconds and date (cal. 351-513)
Width 39 mm

BELOW, RIGHT Pulsar Digital Time Computer, c. 1972.
A gold-filled LED quartz wristwatch
Width 40 mm

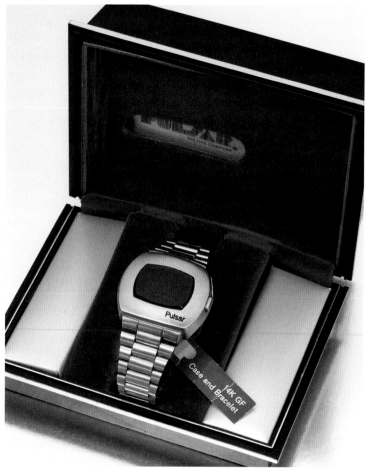

BELOW, LEFT Pulsar Time Computer, launched in 1972, this example c. 1977. A stainless steel digital LED quartz wristwatch
Width 40 mm

BELOW, RIGHT Sekonda LCD, made in 1979.
A gold-plated and steel LCD quartz wristwatch with full calendar, hourly 'beep', split-seconds stopwatch, 24-hour alarm, countdown alarm and musical reminder alarm, set to a gold-plated link bracelet
Width 36 mm

revolutionary watch. The model dispensed with moving parts and, instead of hands, used a screen to display time in the form of illuminated digits. The watch was silent – unlike its analogue electronic competitors, which audibly hummed – and the lack of moving parts meant that it never required servicing or cleaning. Incorporating a light emitting diode (LED), a semi-conductor that emitted light upon connection with electricity, the battery-powered watch had a pusher that, when depressed, displayed time on the screen. The system required considerable battery power for the illuminated display, and even though the screen was only lit up on demand, the batteries were not long-lasting – the model's press release claimed a battery duration of six months. Named the Pulsar and launched to the public in 1972 as an all-gold watch, it was an aspirational model with a price tag to match, selling for $2,100. The modern, space-age look and action of the watch created a sensation, and demand for LED watches soared. Success was so marked that other US electronics companies began to produce their own LED watches; prices resultingly dropped, and by 1977 LED watches were available from $10.[4] However, it was not just the price reduction that left the makers of LED watches exposed. The introduction of the LCD (liquid crystal display) in 1973 had at first not been popular, the screens becoming cloudy after a few months of use. However, improvements in their production and the sheer potential of this genre transformed the market. Far more energy-efficient than the LED, the LCD watch's time display was continually visible, and, crucially, an extraordinary array of 'complications' could be added to their modules. The image below right shows a Sekonda LCD wristwatch introduced in 1979 – this watch had a format that would become commonplace for LCD watches of the 1980s and incorporated a dazzling array of functions, including a split-seconds stopwatch, countdown timer and several alarm functions, one with the tune 'Oh Susannah' – prompting Sekonda to bill the model as 'The first watch you can dance to' (the antiquarian horologist might well

have taken issue with the latter claim, the mechanical musical watch having its own long history).

Although Omega had been heavily involved in the creation of the Beta 21, the watchmaker continued to develop other electro-quartz movements. In collaboration with the Battelle Institute of Geneva, Omega developed their Megaquartz f2.4Mhz (cal. 1510) movement. In 1972, an updated version of the movement (cal. 1511) was tested over a 63-day period at Neuchâtel Observatory, recording a mean daily variation of less than two thousandths of a second, or 0.73 seconds a year.[5] Indeed, so precise was the movement that the observatory awarded the movement the elevated status of 'Marine Chronometer'. To mark this achievement, in 1974 Omega launched a series of 1,000 examples of the Constellation Marine Chronometer Megaquartz. The styling of the watch was unmistakably maritime, with a box-like case, screwed-down bezel and utilitarian-design dial.

Other Swiss watchmakers, some of whom had declined an invitation to be involved in the CEH (Centre Electronique Horloger) project to build the Beta 21, had embarked on the development of their own quartz calibres. Girard-Perregaux, for example, hired the electronics engineer Georges Vuffray and designed their first quartz wristwatch, which was presented at the Basel Watch Fair of 1970.[6] Although the development of the Beta 21 had been an important exercise, there were several drawbacks to the calibre. The size of the movement greatly limited the appeal of the finished watches to a wider audience and the batteries drained relatively quickly, requiring replacement within a year. Furthermore, these watches were the antithesis of the slim dress watches of the 1960s, and the participants in the Beta 21 project quickly realised that the future of the electronic watch lay in smaller and slimmer quartz movements. As a consequence, many of the major brands retreated once again to concentrate on developing their own movements. In 1975 Piaget introduced their calibre 7P quartz movement. Just 3.1 mm in thickness, it was the smallest quartz movement upon release and enabled the brand to further broaden their range of slim dress watches with new battery-operated models. As the decade closed, Ebauches SA and Ebauches-Fabrik ETA launched an extraordinarily slim quartz movement (cal. 999.001) named the Delirium. Integrating the movement into the actual plate of the case back, so that the movement and case back were

BELOW, LEFT Vacheron Constantin Ref. 222, c. 1977.
A stainless steel automatic wristwatch with date and integrated bracelet (cal. VC1120)
Diameter 37 mm

BELOW RIGHT, Le Phare, c. 1970–75.
A steel and chrome manually wound wristwatch with sector indication time dial and date aperture
Width 39.5 mm

one and the same, its designers created a watch with a thickness of just 1.98 mm. This was an astonishing advance: in less than a decade, the Swiss quartz watch had been reduced from the massive case forms required by the Beta 21 movement to the slimmest form imaginable.

All this innovation and change meant that to garner attention, manufacturers of mechanical watches had to offer a range of bold and edgy styles. The electronic watches of the early 1970s were hefty pieces, and to get noticed – to be the one with the latest wrist gadgetry – often demanded big and colourful designs. This was, as we shall see, most visible in the chronograph watches of the period. There was certainly no wholesale move to replace the mechanical watch with the quartz, at least among traditional watchmakers. Even Bulova, the firm that had been so successful with the sale of its electronic 'tuning fork' watch throughout the 1960s, released a new mechanical automatic model in 1970, prominently citing in the product's advertisement that '70% of men prefer self-winding watches.'[7] Indeed, mechanical automatic movements were chosen for a new, modern style of wristwatch that was introduced during the 1970s, one that bridged a gap in the market between the dress-style

wristwatch and the sports watch. Gérald Genta would be largely responsible for this trend, designing iconic models for Audemars Piguet, Patek Philippe and IWC – respectively the Royal Oak, Nautilus and Ingenieur SL (see pp. 234–35). Meanwhile, Vacheron Constantin turned to the designer Jörg Hysek to produce their own hybrid sports/dress-style bracelet watch. Named the 222, the model was launched in 1977 to celebrate Vacheron's 222nd anniversary year. Ergonomically designed, the watch had a sleek integrated bracelet, and the tonneau-shaped case was made from a single block of steel with separate, screw-down, crenelated bezel. The dial featured baton hour indexes and hands, as well as an aperture for date. Made in two sizes, the larger version measured 37 mm in width, and although substantially proportioned the model retained a slim profile, in part achieved by the use of LeCoultre's calibre 920 (the same base calibre as that used in the Royal Oak and Nautilus), which Vacheron Constantin finished in-house and designated the VC1120.

Tonneau-, cushion- and elliptically shaped cases were all popular styles for mechanical watches of the period. Though dial designs varied wildly, the classic watches of the period tended to favour slim baton hour indexes and

hands. Colour was also important, and dials were produced in a range of differing shades, predominantly greys, golds, blues and black but also browns, burgundies, greens, yellows and reds. For the classically styled watch, these colours were usually metallic in finish with a satin-finished ground, while the sportier models tended to be finished with matt surfaces. Stone dials were also used to bring colour and contrast. Experimentation in dial design was also important to manufacturers keen to compete with the space-age designs of the new breed of electronic watches, leading to some novel time indications, including retrograde sector displays.

As in the 1960s, Rolex again made updates to their signature line of models. The majority of changes were relatively nuanced, and apart from the release of the Rolex Quartz with Beta 21 movement in 1970 (see p. 233) and the introduction of quartz versions of the Day-Date and Datejust models in 1977, there were few dramatic changes in the Rolex catalogues. The 1977 quartz models used Rolex's traditional Oyster designs but were more angular in style, with a tonneau-shaped case and flat

(rather than rounded) link bracelet. Otherwise the bezels and dials largely followed established Rolex patterns, with satin finishes and baton indexes and hands. However, one watch that did embrace an entirely new form of styling was the 1971-issued Rolex Explorer II. This model had a modernist design with a matt black dial and block-form luminescent markers around the dial's edge. The bezel was fixed and calibrated for 24 hours and an additional central orange hour hand indicated to it. Coloured hands were occasionally used across a range of models during the decade to clearly demarcate additional central hands, such as that of the Explorer II or for chronographs with multiple centrally set hands. However, they were also used to provide jarring contrast between minute and hour hands. In 1970 Omega released a deep-sea diving model that was massive in size, highly legible and included contrasting white and orange hands. Measuring 54 mm in width, the watch was designed to be waterproof to 600 metres. The bezel was fully graduated for 60 minutes and, for extra protection, the bezel was locked and could only be rotated

BELOW, LEFT Rolex Oysterquartz Day-Date Ref. 19018, c. 1978. An 18 ct yellow gold centre seconds quartz wristwatch with day and date indication and integrated 18 ct yellow gold bracelet (cal. 5055) Width 36 mm

BELOW, RIGHT Rolex Oyster Perpetual Date Explorer II Ref. 1655, c. 1972. A stainless steel automatic centre seconds wristwatch with date, 24-hour indication and bracelet (cal. 1570) Diameter 37.5 mm

OPPOSITE, TOP Omega Seamaster 600 Ploprof Ref.166.077, c. 1970. An oversized diver's stainless steel automatic centre seconds wristwatch with date and bracelet (cal. 1002) Width 55 mm

OPPOSITE, BOTTOM Corum for Rolls-Royce, late 1970s. An 18 ct white gold manually wound wristwatch in the form of a Rolls-Royce radiator grille (cal. 9‴) Width 40 mm

while the large red pusher to the right-hand side was depressed. This system prevented accidental movement of the bezel, and as the calibrations to the bezel were used for timing dives, this helped to ensure that the user could be confident of the displayed duration of their dive – important when calculating the amount of air left in one's tanks. A large orange minute hand contrasted with the white hour hand, the focus on the former designed to ensure that time elapsed could be easily read by the orange hand's indication on the minute graduations of the bezel.

The 1970s had been about modernisation, experimentation and recalibration. After years of sustained growth, a massive correction to the market had taken place. While the Quartz Crisis would see the bankruptcy of many watch firms and the amalgamation of others, it forced the leading players to focus minds, and during the second half of the 1970s the groundwork for the rebirth of the mechanical watch was being laid. It would be a renaissance based both in heritage and mechanical prowess. While it was clear that the electronic watch would continue to enjoy a mass-market appeal, it was the very prevalence of this genre that provided the opportunity by which the mechanical watchmakers could differentiate themselves. In 1976, Corum released a wristwatch in the form of a Rolls-Royce's radiator grille. Designed and produced in partnership with the car manufacturer, the model represented the ultimate in luxury and was fitted with a traditional mechanical, manually wound movement. Despite the eclecticism of its form, this timepiece clearly drew on watchmaking heritage – wristwatches in the style of car radiator grilles had been among the first shaped wristwatches to appear in the 1920s. During the 1980s, brands would continue to dip into the rich seam of watch design history, reinterpreting, adapting and, in some instances, rereleasing vintage forms. Just as the Corum watch was launched, a team of watchmakers at Audemars Piguet were working on one of the most innovative watches of the decade – an extremely slim, mechanically automatic perpetual calendar wristwatch with moon phases (see pp. 240–41). Sophisticated and exceptionally refined, it was models such as this that demonstrated a path to the future for the mechanical watchmakers.

THE BETA 21

The Basel Watch Fair of 1970 saw the Swiss watch manufacturers that had been involved in the development of the Beta 21 release a broad range of quartz models. The Beta 21 movement was an extraordinary collaborative effort by makers that were, in other circumstances, competitors. Grouped under the banner of the CEH (Centre Electronique Horloger), the collective designed the module and integrated circuit, while Ebauches SA (now known as ETA) manufactured the quartz oscillators and the movement's mechanical parts. It was agreed by the participants that 6,000 movements would be produced commercially. Although twenty companies contributed to the movement's development, not all the firms involved released production models.

Beta 21 was huge, and its rectangular shape meant that the overall proportions of the finished watches were necessarily large. For the watchmakers that developed series-produced models incorporating the Beta 21, their watches would seem unashamedly brash by comparison with the pared-down trends of the previous decade. Yet these were fiercely modern watches using the latest technology, and for their owners they were also a statement piece. It is therefore unsurprising that, despite the heft of these models, options were available in heavy 18 ct gold cases, often with integrated bracelets to yet further their aspirational appeal.

Omega, who had developed the micro-motor that drove the hands of the Beta 21, released their Electroquartz Beta 21 model at the Basel Watch Fair of 1970. The watch had a wedge-shaped case with a bulky, thick body. The dials were available with a variety of contemporary-coloured satin finishes. One rather nuanced feature was the placement of the crown at nine o'clock. These watches were phenomenally accurate by the standards of the day, keeping time to within five seconds a month, and so would require only rare adjustment. Since this was not designed as a left-handed watch, it seems that the crown placement was a discreet means of displaying the fact that adjustment was, while not entirely superfluous, at least barely required.

BELOW Omega Constellation Electroquartz Ref. 196.005, c. 1970.
A large and heavy stainless steel electro-quartz wristwatch with centre seconds and date (cal. Beta 21)
Length 42 mm

OPPOSITE, TOP Patek Philippe Ref. 3587/2, introduced in 1970, this example made in 1972.
A large and heavy 18 ct yellow gold electro-quartz bracelet watch with centre seconds and date (cal. Beta 21)
Width 43 mm

OPPOSITE, BOTTOM Rolex Quartz Ref. 5100, c. 1970.
A heavy 18 ct yellow gold electro-quartz bracelet watch with centre seconds and date (cal. Beta 21)
Width 38.5 mm

Patek Philippe launched their Beta 21 watch under reference number 3587 in 1970. Another vast watch, this had a width of 43 mm, at a time when most Patek Philippe watches were 32 to 34 mm wide and a 36 mm case was considered oversized. Made only in yellow or white gold, this was a heavy model, invariably with an integrated thick gold bracelet. Coloured, satin-finished dials also dominated the appearance of these watches. Rolex's version of the Beta 21 was another hefty model. Also released in 1970, Rolex's Quartz wristwatch was a substantial gold bracelet watch that drew its styling from the company's Oyster dress models. Yet this was not itself an Oyster watch, being distinctly more angular in appearance and with a snap-on rather than screw-down back. The dials were, like their competitors, available in coloured satin finishes; however, the Rolex dials took full advantage of the continually sweeping movement of the seconds hand to place enhanced calibrations at the dial's edge. There were elongated, slim minute markers that were interspersed with calibrations to fifths of a second. Rolex's divisions of time gave the dials a visual feeling of precision and were more akin to the layout of a chronograph's seconds track. The sharp chamfers of the Rolex model's case and bracelet also spoke of modernity while retaining the brand's by now classic fluted bezel.

DRESS/SPORTS HYBRID WATCHES

In 1970, Gérald Genta was approached by Georges Golay, the managing director of Audemars Piguet, to design a new waterproof sports wristwatch. Following production of a prototype, the model, to be known as the Royal Oak, was put into production in 1972. In designing the watch, Genta had been inspired by the diving helmet, with its screwed-down viewing window, and this feature was translated into the octagonal bezel of the Royal Oak. The case was seamlessly integrated with a link bracelet, giving the watch a rugged yet perfectly balanced appearance. One of the most important and influential wristwatch designs of the twentieth century, it was a remarkably visionary timepiece and, for Audemars Piguet, arrived at a critical moment, during the turbulent period of the 1970s. The Royal Oak would become Audemars Piguet's signature model and would transform the fortunes of the watchmaker for decades to come.

By the mid-1970s, Patek Philippe, no doubt impressed by the success of the Royal Oak, were keen to develop their own sports-style watch. Once again it was Gérald Genta who designed the model, his genius producing yet another iconic wristwatch. Released in 1976 and this time based on a ship's porthole, the Nautilus, as the new model was to be named, had a large yet sleek case design with an integrated bracelet. The bezel, rather than being screwed down from the top as in the Royal Oak, was instead secured by screws to the protruding 'ears' at the left and right sides of the case.

There was no mistaking the relationship between the Royal Oak and Nautilus: Genta's design DNA was clear to see. Each watch had a textured dial, the Royal Oak with a hobnail finish, the Nautilus with horizontal ribbing; and the baton hands, numerals and date apertures were almost identically styled between the two models. For both Audemars Piguet and Patek Philippe, these new sporty watches were a departure from their traditional dress-style watches. Yet despite their large-sized cases (Royal Oak 39 mm, Nautilus 42 mm), they were surprisingly slim (each approximately 7 mm deep), especially given their rugged looks, and this enabled

BELOW Patek Philippe Nautilus Ref. 3700/1A, introduced in 1976, this example made in 1979.
A stainless steel automatic wristwatch with date and integrated bracelet (cal. 28–255 C)
Width 42 mm

them to be marketed as multipurpose watches that would be as well matched to a dinner suit as to a wetsuit. Their slender profiles were in large part achieved by the movement each incorporated. Both the early Royal Oak and Nautilus watches were fitted with Jaeger-LeCoultre's ultra-slim automatic calibre 920, with the finishing of the movements completed in-house, respectively by Audemars Piguet (cal. 2121) and Patek Philippe (cal. 28-255 C). The movement had a height of just 3.05 mm and was wound via a central rotor with a 21 ct gold rim to enhance its velocity.

One further watch to enter this particular style arena was the Ingenieur SL. By 1975 the International Watch Company had ceased production of their classic Ingenieur model; however, they made an approach to Gérald Genta to update the model and transform it into a modern, sporty bracelet watch. In 1976 the new model was launched with its unmistakable Genta design. Size-wise, with a case width of 40 mm, the Ingenieur SL was again a very broad watch, but at approximately 12.5 mm deep it was also substantially thicker than the Royal Oak and Nautilus, the extra depth necessitated by IWC's larger calibre 8541 movement. However, like the Royal Oak and Nautilus, the classic black dial with slim baton indexes and hands, combined with the angularity of the watch's case and bracelet, once again made the Ingenieur SL a multipurpose watch.

The radical new styling of these watches was perfectly suited to the period. With their modern, avant-garde looks, the Royal Oak, Nautilus and Ingenieur SL challenged the conventions of watch design at precisely the moment when the mechanical watch's future was being called into question. The legacy of the introduction of these models would ultimately last far beyond the darkest days of the Quartz Crisis – indeed, for Audemars Piguet, the Royal Oak would be seen as the very saviour of the brand.[8]

CHRONOGRAPHS

Having invested heavily in the development of new automatic chronograph movements during the 1960s, brands such as Breitling, Heuer, Omega and Zenith released a slew of new and varied chronographs in the early years of the 1970s. For watchmakers, the chronograph's great advantage was that it lent itself to innovative and elaborate dial design. As electronic watches both in analogue and LED formats were taking the world by storm with their massive cases and space-age looks, the mechanical chronograph offered traditional watchmakers the opportunity to follow these trends by producing watches with equally outlandish designs. At the start of the 1970s, the mechanical watchmakers still had the advantage that their models could incorporate a range of indications that could not be replicated on the early electronic watches, though this would soon change with the introduction of the LCD wristwatch in the middle of the decade.

Heuer's Monaco wristwatch, first released in 1969, became one of the defining chronograph models of the

1970s. The sharp lines of the case were reflected in the horizontal, linear, raised-hour indexes to the dial. The subsidiary recording dials for hours and minutes also followed the shape of the case and were square with rounded corners. The placement of the crown at nine rather than three o'clock served to reinforce the fact that this was one of the new breed of automatic models and therefore, unlike the traditional chronograph, did not require winding. While there was certainly something of the 1960s in the Monaco's pared-down design, the colourful blue dial with its red highlights, eccentric applied hour indexes and the large cushion shape of its case spoke of a new 1970s aesthetic.

During this period, Omega used colour and innovative dial displays to create unusual and eye-catching models. Having developed an automatic chronograph calibre together with Lemania, Omega introduced a suite of contemporary models in the early years of the 1970s, of which the Ref. 176.005, shown opposite, is a typical example. The case of the watch is both chunky and large,

BELOW, LEFT Zenith El Primero Ref. 01-0200-415, c. 1975.
A stainless steel cushion-form automatic chronograph wristwatch with date, subsidiary dials for constant seconds, 30-minute and 12-hour registers, aperture for date, inner bezel calibrated for tachymeter, steel bracelet (cal. 3019PHC)
Width 40 mm

BELOW, RIGHT Heuer Monaco Ref. 1133B, c. 1971.
A stainless steel cushion-form automatic chronograph wristwatch with blue dial, subsidiary dials for 30-minute and 12-hour registers, and aperture for date (cal. 11)
Width 40 mm

Omega Seamaster Ref
176.005, c. 1972.
A stainless steel cushion-form automatic
chronograph wristwatch with date, blue
dial, central chronograph minute-
recording hand and subsidiary dials for
hour recording and constant seconds
combined with 24-hour indicator
(cal. 1040)
Width 42 mm

Omega Chrono-Quartz
Montreal Olympics Ref. 196.0052/
396.0839, c. 1976.
A stainless steel quartz wristwatch with
dual LCD stopwatch display and analogue
time with date (cal. 1611)
Width 47 mm

measuring 42 mm by 49 mm – this was a giant by
comparison with the watches of the previous generation.
In layout, the dial dispensed with the traditional
chronograph format with its standardised subsidiary
dials. Most noticeable was the use of a central minute-
recording hand: when at rest this winged, orange-tipped
hand sat beneath the central chronograph seconds
hand, and when the chronograph was running the hand
would advance to count minutes at the edge of the dial.
A standard hour-recording dial was placed at six o'clock,
and at nine o'clock a constant or subsidiary seconds dial
was combined with a 24-hour indicator that was itself
divided into day and night hours.

Reinterpreting the chronograph took another bold step
with Omega's 1976 release of a hybrid electronic wristwatch
with both an analogue and an LCD display. A remarkable-
looking and large wristwatch, the rectangular-shaped
case lay horizontally on the wrist. Its size (45.3 mm wide,
12.8 mm thick) and unique displays lent the watch the
feeling of a miniaturised computer. To the left, two

stacked LCD screens displayed the chronograph functions
in minutes, hours and hundredths of a second. The 1976
launch of the model, which was dubbed the Seamaster
Chrono-Quartz, was timed to coincide with the Olympic
Games in Montreal.

All this modernity was of course tempered by more
standard offerings, but the classic chronographs of
yesteryear were becoming increasingly scarce. Rolex
continued to offer their Daytona models, which
stylistically remained little changed from those of the
1960s. Others such as Breitling and Omega kept their
respective Navitimer and Speedmaster designs alive,
while also offering additional variants of these models
with more modernist styling. By contrast, however,
Patek Philippe almost entirely retreated from the
chronograph field, ceasing production of their last
standard chronograph, the Ref. 1463, in 1969 and their
split-seconds chronograph Ref. 1436 in 1971 (although
the company continued to offer their Ref. 2499 perpetual
calendar chronograph wristwatch throughout the 1970s).

It is one of the great ironies of watchmaking history that what has become one of the most coveted of all vintage chronographs, the Rolex Daytona, was, according to anecdotal evidence, a difficult model to sell during the 1970s. This combined with fact that Audemars Piguet, Patek Philippe and Vacheron Constantin were all drawing away from the chronograph market suggests that, by the mid-1970s, demand for the classic chronograph wristwatch was at its lowest ebb. Indeed, Patek Philippe, traditionally a leader in the classic chronograph field, would not reintroduce a standard chronograph model (without perpetual calendar) until 1998.

RIGHT Breitling Chrono-Matic
Cosmonaute Ref. 1809, c. 1970.
A stainless steel automatic chronograph
wristwatch with 24-hour dial calibrated
with luminescent hour indexes, luminous
hands, subsidiary dials for 30-minute
and 12-hour registers, aperture for date,
outer scales for flight-specific slide rule
with rotating bezel (cal. 14)
Diameter 48 mm

OPPOSITE Rolex Oyster Cosmograph
Daytona Ref. 6265, c. 1978.
An 18 ct yellow gold manually wound
chronograph wristwatch with subsidiary
dials for constant seconds, 30-minute
and 12-hour registers, bezel calibrated
for units per hour, gold bracelet (cal. 727)
Diameter 37 mm

AUDEMARS PIGUET PERPETUAL CALENDAR

In the midst of the Quartz Crisis, three watchmakers at Audemars Piguet, horrified by the damage being wrought across the mechanical watch industry, devised an audacious plan to reignite a passion for traditional watchmaking. The aim was to create an automatically wound, perpetual calendar wristwatch that would be both sleek and refined. The watchmakers, Michel Rochat, Jean-Daniel Golay and Wilfred Berney, completed their prototype in 1977. Georges Golay, Audemars Piguet's managing director, was convinced of the project's merits. Quite extraordinary is the fact that Georges Golay commissioned the production of 159 examples of the watch – while this may seem a small number, the investment of time and labour in the construction of the watches was an enormous commitment. Remembering that the age of the full-calendar mechanical watch appeared to have passed by the end of the 1960s, the risks, especially during the turbulent years of the second half of the 1970s, were hard to dismiss. Indeed, to put the initial quantity commissioned into perspective, 159 perpetual calendar watches was almost as many as the total number of calendar watches produced by Audemars Piguet since 1924.[9]

Audemars Piguet presented their new model, named the Ref. 5548 Quantième Pérpétuel, at the Basel Watch Fair of 1978, where it claimed the title as the world's thinnest automatic movement with perpetual calendar and moon phases. Comprising a total of 292 parts, the movement (cal. 2120 QP), which used a LeCoultre 920 ébauche as its base, had a thickness of just 3.95 mm. The external design was elegant and classic. Designed by Jacqueline Dimier, who had arrived at Audemars Piguet in 1975, the dial was white with slim baton indexes and hands; the calendar indications were calibrated in black, while the disc for the phases of the moon was gold, heightened with blue enamel.[10] The case was circular with a rounded, stepped bezel and discreet lugs. With a diameter of 36 mm and total depth of just 7 mm, the watch was an assured return to the traditionally sized mechanical wristwatch and stood in stark contrast to the giant watches that the electro-quartz age had ushered in.

In the darkest days of the Quartz Crisis, few would have predicted the possibility of a renaissance for the mechanical watch. Yet Audemars Piguet's Quanitème Pérpétuel in many ways showed a path to the future: the sophistication and refinement of the watch's mechanical movement and the classic beauty of its styling would be a theme adopted by many makers during the following decade.

BELOW Audemars Piguet 12½‴ calibre 2120/2800, as used in the model Ref. 5548 and launched in 1978. Detail of movement backplate/rotor and under–dial
Diameter 28 mm, thickness 3.95 mm

OPPOSITE Audemars Piguet Ref. 5548, introduced in 1978.
An 18 ct yellow gold automatic perpetual calendar wristwatch with moon phases (cal. 2120)
Diameter 36 mm

COLOURED DIALS

Watches with dials made from stone began to appear in the 1960s, but it was during the 1970s that the coloured dial found its fullest expression. Piaget led the field in this particular genre, producing an extraordinary array of watches that continued to break with traditional watch styles. In 1969, under the direction of Valentin Piaget, the watchmaker created the 21st Century Collection, a new form of avant-garde watch design that saw the release of an incredible array of timepieces, including innovative cuff watches and intricate pendant watches that played with colour, texture and asymmetry. At the Basel Watch Fair of 1970, Piaget displayed a kaleidoscope of coloured dials made from coral and hardstones, including jade, lapis lazuli, opal, turquoise and tiger's eye.[11] With natural inclusions and striations, the polished stone dials enhanced the feeling of the unique. Among the most captivating watches created by Piaget during this decade were a series of cuff-form watches that were made under the direction of Jean-Claude Gueit, who had trained at the Geneva School of Decorative Arts. These

large-sized watches followed both the curvature and taper of the wrist to form a comfortable, bangle-form bracelet. The stone dials of the period were perfectly matched to these designs, allowing a stark contrast between the large gold meshwork of the bracelets and the coloured dials, which were left entirely free of hour and minute calibrations.

In 1970, Corum introduced novel coloured detailing with the release of a range of watches with dials made from birds' feathers.[12] These were often fitted to broad-cased models where the dial was large, allowing the feathers maximum visual impact. The feather dials were usually left 'blank', save for the Corum logo applied at the twelve o'clock position, although occasionally the quarter hours were also marked. The natural banding of the feathers created a look not entirely dissimilar to the stone dial, but their more muted sheen and subtle surface textures gave them their own distinctive appearance.

During the 1970s, the production of watch and jewellery sets by makers such as Piaget and Patek

Philippe enabled the brands working at the most luxurious end of the market to emphasise yet further the exclusivity and exceptional quality of their art. This, at a time of challenge from many newcomers to the watch market, including technology companies that had no history of watchmaking, helped to reinforce the very meaning of *haute horlogerie*. To further decorate the bracelets, earrings and rings that formed these ensembles, these sets often incorporated the coloured hardstones that were being used to make dials. The image opposite shows an especially fine watch and jewellery set that dates to 1977. The pavé diamond-set dial of this watch represented a new trend that was beginning to emerge, one that would become increasingly fashionable during the 1980s.

RIGHT Corum, made in the 1970s.
An 18 ct white gold broad tonneau-form
wristwatch with feather-set dial and
diamond-set bezel (cal. 7001)
Width 42 mm

OPPOSITE Patek Philippe Ref. 4363/1,
made in 1977.
An 18 ct yellow gold turquoise- and
diamond-set suite comprising a
wristwatch, pair of earrings and a ring
(cal. 16.250)
Width 32 mm

COMPOSITE MATERIALS

In 1970, Tissot had recently introduced a range of fibreglass models within their Sideral range. Marketed as youthful and sporty models, contemporary Tissot advertising material explained that 'the novelty and originality of the watch results from the ultramodern design of its case.'[13] Tissot emphasised the attributes of fibreglass, explaining that the material was not susceptible to ageing, deforming or rusting and that it was impermeable and had excellent resistance against shocks. A trailblazing design, Tissot's use of fibreglass foreshadowed the use of plastics that would, in tandem with the wider use of quartz movements, revolutionise watch design right into the 1980s, heralding a change that would bring down prices and open up a new 'fashion' watch genre. Such composite cases also avoided the use of chrome- or gold-plated finishes, which were especially susceptible to wear and damage. Other brands to experiment with composite cases included Breitling and Heuer, both of whom produced a range of mechanical chronographs with composite cases.

BELOW Tissot Sideral, c. 1970.
A fibreglass, rubber and steel automatic diver's wristwatch with date and rotating bezel calibrated for 60 minutes (cal. 784-2)
Width 40 mm

At the Basel Watch Fair of 1971, Tissot took the use
of plastics a step further by presenting an entirely new
mechanical movement in which almost all parts were
made from injection-moulded plastic, including the
plates, bridges, gear train and escapement. Under
development since 1964, the movement was named
the Astrolon. Designed to be cheap to manufacture and
assemble, the plastics used did not require lubrication,
were not susceptible to corrosion and were entirely
anti-magnetic and highly shock-resistant. With many
traditional steps such as oiling and tightening of screws
removed from the assembly process, the production line
was largely automated. It was even claimed that, with
some adjustments and additional fixings, the movement
could be made to run to chronometer standards.[14]

GEORGE DANIELS

Despite the dark clouds of the Quartz Crisis, there were a determined few who believed in the future of the mechanical watch. While it was now pointless for traditional movement manufacturers to attempt to compete with the accuracy of the quartz watch, it was recognised that the mechanical watch could still offer an exclusivity, individuality and a quality of workmanship that could never be replicated in the circuit boards of an electronic watch. And it was among the melee of the electronic watch's rise that one name emerged to reassert the relevance and importance of the watch, a name that would, perhaps more than any other, lead the way for the rise of a new breed of watchmakers, the so-called independents.

The English watchmaker Dr George Daniels began his career as a trade watch repairer. It was a chance encounter with Cecil Clutton, like Daniels a fellow car enthusiast, that would change the direction of Daniels's career. Clutton was a renowned antique watch collector and his passion for the subject captured Daniels's imagination. During the 1960s Daniels developed a passion for the work of Abraham-Louis Breguet, and when he turned to making his own watches, it was his study and understanding of Breguet's work that would most heavily influence his own. In 1969 Daniels created his first watch, which he made for Cecil Clutton. The watch was a gold and silver one-minute, pivoted-detent chronometer tourbillon. From 1970 to 1974, Daniels made and sold seven further watches based on the original watch he had made for Clutton. Shown opposite is the fourth watch made by Daniels, which he sold to the collector Edward Hornby in January 1971. Hornby later recollected: 'I well remember the day when he [George Daniels] said to me that he was going to start to make his own timepieces, [Daniels remarked,] "you are down to have one of them." "Just a minute" I said, "that's fine but how much are they going to cost?" – "A great deal" he said, "But you're going to have one just the same."'[15]

Aside from the exceptional quality of Daniels's watches, the most remarkable fact about them was that he made almost every component himself. This stood in stark contrast to the rest of the watch industry, which relied on the sourcing of components from a variety of different companies – cases and dials from specialist makers, parts or even whole movements from specialist suppliers. It was Daniels's determination to design and make his watches almost entirely alone that immediately set him apart. From the outset, Daniels made the important decision to produce only watches of his own design that would incorporate interesting mechanical features and, notwithstanding his admiration for the work of Breguet, exude a uniquely Daniels aesthetic.

Each of the early series Daniels watches had a silvered dial that was engine-turned with three different decorative designs, and an eccentric, satin finished sector displayed the hours in Roman numerals. The clarity of the design was superb: the outer minute track, which was indicated on a satin-finished ring to the edge of the dial, was clearly delineated, crossed over only by the slim ring of the subsidiary seconds calibrations at the base of the dial. An impressive retrograde action saw the hour hand 'fly' back to the left side of its sector as the hour reached one o'clock. The movement itself incorporated an Earnshaw-type spring-detent escapement that was mounted within a polished steel tourbillon carriage. A feature that has been long prized, the intricacy of the tourbillon's mesmerising action and the extreme complexity of its construction excites the greatest admiration in the eyes of the watch collector. Daniels's choice of the tourbillon was prescient, for it was the application of the tourbillon within the confines of the wristwatch case that would do much to reignite the mechanical watch's appeal in the 1980s.

Edward Hornby, who owned the watch illustrated opposite, was an avid collector of antique watches, but he also purchased one of the newly released quartz watches of the 1970s. George Daniels later recounted how Hornby was curious to see how his Daniels watch would perform against his recently purchased quartz watch and decided to test the two together: 'The test lasted 8 months before the battery went flat and he cheerfully awarded the honour to the tourbillon. Its daily variation rate at room temperature averaged 0–3 seconds per day.'[16]

THE NEW SWATCH. GRANITA DI FRUTTA
THE ONLY WATCH THAT MAKES SCENTS.

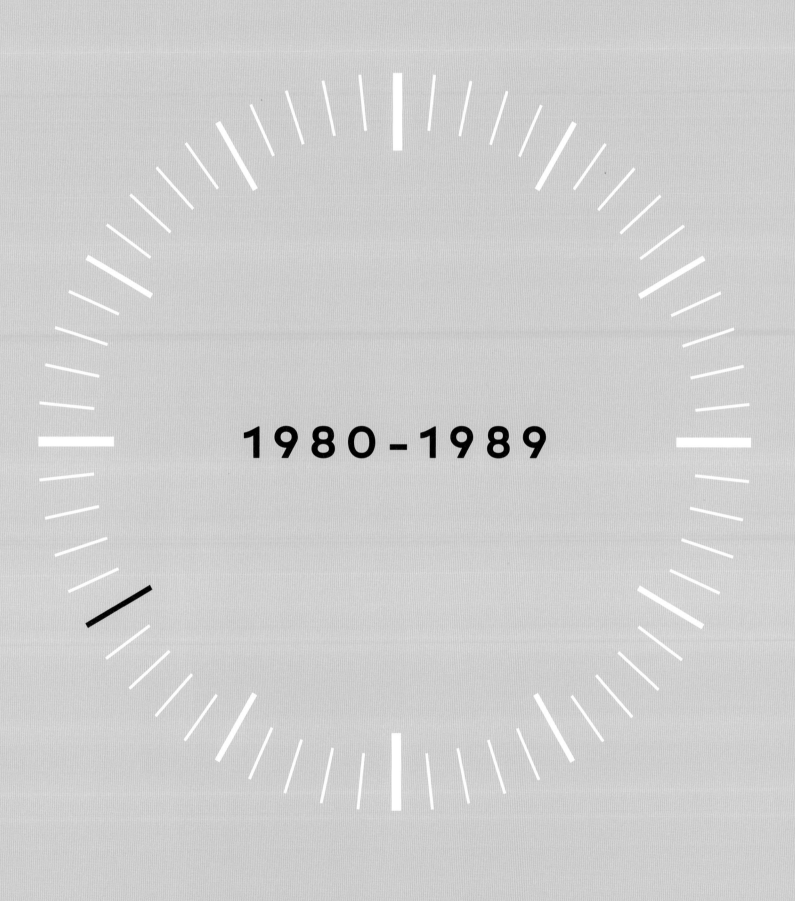

1980-1989

THE 1980s

By the early years of the 1980s, the initial excitement that had greeted the introduction of the electronic wristwatch was beginning to fade. Though it was clear that the mass-market watch would continue to be dominated by the quartz movement, the green shoots of the mechanical renaissance were beginning to appear. Two main themes would dominate the decade at entirely opposing sides of the style spectrum – one would represent the watch as an item of opulent luxury, while the other would reflect a nostalgia for watches of the past. The difficult years of the 1970s had seen many traditional watch brands swept away, and others had been amalgamated or mothballed. At the beginning of the new decade, the crisis was far from over, but enterprising watchmakers and investors who still believed in the mechanical watch's potential would spectacularly turn around the fortunes of some of the oldest watchmaking firms.

For the traditional watchmakers, there was no better way to emphasise the quality and exclusivity of their watches than by visibly displaying their movements. One of the great ironies of the luxury mechanical watch lay in the fact that the inner workings were entirely hidden from view, despite the fact that they were beautifully finished. Skeletonised watches that allowed the wearer to see into the movement of their watch were scarce prior to the 1980s, yet with a renewed interest in the mechanical movement, several brands introduced variations of the skeleton watch to an eager clientele. At the Basel Watch Fair of 1980, the International Watch Company exhibited skeletonised pocket and wristwatches; heightened with diamond-set bezels, these pieces emphasised the exclusivity of the traditional mechanical timepiece. To further stress their uniqueness, the movements of a limited series of these watches were engraved with the signature of the individual IWC watchmaker who had created them.[1] In 1980 Corum also launched a new skeletonised model, which they named the Golden Bridge. The watch had transparent crystals to the front and back of the case and the movement was arranged linearly, the spring barrel at one end and the balance directly opposite at the other. This was a highly effective design since the casing made the movement appear somewhat akin to an exhibit suspended in a museum cabinet, the movement itself allowed to become an object of wonder.

Glazed case backs that acted as a window into the movement were also extremely rare before the 1980s, being almost exclusively reserved for watches designed for exhibition purposes. However, this too was an excellent way for the watchmaker to display the quality of their workmanship and also had the potential benefit of acting as an additional selling tool for the retailer – the salesperson being able show a customer the movement of a watch by simply turning it over. There was initially some reluctance to fully exploit the glazed case back – no doubt there was concern that the feature might lessen the aesthetic refinement of the watch case or, perhaps worse, appear something of a gimmick. When Patek Philippe released new perpetual calendar and perpetual calendar chronograph models in the mid-1980s, they offered two versions of each – these were under separate reference numbers: the 3940 and 3970 were fitted with solid case backs, while the 3941 and 3971 were fitted with sapphire crystal transparent backs. With opinion split on which option was the most appropriate for such

technically refined models, at the end of the 1980s the watches were standardised under reference numbers 3940 and 3970, but each model was now accompanied by two case back options: one solid and one glazed. As fascination with the mechanics of the watch gained momentum once more, display backs would become increasingly visible during the following decades.

Part of the drive to emphasise brand heritage resulted in a range of vintage designs being reintroduced. In 1979 Jaeger-LeCoultre had reissued their famous Reverso wristwatch – the challenging era of the late 1970s being a somewhat fitting period in which to bring back this most iconic model, since the Reverso's first appearance was during the economic depression of the 1930s. In 1985 Cartier oversaw the reintroduction of the Pasha wristwatch: a model originally designed in 1943, it was updated for a new era by the designer Gérald Genta. Another Cartier model that would return to prominence was the Santos, which had been relaunched in 1978, and it was this model that would be ideally suited to the popular 1980s trend

BELOW, LEFT Patek Philippe Ref. 3971, introduced in 1986.
An 18 ct yellow gold perpetual calendar chronograph wristwatch with subsidiary dials for 30-minute register combined with leap year indication, date with aperture for moon phases and constant seconds with 24-hour indicator (cal. CH27-70 Q)
Diameter 36 mm

BELOW, RIGHT Cartier Pasha, c. 1988.
An 18 ct yellow gold automatic centre seconds wristwatch with date (cal. 20)
Diameter 38 mm

OPPOSITE The transparent sapphire crystal display back of the Patek Philippe Ref. 3971

for bi-metal cases and bracelets. While mixed-metal watches had begun to appear with increasing frequency in the catalogues of watch brands during the 1970s, it was throughout the 1980s that the trend for steel and gold wristwatches reached its height. Some firms also used combinations of precious metals as a means to further enhance the prestige of models. In 1985 Rolex launched their Tridor bracelet; as the name suggests, three colours of gold were used in the design. The outlying links were made in a grey tone of white gold, while the central links were composed of bands of yellow, pink and white gold. Experimentation was also made with other materials, such as ceramic, titanium and aluminium. The International Watch Company worked with the designer Ferdinand Alexander Porsche to create a new, modern line of wristwatches, producing a blackened aluminium wristwatch with compass in 1978, followed by a range of models including, in 1984, the first all-titanium diver's wristwatch. By the end of the 1980s IWC were using zirconium oxide ceramic for a special version of their Da Vinci perpetual calendar wristwatch (see p. 277).

In keeping with the traditional wristwatch, classically styled models of the period invariably had rounded bezels and short lugs. Sizes were, for the most part, modest, with the large, chunky sports watches of the 1970s largely phased out. Coloured dials were still to be found, but pure white dials were an increasingly common option and the dial maker's palette was largely devoted to silvers, champagnes, blacks and deep blues. Satin finishes were common for silver, champagne and blue dials. White dials were occasionally matt in finish, although they were frequently found with a high sheen or gloss finish in imitation of the traditional enamel dial. Black dials could be found with gloss, matt or, occasionally, satin finishes. Numerals remained largely slim, with baton and Roman numerals especially popular.

Gold bracelet watches were a common offering during the decade, with popular models including Cartier's Panthère and the heavy models of Rolex's Day-Date and Piaget's Polo. The Polo seamlessly combined the watch's dial with an integrated bracelet. Panels alternately set with satin and polished finishes formed the bracelet's

BELOW, LEFT Cartier Santos, 1980s.
A ladies' steel and gold automatic centre seconds wristwatch (cal. 8''')
Width 23.5 mm

BELOW, RIGHT International Watch Co. Ocean, c. 1984.
A titanium automatic centre seconds wristwatch with date (cal. 375)
Diameter 43 mm

OPPOSITE, TOP Rolex Oyster Perpetual GMT-Master Ref. 16753, so-called 'Root Beer', c. 1984.
A stainless steel and gold automatic dual-time wristwatch with date and bracelet (cal. 3075)
Diameter 40 mm

OPPOSITE, BOTTOM Rolex Oyster Perpetual Day-Date Tridor, Ref. 18039, c. 1985.
An 18 ct white gold automatic centre seconds wristwatch with yellow gold fluted bezel and an 18 ct three-colour gold link bracelet, the dial with day and date indication (cal. 3055)
Diameter 36 mm

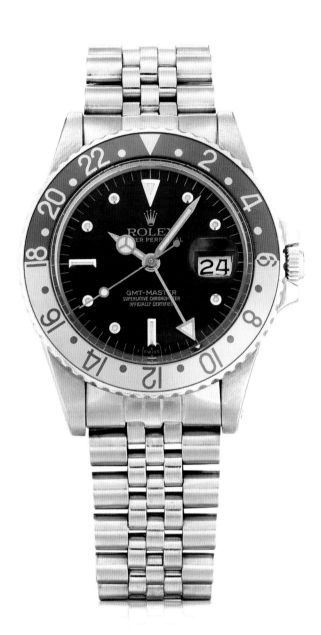

links and continued across the case and dial surface. These models were often embellished with pavé diamond settings. It was models such as these that served, for many owners, as an outward expression of wealth and success.

Complication watches made a return to the fore. A significant part of the industry recognised the marketing appeal of the calendar watch, especially those models that carried indication for the phases of the moon. The 1980s would see a stream of releases within this genre, many with traditional styling. In 1987, the famous watch house of Breguet was purchased by Investcorp. The Breguet brand, which had been reinvigorated by its previous owners, the brothers Jacques and Pierre Chaumet, was poised to make a renewed and spectacular rise to prominence. The distinctive style of Breguet watches had been admired for generations, and the classic nature of their design meant that they were ideally suited to the renaissance period of the mechanical wristwatch. The firm's watches featured distinctive cases with rounded bezels, milled case sides and straight, screw-set lugs.

It was the firm's calendar dials, however, with their elegant yet sophisticated engine-turned patterns, that were especially well suited to the classic luxury dress watch. Although Breguet wristwatches had been produced throughout much of the twentieth century, a new commercialisation of the marque dramatically increased the brand's visibility and availability. Furthermore, the Breguet style had a history of influencing other watchmakers, and this would be particularly in evidence during the 1980s and '90s.

The battle to draw attention also resulted in some daring and innovative designs within the complication watch genre. In 1982 the Swiss businessman Rolf Schnyder acquired a majority shareholding in the watchmaking firm Ulysse Nardin. By the early 1980s, the mechanical Marine Chronometer, on which so much of Ulysse Nardin's business had depended, had been superseded by modern navigational equipment. Schnyder was determined to reinvigorate the firm and sought to produce an entirely new form of wristwatch that would

BELOW, LEFT Cartier Panthère, c. 1985. An 18 ct yellow gold bracelet wristwatch with date and quartz movement Width 27 mm

BELOW, RIGHT Piaget Polo, c. 1985. An 18 ct yellow gold bracelet wristwatch with date and quartz movement Diameter 35 mm

OPPOSITE Breguet Ref. 3330, c. 1988. An 18 ct yellow gold automatic wristwatch with day, date and moon phases (cal. 12½''') Diameter 36 mm

reaffirm Nardin's position as a maker of exceptional mechanical timepieces. The new model, a wristwatch, was named the Astrolabium Galileo Galilei and was released to the public in 1985. A remarkable model, in addition to standard time the watch showed the position of the sun, moon and stars as viewed from earth. The watch's complex dial also displayed a perpetual calendar, the phases of the moon, moonrise and moonset, sunrise and sunset, dawn and dusk, the signs of the zodiac and solar and lunar eclipses. Indeed, so complex was the display that the instruction manual for the watch had to be rewritten three times in an attempt to make it intelligible to the user.[2] The model was housed in a typically 1980s-style case with rounded bezel and case sides and was available on a leather strap or with an integrated bracelet.

In 1986 Audemars Piguet released the world's thinnest automatic tourbillon wristwatch under reference number 25643. Wristwatches with tourbillons were exceptionally rare before the 1980s, with only a very small number of pieces made during the preceding decades by watchmakers such as Omega, Patek Philippe and Lip. Audemars Piguet's tourbillon wristwatch was designed by Maurice Grimm and André Beyner, the same pair responsible for the design of the Delirium, the world's thinnest watch at the end of the 1970s (see pp. 228–29). Although this new tourbillon wristwatch was a far cry from the circuitry of the Delirium's quartz movement, Grimm and Beyner were able to adapt some of the principles of the latter's design. Like the Delirium, the movement for the new tourbillon watch was integrated into the back of the watch's case, and much of the mechanical watch's traditional bridgework was removed. Rather than incorporate a rotor to wind the watch, a heavy swinging weight made of a platinum-iridium alloy was used instead (a full rotor would have compromised the watch's super-slim design, yet if the swinging mass was not appropriately weighted – given the limited space available – it would have failed to engage the automatic winding system effectively). Following production of a prototype, Audemars Piguet purchased the rights to the design. The finalised watch had a radical look, the dial featuring gold sunrays rippling across the surface, these appearing to emanate from the tourbillon carriage, which was visible to an aperture at the top left of the dial. A further aperture to the base of the dial revealed part of the automatic weight within: this was emblazoned with the firm's initials and, when in motion and viewed through its aperture, had the appearance of a mock pendulum. Like many watches of the period, this Audemars Piguet model had a rounded bezel and short lugs. Ultra-thin, the watch had a depth of just 4.8 mm.

BELOW Ulysse Nardin Galileo Galilei, launched in 1985, this example c. 1989. An 18 ct yellow gold automatic astronomical bracelet watch (cal. UN-97) Diameter 40 mm

During the early years of the 1980s, a management consultant, Nicholas Hayek, was approached by a group of Swiss bankers to organise the liquidation of the SSIH[3] (which included the brands of Omega and Tissot) and ASUAG (the world's largest producer of watch parts and movements).[4] In 1983, SSIH and ASUAG were merged into a holding company, and this was subsequently taken private by Hayek in 1985 with the support of a group of Swiss private investors. The business was renamed the SMH[5] in 1986 before taking on its new title, the Swatch Group, in 1998. Hayek's exceptional ability to reorganise, streamline and modernise the companies that had formed the ASUAG & SSIH helped to transform the industry, and by the end of the 1980s the newly formed SMH was the world's most valuable watchmaking group. An important part of SMH's success was owed to the group's movement-manufacturing arm, ETA, which had introduced the Swatch watch in 1983. The Swatch watch gave the SMH an effective weapon with which to challenge the mass-produced electronic watches that were, at that time, flooding the marketplace, and it was the Swatch that would become an icon of the Swiss watch industry's revival. Under Hayek's leadership, the SMH/Swatch Group would go on to acquire a range of historic watch brands throughout the 1990s, including Blancpain in 1992 and Breguet in 1999.

By the end of the 1980s, the future of the mechanical watch seemed assured once again. A fresh confidence was breathing new life into the traditional world of the watchmaker. While the Quartz Crisis had wreaked havoc across the traditional watchmaking industry, it had also enabled a spotlight to be placed on the genius of the fine mechanical timepiece, and it was through this new appreciation of the watchmaker's art that unique opportunities were opening for skilled independent makers. In 1985 the watchmakers Svend Andersen and Vincent Calabrese launched the AHCI (Académie Horlogère des Créateurs Indépendants). The AHCI's mission was, and is, to promote independent watch- and clock-makers and help them to develop their own brands. The academy's members would include the legendary watchmakers François-Paul Journe and Philippe Dufour, both of whom would rise to prominence during the 1990s.

SWATCH

Traditionally, a watch's reliability and accuracy had largely been reflected in its price point. As the 1980s opened, the quartz wristwatch was already a mass-market item that put phenomenally accurate timekeeping on the wrist of any who desired it. For the Swiss movement manufacturer ETA, the Delirium wristwatch, which had been released at the end of the 1970s, opened a pathway for the development of a new mass-market model that could be sold cheaply and on a scale hitherto unknown in Swiss watchmaking. Ernst Thomke, the CEO of ETA, led the project to develop a new type of mass-market wristwatch under the project name Vulgaris Calibre 500.121. Initial planning for what would eventually become known as the Swatch watch was carried out in January 1980. By October 1981, Thomke's principal team consisted of Jacques Müller, designer of the motor and mechanical parts of the movement; Elmar Mock, engineer for the plastic components; Marlyse Schmid and Bernard Müller, the chief stylists; and Franz Sprecher, head of marketing.[6] Among the primary aims were that the new watch should be Swiss-made, strong, accurate, waterproof and have a production cost of no more than 10 Swiss francs.[7]

The key to Swatch's success was the exploitation of the dial and the execution of the case in plastic. While there had been experimentation with fibreglass and other composite materials during the 1970s, the results had tended to be plain and muted in colour. By contrast, Swatch's case would encompass a kaleidoscope of colours, and the prototypes of 1981–82 already showed a rich variety of brightly coloured cases, from greens and blues to yellows and reds. Early dials played with colour and simulated textures, such as imitation stone dials that reflected the continued popularity of that genre at the luxury end of the market. Colour would play an ever more important role in defining the Swatch watch as the decade progressed. The sheer volume of sales and the cheap manufacturing costs meant that a huge range of models could be produced; these varied from minimalist, plain-coloured dials without calibrations to vintage-inspired designs and, increasingly, bright designs with brash colours that were reflective of 1980s pop culture.

The Swatch quickly became a fashion icon. Crucial to this was the fact that, although it was originally conceived as an owner's 'second watch', its designers had managed to produce a wristwatch of such variety that it could be as easily worn in the boardroom as on the playing field. The models allowed the owner to express their individuality, and the affordable price tag meant that it was possible to own a range of different styles for a multitude of occasions. A collectors' market quickly sprang up, and Swatch mania followed. Despite its mass-market availability, the Swatch still felt like an aspirational brand, and securing the rare, limited-edition pieces further enhanced the brand's desirability. The speed of the brand's growth was extraordinary: officially launched in 1983, production had already reached 1 million units in 1984, and by 1990 more than 75 million Swatch watches had been manufactured.[8]

OPPOSITE, LEFT Swatch Jelly Fish, Ref. GZ010, made in 1983. A transparent plastic quartz wristwatch Diameter 34 mm

OPPOSITE, MIDDLE Swatch Yellow Racer, Ref. GJ400, made in 1984. A yellow plastic quartz wristwatch with multicoloured dial Diameter 34 mm

OPPOSITE, RIGHT Swatch Granita di Frutta, Ref. LW105, made in 1985. A ladies' plastic quartz wristwatch with scented casing Diameter 25 mm

ART WATCHES

OPPOSITE Movado and Andy Warhol Times/5, released in 1988.
A blackened steel limited-edition bracelet watch composed of five watch heads with quartz movements, each dial depicting different photographic images of New York City
Length of watch heads 38 mm each

BELOW Movado and Yaacov Agam, Rainbow Collection, released in 1989.
A collection of timepieces with blackened cases, quartz movements and multicoloured discs and bezel calibrations
Diameter of wristwatches 31 mm and 32 mm
Diameter of pocket watch 46 mm

In 1983 Gedalio Grinberg, the chairman of the North American Watch Corporation, took over the watch brand Movado, which like many other watch firms had been suffering due to the Quartz Crisis and the turbulent worldwide economic situation. As an avid collector of modern art, part of Grinberg's plan to revitalise Movado was to produce a series of limited-edition watches designed by artists. Andy Warhol, a personal friend of Grinberg, was the first artist to be approached. Experimenting with round and square shapes, Warhol eventually settled on a rectangular case. Early on, he had the idea of joining several watch cases together, showing Grinberg a string of five watches wired together as a prototype. Rather than produce 'painted' scenes for the dials – which Warhol feared would give the watch 'a department store fashion watch feeling'[9] – he instead settled on black-and-white photographic scenes of New York. Warhol died in 1987 before the project was completed; however, he had already selected the photographs to be used for the dials, and Vincent Fremont, who was the

executive manager of Warhol's studio, was able to report to Grinberg that the Movado watch project was 'complete and ready to go'.[10]

Warhol was himself a collector of watches and was often to be seen wearing a Cartier Tank. Tellingly, Warhol has been quoted as saying, 'I don't wear a [Cartier] Tank to tell the time, in fact, I never wind it. I wear a Tank because it's the watch to wear.' It is therefore unsurprising that Warhol should have chosen the classic rectangular form of watch case as the basis for his design for Movado – and also unsurprising that the dials should be entirely devoid of time calibrations. Warhol's watch was to be a statement piece, first and foremost an artwork, with the dials forming the canvases on which to show his five black-and-white cityscapes. The bracelet was a fixed length and measured around 22 cm, meaning that it acted as a loose-fitting bangle. The cases were made from blackened steel, ensuring that the watches had an entirely monochromatic look that was only punctuated by the red hour and minute hands. Perhaps for Warhol the hands

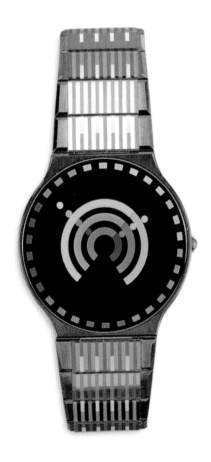

were primarily a visible sign of the passage of time rather than a means by which to tell the hour of the day; in any event, each was fitted with a quartz movement, ensuring that the perpetual motion of the hands was of no issue.

Named the Times/5, Warhol's Movado watch was released in 1988 in a limited edition of 250 pieces and with a price tag of $13,500. The following year, in 1989, Movado continued their Artists' series with a small collection of four timepieces by the Op and kinetic artist Yaacov Agam. These pieces included a wristwatch model with leather strap, a similar wristwatch with blackened steel bracelet, a pocket watch and a desk clock. Three collections were released by Agam for Movado, named the Rainbow, Love Star and Galaxy. The timepieces all featured blackened cases. The Rainbow collection had coloured rings mounted on glazed discs that rotated, forming a semi-circle and a full circle once an hour; beneath these, a series of dots formed the hour and minute hands, which indicated to a rainbow-coloured minute track shown on the watch's bezel. Agam took his abstracted designs further, with triangles in place of hands on the dials of his Love Star collection and swirling rings of colour to the dials of the Galaxy range.

The transformation of the watch into a work of art was not restricted to the luxury end of the market. In 1985, Swatch announced the release of a new line of 'Art' watches. The first artist to collaborate with Swatch on the project was the French designer Christian Chapiron, working under his artist name, Kiki Picasso. Chapiron was soon followed by Keith Haring, who produced four Swatch models in limited series that were numbered from 1 to 9999;[11] at least one of Haring's models was already available in December 1985 in New York, retailing for $50.[12] Haring's graffiti art has become synonymous with the 1980s, and the bold colours and youthful feel of the designs perfectly complemented Swatch's modern vision. The following years would see further artists commissioned to produce artwork for Swatch, including the Belgian surrealistic painter and illustrator Jean-Michel Folin in 1987 and the renowned Japanese graphic artist Tadanori Yokoo. Yokoo was commissioned to produce a limited-edition model in 1988 to celebrate both the fifth anniversary of Swatch and the production of the 50 millionth Swatch.[13]

LEFT Swatch and Kiki Picasso Ref. GZ008, made in 1985.
A plastic limited-edition quartz wristwatch
Diameter 34 mm

OPPOSITE, LEFT Swatch and Keith Haring Personnage, Ref. GZ100, made in 1985–86.
A plastic limited-edition quartz wristwatch
Diameter 34 mm

OPPOSITE, MIDDLE Swatch and Jean-Michel Folin Perspective, Ref. GZ106, made in 1987.
A plastic limited-edition quartz wristwatch
Diameter 34 mm

OPPOSITE, RIGHT Swatch and Tadanori Yokoo Ref. GZ107, made in 1988.
A plastic limited-edition quartz wristwatch
Diameter 34 mm

HIGHLY GEM-SET WATCHES

In 1979, Vacheron Constantin received a commission to create a remarkable gem-set wristwatch of extreme opulence. Named the Kallista, from the Greek *kalos*, meaning 'beautiful', the watch was designed by Raymond Moretti. The case was carved from a single gold ingot weighing 1 kilogram and had a finished weight of 140 grams. One hundred and eighteen emerald-cut diamonds of identical colour and clarity were sourced, allowing the case, bracelet and dial to be entirely covered with the stones. Carrying a price tag of $5 million,[14] the commission came at a critical time for Vacheron Constantin, who had seen sales collapse during the turbulent years of the 1970s. Although the Kallista was a unique piece, closely related watches were produced by Vacheron Constantin during the 1980s. These gold bracelet watches followed the same opulent format as the original Kallista, with integrated gold bracelets and every upper surface covered in diamonds. The largest and most imposing model was known as the King Kalla.

Particularly noteworthy was the fact that the King Kalla was made to be worn by a man. While elaborate gem-set watches for women had been a feature of wristwatch production for much of the twentieth century, there was now, in the 1980s, an increasingly large range of jewellery watches for men. During this period, Rolex became well known for the extravagant range of gem-set watches they offered, especially those produced as variants of the heavy gold bracelet watches within the Day-Date range. These watches have in many ways become synonymous with the 1980s, when, for some, the ability to openly express wealth and success was embodied in the dazzle of the jewellery-form bracelet watch.

Predominantly produced in yellow gold settings, the jewellery watches of the 1980s were often pavé-set, the upper surfaces of the cases and bracelets almost entirely mounted with precious stones. Jewellery watches for women continued to be produced by a wide variety of makers. The pavé-set watches by the leading manufacturers of the period were beautifully executed, usually with round-cut stones that were mounted flush with the surface of the case and/or bracelet and dial. These watches were ideally suited to the styles established during the second half of the 1960s and the 1970s, when the integrated, flexible bracelet had been brought into favour.

Chopard continued to develop their series of Happy Diamonds models. First introduced in 1976, the patented design, with its free-floating diamonds set between two sapphire crystals, would become a signature model of the brand and its innovative, quirky look matched well with the fashions of the 1980s.

BELOW, LEFT Rolex Oyster Perpetual Day-Date Ref. 18048, c. 1985.
An 18 ct yellow gold automatic wristwatch with day and date indication, diamond-, ruby- and sapphire-set dial, diamond-set bezel and gold and diamond-set bracelet (cal. 3055)
Diameter 37 mm

BELOW, MIDDLE Patek Philippe Ref. 3817/4, made in 1984.
An 18 ct yellow gold and diamond-set quartz wristwatch with integrated diamond-set gold bracelet (cal. E19)
Width 25 mm, length 30 mm

BELOW, RIGHT Chopard Happy Diamonds, c. 1980.
An 18 ct white gold manually wound bracelet watch, the black outer dial with free-floating diamonds (cal. 2446)
Width 32 mm

OPPOSITE Vacheron Constantin King Kalla, released in the 1980s.
An 18 ct white gold manually wound bracelet watch set with 160 emerald-cut diamonds, total diamond weight 101.27 carats (cal. 1052)
Width 27.5 mm

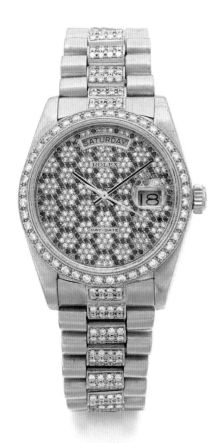

CHRONOGRAPHS

Between 1980 and 1993, Audemars Piguet produced a small number of manually wound chronograph wristwatches that followed in the footsteps of the firm's vintage production. However, these new chronographs featured skeletonised dials, allowing the viewer to see right through the movement. Even the spring barrel's cover was cut away to show the coils of the spring beneath. Such delicate openwork designs, with beautifully finished bridgework, emphasised the skill of the watchmaker's art and were a perfect means by which to further the mechanical watch's renaissance. In 1986 Audemars Piguet launched their first automatic chronograph model, which had subsidiary dials for 30-minute and 12-hour registers. The case was typical of the period: circular in shape with a rounded bezel and short lugs. The dial was asymmetrically arranged with the three subsidiary dials at six, nine and twelve o'clock, while the three o'clock position was taken by an aperture for the date. Dial colour was of a single tone that carried through to the subsidiary dials, these bordered with slim, metallic rings.

In 1987 Jaeger-LeCoultre developed a new 'Mecha-quartz' calibre (cal. 630), which combined traditional watchmaking with quartz technology. Although comprising 233 parts, the movement was one-third the size of a normal mechanical chronograph movement and, when launched, was 40 per cent smaller than the smallest quartz chronograph (with analogue display) available on the market.[15] Powered by a battery and with a quartz oscillator, the chronograph was otherwise a relatively traditional mechanical module. The movement was used by Jaeger-LeCoultre in their ultra-slim Odysseus chronograph, launched in 1988 with the additional functions of date display and moon phases.

Rolex introduced their first major chronograph update since the 1960s with the launch of a new automatic Cosmograph Daytona model in 1988. Measuring 39 mm in diameter, the watch was slightly larger than its predecessors (Refs 6263 and 6265), which Rolex had introduced at the end of the 1960s and which were still available until the introduction of the 1988 model. The

BELOW, LEFT Audemars Piguet Ref. 25563, introduced in 1981. An 18 ct pink gold skeletonised chronograph wristwatch with 30-minute register (cal. 5030) Diameter 36 mm

BELOW, RIGHT Jaeger-LeCoultre Odysseus, introduced in 1988. An 18 ct yellow gold quartz/mechanical hybrid chronograph wristwatch with subsidiary dials for constant seconds, 30-minute and 12-hour registers, apertures for date and moon phases, outer pulsometer scale (cal. 630) Diameter 35 mm

RIGHT Audemars Piguet Huitième Ref.
25644, introduced in 1986.
An 18 ct yellow gold automatic
chronograph wristwatch with subsidiary
dials for constant seconds, 30-minute
and 12-hour registers, aperture for date,
outer tachymeter scale (cal. 2126)
Diameter 40.5 mm

new Cosmograph Daytonas were given a completely fresh look, with dials of white or black gloss for the stainless steel and stainless steel and gold versions, while the all-gold version was available with a satin-finished champagne dial. A major change was the layout of the dial itself, which now featured a single tone across the full surface of the dial. Rather than subsidiary dials of starkly contrasting colour to the main dial surface as had been found in the previous generation of Daytona watches, only the calibrated chapter rings of the subsidiary dials were now differently toned. The crown was 'protected' with shoulders, or guards, an inheritance from Rolex's other tool watches such as the Submariners and GMTs, and the new Daytonas were fitted with a sapphire crystal. However, another significant change was in the type of movement used. Somewhat surprisingly given the popularity of the automatic chronograph in the 1970s, Rolex waited until the introduction of their 1988 Daytona before releasing an automatic chronograph. The movement was based on Zenith's calibre 400, the El Primero calibre that was generally recognised as the finest series-produced automatic chronograph calibre available. Rolex made some 200 modifications to the movement, including reducing the beats per hour from 36,000 to 28,800, the incorporation of a Rolex balance with Breguet hairspring and Microstella regulation system, and the removal of the date indication.[16] The movement was refined to such a degree that all new models of the Daytona were able to achieve chronometer-rated standards.

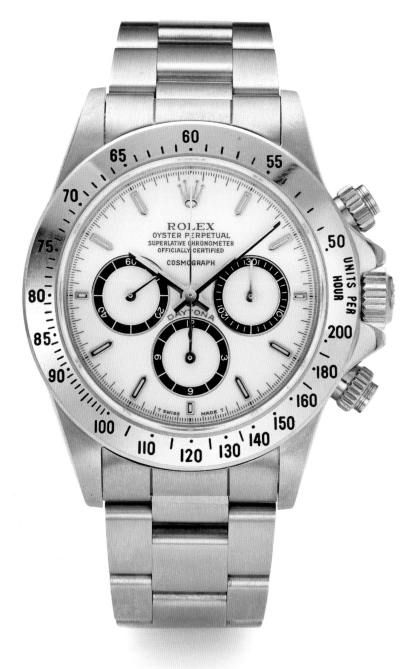

RIGHT Rolex Oyster Perpetual
Cosmograph Daytona Ref. 16520,
introduced in 1988.
A stainless steel automatic chronograph
wristwatch with subsidiary dials for
constant seconds, 30-minute and
12-hour registers, bezel calibrated for
units per hour, steel bracelet (cal. 4030)
Diameter 39 mm

BELOW Blancpain Chronographe
Rattrapante, first released in 1989.
An 18 ct yellow gold automatic split-
seconds chronograph wristwatch
with subsidiary dials for constant
seconds, 30-minute and 12-hour
registers, aperture for date (cal. 1186)
Diameter 33.5 mm

During the 1980s, Blancpain held an enviable position
from which to develop a new series of complication
watches using the expertise of the owners, former Omega
director Jean-Claude Biver and the watchmaker Jacques
Piguet. The latter came from the famous calendar and
chronograph movement-making dynasty of Frédéric
Piguet (formerly Louis-Elysée Piguet), and it was using
Jacques Piguet's expertise that Blancpain were able to
develop a range of completely new chronograph models.
At the end of the decade, in 1989, Blancpain announced
the production of the first split-seconds chronograph
wristwatch with automatic winding (cal. 1186). This was
an extraordinary achievement, since the extra depth usually
required to incorporate the split-seconds mechanism had
previously hampered efforts to automate this extremely
complex variant of the chronograph genre. In addition
to the split-seconds complication and automatic winding,
a date aperture was also added, yet the depth of the
movement was still only 6.75 mm and its diameter just
27 mm. Once again, following the classic circular-cased
aesthetic, the model was released with a rounded bezel
and plain white dial which, in place of slim baton hour
indexes, was calibrated with discreet Roman numerals.
In keeping with the classic style of the vintage mechanical
wristwatch that Biver and Piguet both so admired,
the case of the watch was traditional in its proportions,
with a diameter of 33.5 mm.

CALENDAR WATCHES

While the LCD watch had ensured the cheap and easy availability of the self-adjusting calendar wristwatch, the mechanical perpetual calendar wristwatch had long been a means to demonstrate the skill of the watchmaker. The complex and attractive display of the perpetual calendar, with moon phases, was another perfect genre through which to reinvigorate the public's desire for the mechanical timepiece.

Audemars Piguet's release of their slim automatic perpetual calendar wristwatch in 1978 would be followed by a great variety of mechanically powered calendar watches during the 1980s, including their own Royal Oak perpetual calendar, which was officially launched in 1984. Patek Philippe, the traditional leaders in this field, released a new perpetual calendar wristwatch in 1981. Named the Ref. 3450, this was the firm's first new perpetual calendar model for almost twenty years. Although the new Ref. 3450 was little changed aesthetically from its predecessor, the model had one crucial addition that would become a feature to be found on many perpetual calendar watches

of the 1980s and beyond: the leap year indicator. A circular aperture between three and four o'clock on the dial of the 3450 displayed the leap year cycle – this showed numerals for years one, two and three within the cycle and finally a red dot during the leap year itself (later versions of the model showed all four years of the cycle in Roman numerals). As has been seen, while the perpetual calendar pocket watch was often calibrated for leap year indication, the leap year was seldom displayed on the smaller surface of a wristwatch dial. The potential inconvenience for the user was in there being no visible way of telling which year of the leap year cycle the perpetual calendar wristwatch was currently in – perfectly fine if the watch was in daily use and had been set up to the correct cycle by the watchmaker, but not if the watch had been stored for a long period of time. Considering part of the thrill of owning a perpetual calendar is in witnessing the watch's self-adjustment once every four years, when the calendar work accounts for the extra day of 29 February, it would seem natural for the owner to wish to have the full

cycle indicated. Indeed, when Patek Philippe again updated their perpetual calendar wristwatches in 1984–85, the leap year cycle was displayed in full within a subsidiary dial.

In 1985 the International Watch Company took the leap year indicator one stage further with the launch of a new model named the Da Vinci. An automatic perpetual calendar watch, this was the first wristwatch to mechanically indicate the complete year on the watch's dial. Indeed, the model was designed to continue telling the correct date until 2499. As part of the accessories supplied with the watch, a vial sealed with wax contained spare century indicators for the 22nd, 23rd and 24th centuries. Although of course somewhat tongue in cheek, such a feature allowed IWC to capitalise on the quality and projected longevity of the fine mechanical wristwatch. In addition to the calendar and moon phase indications, the Da Vinci also incorporated a chronograph with register for periods of 30 minutes and 12 hours. The model's case had distinctive rounded sides and hinged, hooded lugs.

By the 1980s, Gérald Genta, already well known for producing iconic watch designs for other brands, was creating his own distinctive wristwatches. Largely focusing on watches with complications and unusual displays, Genta produced a range of perpetual calendar watches that also indicated the leap year cycle to the dial. To the centre of Genta's subsidiary month dial, a smaller dial had four wedge-shaped apertures, and a coloured disc beneath would fill the aperture to display the current year within the leap year cycle. Another notable feature was the distinctive blue disc set to the top of the dial, with an off-set aperture to its base through which the phases of the moon were displayed. These models were housed in distinctive cases, predominantly octagonal or round in shape.

Audemars Piguet dramatically increased production of their perpetual calendar watches during the 1980s. In the fifteen-year period following the launch of the company's 1978 automatic perpetual calendar Ref. 5548, Audemars Piguet made over 7,000 perpetual calendar watches, comprising more than 70 different models.[17]

During the 1980s the watchmaker also introduced their
new Grande Complication; an open-faced pocket watch,
this model combined perpetual calendar with moon
phases, a split-seconds chronograph and minute repetition.
At the time of its launch it was reportedly the most
expensive series-produced watch in the world, with just
one example made each year.[18] The model had a dress-
style case and traditional dial layout, and the slim baton
numerals, fonts and calibrations followed the general
1980s aesthetic.

By the end of the decade, the growing popularity of the
skeletonised wristwatch saw the release of 'transparent'
perpetual calendar wristwatches, the dials reduced to slim
chapter rings for calendar indications and minimal
calibrations for the hours and minutes. Such a treatment
was ideally suited to a watch of such complexity, allowing
the exceptional finishing of the movement and the
astonishing intricacy of the operating system to be clearly
viewed by the owner and, of course, the admiring spectator.
Both Audemars Piguet and Vacheron Constantin released
skeletonised versions of their perpetual calendar models
before the close of the decade.

RIGHT Audemars Piguet Grande
Complication Ref. 25570, c. 1984.
An 18 ct yellow gold manually wound
pocket watch with perpetual calendar,
moon phases, minute repetition
and split–seconds chronograph
with 30-minute register (cal. 2860)
Diameter 52 mm

OPPOSITE Vacheron Constantin Ref.
43032, c. 1988.
An 18 ct yellow gold automatic skeletonised
wristwatch with perpetual calendar
and moon phases (cal. 1120QP)
Diameter 36 mm

INNOVATIVE COMPLICATIONS

Throughout the 1970s, George Daniels had continued to produce a remarkable series of watches. These had included the first Daniels watch to include an escapement of the maker's own invention – the Daniels independent double-wheel escapement – which was incorporated into a gold open-faced pocket watch and sold to the collector Seth Atwood in 1976. In 1982, Daniels completed the first of his Space Travellers' watches. Two years later, in 1984,[19] a second, more complex watch, the Space Traveller II, was finished by Daniels, this time with the addition of a chronograph function. The exceptionally complex movement was captivating in appearance, with its symmetrical trains, twin escape wheels and exposed chronograph bridges. Designed to show both mean solar and sidereal time, the handmade silver dial had multiple engine-turned finishes and displayed sidereal time to the left dial and mean solar time to the right, each with their own subsidiary seconds immediately below. A sector for the equation of time appeared at the top of the main dial, and an aperture for moon phases was placed within the sidereal

time dial; further apertures within the chapter rings displayed the moon age and annual calendar. The watch had a chronograph function that could be switched to either the mean solar or sidereal time trains to measure time elapsed. This was an extraordinarily complex watch and Daniels's most sophisticated to date. The Space Traveller II was retained by George Daniels until his death in 2011 and during his lifetime was invariably his dress watch of choice. Significantly, the case back was glazed. Enthusiasts were, unsurprisingly, always keen to see what watch Dr Daniels was wearing – the design of this watch meant that not only could the viewer marvel at the beauty of its dial, but they could be equally mesmerised by the complexity and wonder of the movement, clearly visible through the 'exhibition' back.

One of George Daniels's closest horological friends was the English watchmaker Derek Pratt. In 1965 Pratt had relocated to Switzerland, where he worked as a freelance watchmaker and watch restorer. It was here that Pratt met Peter Baumberger, and the pair would

BELOW The glazed 'exhibition' back of the George Daniels Space Traveller II

OPPOSITE George Daniels Space Traveller II, made between 1982 and 1984. An 18 ct yellow gold chronograph watch with Daniels independent double-wheel escapement, mean solar and sidereal time, annual calendar, age and phases of the moon, equation of time indication Diameter 63 mm

go on to collaborate on the production of an exceptional collection of pocket and wristwatches at the watchmaking firm of Urban Jürgensen & Sønner throughout the 1980s and beyond. In fact, Baumberger would himself acquire the firm of Urban Jürgensen in 1985. Prior to this, during the second half of the 1970s, Pratt and Baumberger had embarked on a project to produce a small series of tourbillon pocket watches. In 1979 Gerhard Scheufens, then owner of Urban Jürgensen & Sønner, gave permission for these new tourbillon watches to be signed with the full company name. One of the first of these tourbillon pocket watches, completed around 1982, is shown opposite. The watch employs Derek Pratt's one-minute tourbillon carriage with one-second remontoire mounted within – this design marked a first in tourbillon production and achieved Pratt's goal of providing greater accuracy. The design of the dial and case of the tourbillon watch shared stylistic similarities with pocket watches of the 1920s and '30s.

Like George Daniels, the aesthetic style that Baumberger and Pratt developed together was heavily influenced by the work of Abraham-Louis Breguet, and their watches would increasingly feature exceptional engine-turned dials with multiple, contrasting finishes. Such dials were made for a small range of highly complex but unfinished movements that Baumberger acquired with his purchase of the Urban Jürgensen firm. These watches were completed and regulated by Pratt during the 1980s. Baumberger recognised that, in order to increase sales, it would also be necessary to manufacture a range of wristwatches. At the end of the 1970s, just as mechanical movements were falling out of favour, Baumberger had purchased a batch of Zenith El Primero chronograph movements. With these, he would introduce a new wristwatch model. Named the Ref. 1, the watch was an automatic triple-calendar chronograph wristwatch with moon phases and was produced between 1982 and 1986 in 186 examples.[20] The dial of the Ref. 1 was made of silver and was engine-turned by hand. Stylistically the dial was, once again, heavily influenced by the Breguet aesthetic. A mid-century design was used for the case, with teardrop lugs, rectangular chronograph pushers and rounded case sides.

PATEK PHILIPPE'S 1989 ANNIVERSARY

OPPOSITE AND BELOW Patek Philippe Calibre 89, made between 1980 and 1989. A yellow gold double-dialled and double open-faced minute repeating *grande* and *petite sonnerie* clock-watch with Westminster chimes, tourbillon, split-seconds chronograph, registers for 60 minutes and 12 hours, perpetual calendar, retrograde date, indications for year, leap year cycle, seasons, second time zone, date of Easter, astrological indications, moon phases, equation of time, power reserves for striking and going trains, mean and sidereal time, alarm, temperature, indications for times of sunrise and sunset, and celestial chart for the night-time sky over Geneva, Switzerland, at latitude 46° 11′ 59″ N (cal. 32‴ 89)
Diameter 88.2 mm

In 1979, at the end of a decade of turbulence both for the world economy and the watchmaking community, Philippe Stern, honorary president of Patek Philippe, had an eye on the future. In ten years' time the company would be celebrating its 150th anniversary, and Stern wished to ensure that Patek Philippe was well prepared for the occasion. Stern discussed with Patek Philippe's technical director, Max Studer, the possibility of re-creating the Henry Graves Supercomplication[21] (see pp. 106–9). This must have seemed an appropriate project in so many ways, for the Supercomplication was born in similarly challenging times, completed as it was in 1933 during the Great Depression. However, Studer was keen to take the project further, suggesting that Patek Philippe aim to create an even more complex watch, the most intricate the world had ever seen. This was an extraordinary project to conceive – the requirements in terms of designers, watchmakers and artisans would mean committing a significant proportion of the company's resources for the next few years. However,

Stern was adamant, and with Paul Buclin appointed as the lead watchmaker, the project was silently but officially launched.

Completed in 1989 and appropriately named the Calibre 89, the watch weighed 1.1 kg, and it had required 1,728 components to produce the watch's 33 mechanical complications (nine more complications than incorporated in the Henry Graves Supercomplication). The functions included a star chart, a perpetual calendar, times of sunrise and sunset, split-seconds chronograph, minute repetition, *grande* and *petite sonnerie* and alarm functions, and even an indicator for the date of Easter. It was an astonishing achievement and cemented the watchmaker's position at the pinnacle of high horology. The watch's external design echoed that of the Henry Graves Supercomplication: the case was of similar bassine form, with open-faced dials to both sides of the watch. However, the calibrations to the dial, while traditional, were clearly influenced by the 1980s aesthetic in their fonts and styling.

The parallels drawn between the Henry Graves Supercomplication and the Calibre 89 were intended to rekindle the market's appreciation and desire for the classic mechanical watch. Just four examples of the Calibre 89 were made – the watch was of course a statement of mechanical prowess and never intended for series production. However, alongside the Calibre 89, Patek Philippe also released a selection of wristwatches that were designed to further highlight the watchmaker's heritage as well as their continuing commitment to fine watchmaking. Chief among these models were two minute-repeating wristwatches. The first of these was the Ref. 3979, a minute-repeating wristwatch with automatic movement and a porcelain white dial with Roman numerals. The epitome of the classic wristwatch, it was a wonderfully understated model that housed one of the most intricate forms of movement in watchmaking. From the front, the only guide to the watch's immense complexity was a slide to the left case side that would, when activated, chime the hours, the quarters and minutes past each hour. This model was joined by an even more complex minute-repeating wristwatch, the Ref. 3974, which additionally incorporated a perpetual calendar and moon phases.

Patek Philippe released commemorative, limited-edition models to celebrate their 1989 anniversary. These included two significant models based on two of the earliest wristwatch styles to have emerged. The first was the so-called 'Officer's' watch (Ref. 3960), which was closely based on early wristwatches from the 1910s, and the second was a tonneau-shaped wristwatch with jump hours (Ref. 3969) that was a clear descendant of the Art Deco originals. These pieces were especially significant for they channelled the very essence of Patek Philippe, at once emphasising the watchmaker's long history and simultaneously creating a desire for the collector's watch. Drawing on, updating and reissuing vintage models would become an increasingly large and important part of the mechanical watchmaker's oeuvre in the years and decades ahead.

BELOW Patek Philippe Officier, Ref.
3960, formally released in 1989.
An 18 ct yellow gold wristwatch with
hinged case back revealing cuvette
with engraved commemorative dedication
(cal. 215PS)
Diameter 33 mm

OPPOSITE Patek Philippe Ref. 3969,
formally released in 1989.
An 18 ct pink gold tonneau-form
jump-hour wristwatch (cal. 215HS)
Length 38 mm

ROYAL OAK OFFSHORE.
SEMPLICEMENTE INIMITABILE.

AP
AUDEMARS PIGUET

Le maître de l'horlogerie.

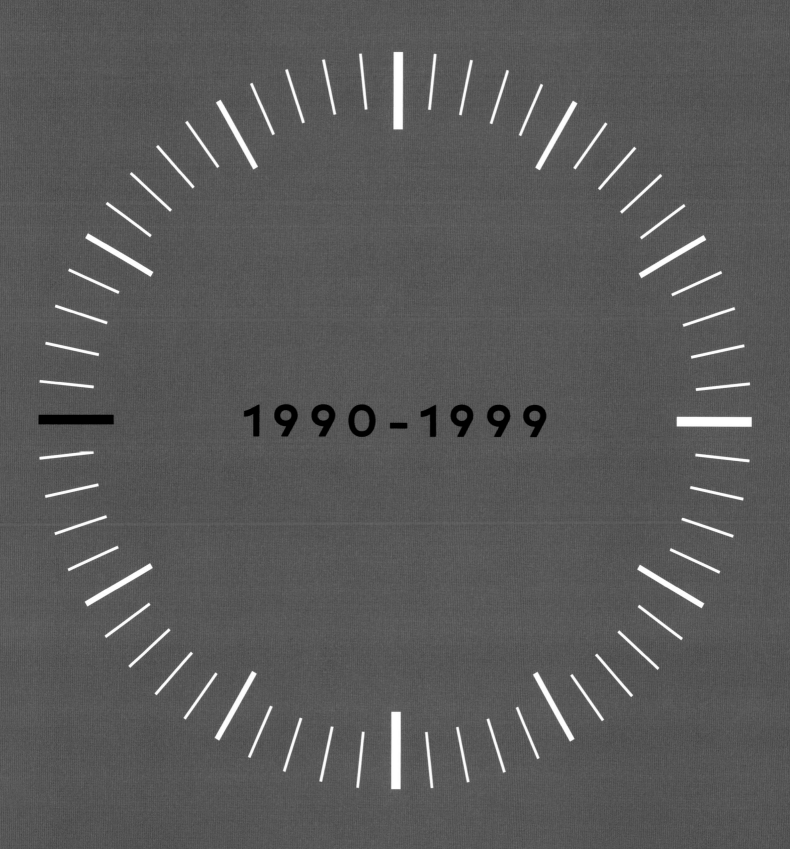

1990-1999

THE 1990s

The hunger for mechanically complex watches that had been fed by a resurgent watch market in the second half of the 1980s continued to be dominant throughout the 1990s. Indeed, while the economic turbulence of the early 1990s would impact the industry, the ability of watchmakers to create new and innovative timepieces ensured the decade was supplied with a huge variety of models.

In December 1990, following the reunification of Germany, the historical watchmaking firm of A. Lange & Söhne was re-established by Walter Lange, great-grandson of the firm's founder. Financed by the Mannesmann group and with technical support from the International Watch Company, A. Lange & Söhne presented their first series of modern watches in October 1994. The firm entered the market with a unique offering that combined outstanding workmanship with innovative yet fundamentally classic design. Every detail of the watches was thoroughly considered and their exceptional quality was clear to see, from the precision and clarity of the dials to the highly engineered movements and cases.

Among the first models released was the Lange 1, and this immediately became an iconic watch in its own right. The design of the dial was highly original, with separate sections for time, seconds and power reserve, designed so that there was no interference or overlapping between one display and another. An oversized date was also created for clarity and ease of use, with a single pusher to the case side above the ten o'clock position allowing the date to be quickly adjusted when required. The watch had an impressive weight to it, and the movement, which was made from German silver, was highly distinctive – the three-quarter plate design followed the traditional aesthetics of the firm's historical production pocket watch movements. The jewels were set within screwed rings, while the backplate itself was beautifully finished with damascened stripes to the surface. The exceptional movement finishing could be viewed through the sapphire crystal display back.

For the watchmakers that had survived the ravages of the Quartz Crisis, an increasing emphasis was placed on

BELOW, LEFT Alain Silberstein Krono 2,
c. 1995.
A blackened steel automatic triple-
calendar chronograph wristwatch with
registers, moon phases and 24-hour
indication (cal. ETA–Valjoux 7751)
Diameter 38 mm

BELOW, RIGHT Patek Philippe Ref. 5015,
introduced in 1993.
An 18 ct yellow gold automatic wristwatch
with sector for power reserve and
aperture for moon phases (cal. 240PS)
Diameter 35 mm

brand heritage. Many firms would dip into their archives
to draw inspiration from designs of the past. For Jaeger-
LeCoultre, 1991 saw the sixtieth anniversary of their
signature model, the Reverso, and the watchmaker
produced a special limited-edition model to celebrate
the occasion. Named the 60ème ('60th'), the anniversary
Reverso had a guilloché dial with indications for date and
a fan-form sector for power reserve. The watch 'reversed'
to a sapphire crystal display back that revealed the manually
wound movement, the plates and bridges of which
were made from solid 14 ct gold, finished with decorative
Geneva stripes. The watch's casing itself was made from
18 ct pink gold. Produced in 500 examples, the 60ème
quickly sold out, and Jaeger-LeCoultre followed this model
with further limited-edition Reverso wristwatches, these
incorporating popular complications such as the tourbillon
and minute repeater.

One of the most distinctive brands of the 1990s was
that of Alain Silberstein. Silberstein, a French artist and
designer, was a marketing consultant for French fashion

watches during the 1980s. Having experimented and
successfully designed a chronograph wristwatch using
a Valjoux calibre 7750, Silberstein, together with his
wife, launched his own watch brand, Alain Silberstein
Creations, in 1989.[1] Using movements supplied by ETA,
Silberstein designed a range of highly unusual and
eccentric mechanical wristwatches, concentrating
especially on models with chronographs, calendars and
tourbillons. Silberstein's watches drew on his artistic flair
and reinterpreted the fashion watch genre for the high-end,
luxury wristwatch market. Influenced by the work of
the artist Joan Miró, Silberstein's watches challenged
the accepted perception of the luxury watch as an item
of understated, clean design, a theme that had dominated
much of 1980s mechanical watchmaking. The success
of the Swatch watch and its appeal to a wide demographic
had created a gap in the market for a higher priced, luxury
wristwatch that mixed playful and colourful designs with
high-grade materials and quality finishing. The majority
of Silberstein's watches were circular with slim bezels

and relatively thick cases, giving the watches a somewhat cylindrical appearance.

As watchmakers vied with one another to create captivating dial designs, many developed unusual forms of time display, among which the jump hour and wandering hour watches featured prominently. Watches with sector displays for functions such as power reserve or date were popular throughout the 1990s. However, sectors were also used for time-telling itself. The year 1994 marked the 400th anniversary since the death of Gerardus Mercator (1512–1594), the Dutch cartographer famous for introducing a world map using his projection system. Vacheron Constantin marked this anniversary by releasing a new model named the Mercator in his honour. The case of the watch was inspired by vintage designs of the late 1940s and 1950s, but the dials were modern and vibrant. Two sectors indicated hours to the left and minutes to the right, each of retrograde format; and the two hands were in the form of mapping callipers – the minute hand would spring back to zero at the end

of each hour, while the hour would jump back to one o'clock at the end of each twelve-hour period. The dials were decorated with maps either in gold or silver; however, a small number of polychrome enamel painted dials were also produced for Vacheron Constantin by the artists Lucie and Jean Genbrugge, using Mercator's maps as inspiration.

Franck Muller, the self-styled 'Master of Complications', launched his own brand in 1991 and throughout the decade introduced an extraordinary number of complication wristwatches that posed a direct challenge to the established watch houses. His models were highly innovative, and through inspired styling he managed to capture the elegance of the Art Deco period while successfully modernising his designs for the contemporary market. Muller had spent the 1980s working as both a restorer and maker of watches, and his passion for and understanding of the complication watch formed the basis of his company. One of this maker's most enduring designs was the Cintrée Curvex, a tonneau-shaped

BELOW, LEFT Vacheron Constantin Mercator Ref. 43050, introduced in 1994. An 18 ct yellow gold automatic wristwatch with two retrograde sectors indicating hours and minutes, the dial decorated with a polychrome enamel map painted by Jean and Lucie Genbrugge depicting the South China Sea / Taiwan and the east coast of China (cal. 1120) Diameter 36 mm

BELOW, RIGHT Franck Muller Curvex Cintrée Ref. 2850, first introduced c. 1992. An 18 ct white gold automatic perpetual calendar wristwatch with curved tonneau–form case (cal. 2800) Length 45 mm, width 31 mm

OPPOSITE Ulysse Nardin San Marco 'Répétition Minutes Jacquemart Forgerons' Ref. 701–22, introduced in 1989, this example c. 1991. An 18 ct yellow gold automatic wristwatch with minute repetition and jacquemart automaton (cal. 11) Diameter 39 mm

wristwatch with a gently curved case back, directly influenced by similarly styled watches of the 1910s and '20s, and this model also invariably featured the stretched Arabic numerals that had epitomised the Art Deco era. Muller deployed the minute-repeating function in many of his models, and he was by no means alone. Throughout the 1990s, the leading makers of complication watches increasingly incorporated minute repetition within their premier models, often in combination with additional complications. While the minute-repeating mechanism is among the most complex of mechanical complications, an activation slide to the side of the case is usually the only indication that a watch contains this particular function. Ulysse Nardin used a historical design to produce a very visible version of the minute-repeating watch. Nardin created a series of minute-repeating wristwatches that harked back to the striking *jacquemart* figures that were found on some repeating pocket watches in the nineteenth century, themselves influenced by the striking figures found on some early

European clocks. Two figures were fitted to the dial of Ulysse Nardin's model, and when the slide to the case side was moved to activate the repeating work, the automated *jacquemart* figures would appear to strike the bell at the same time as hammers within the movement struck their gongs. The dials were invariably finished with translucent enamel over an engine-turned ground, again a style of decoration that had been popular during the nineteenth century.

The range of sports-style watches increased throughout the decade. While Rolex retained their standard sports models such as the Submariner, Daytona and Explorer, in 1992 they introduced a new rugged model named the Yacht-Master. Launched in 18 ct gold, this was a large and heavy wristwatch measuring 40 mm in diameter. With robust styling, the model had a broad rotating bezel with a matt, stippled finish. Vacheron Constantin introduced their own new sports model in the mid-1990s: named the Overseas, it drew inspiration from the firm's Hysek-designed Ref. 222 of the 1970s (see p. 229)

(see p. 229)

BELOW LEFT Rolex Oyster Perpetual Date Yacht-Master Ref. 16628, introduced in 1992.
An 18 ct yellow gold automatic centre seconds wristwatch with date, rotating calibrated bezel and gold bracelet (cal. 3135)
Diameter 40 mm

BELOW RIGHT Vacheron Constantin Overseas Ref. 49140, late 1990s.
A stainless steel automatic chronograph bracelet watch with registers and oversized date (cal. 1137)
Width 40 mm

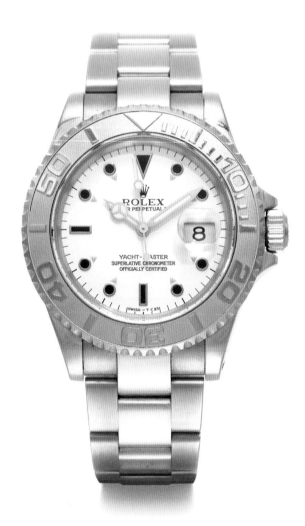

BELOW Omega Co-Axial Chronometer,
made in 1999.
An 18 ct yellow gold limited-edition
automatic centre seconds wristwatch
with date and co-axial escapement.
This example presented to George Daniels
on 30 April 1999 to commemorate Omega's
launch of the co-axial escapement at
the 1999 Basel Watch Fair (cal. 2500)
Diameter 38 mm

and the more recently introduced Phidias model of the early 1990s. The model was made in three sizes, but its largest, chronograph version, with a width of just over 40 mm, was a reflection of the growing demand for oversized cases.

As the 1990s progressed, the traditional default of the luxury wristwatch being predominantly produced in yellow gold began to change. In large part this reflected the influence of the vintage watch market, where pieces in yellow gold were generally more widely available than those in pink gold, white gold or platinum. The consequent disparity in pricing within the vintage market between examples of the same model in yellow gold and those in the rarer metals resulted in a perception that yellow gold was the least desirable of the precious metals. As a consequence, a greater proportion of watch models began to be manufactured in pink gold and the monochromatic metals of white gold and platinum. Mixed-metal watches were still in demand during the 1990s, but the market increasingly favoured watches made in a single metal tone.

At the Basel Watch Fair of 1999, Omega announced the release of their first wristwatch model to incorporate the co-axial escapement. Invented by George Daniels, the co-axial escapement was developed by Daniels over a number of years, with designs completed by 1974 and a patent acquired in 1980. Its genius lay in the reduction of friction, which almost entirely removed the need for lubrication, thereby improving efficiency and extending servicing intervals. To place this event in context, Omega's use of the co-axial marked the first successful commercialisation of a new escapement since the introduction of the lever escapement, the latter invented by the English watchmaker Thomas Mudge in 1754. Stephen Urquhart, president of Omega at the time of the co-axial's launch, later wrote: 'There's no question that the industrialisation of the Co-Axial escapement marked a true turning point for the brand and laid the foundation for Omega's return to its rightful role as producer of fine mechanical watches.'[2] Daniels's contract with Omega's parent company, the Swatch Group, ensured that he could continue to use the escapement in his own watches. It was also agreed that a small number of ébauches made for the co-axial and manufactured by the Swatch Group's movement manufacturer ETA would be supplied to Daniels for his own use. These movements were refinished in the English style, with gilded plates and blued steel screws by Daniels and his exceptional apprentice, the watchmaker Roger Smith. The movements were given handmade, engine-turned dials and the circular cases had rounded, stepped bezels and an eccentrically placed crown to the lower-left case side; a sapphire crystal display back revealed the movement and its decoratively engine-turned gold rotor.

The impact of Daniels was also to be found on another stand at the Basel Watch Fair of 1999, that belonging to the rising watch star François-Paul Journe. In a tribute to George Daniels following his death in 2011, Journe wrote, 'Without you I would most certainly never have started to make my first watch … [You] showed us the path back to authentic watchmaking with innovation.'[3] Journe's exhibit at the Basel fair included his Tourbillon Souverain. Journe had been exposed at a young age to the work of Abraham-Louis Breguet and Antide Janvier while working for his uncle, Michel Journe, an antique clock restorer from Paris. François-Paul's extraordinary creativity, infused with the influence of Daniels and the work of makers such as Breguet and Janvier, led to the creation of his own highly individual style. Journe's Tourbillon Souverain was the first wristwatch to incorporate a constant-force remontoire in a wristwatch – this feature ensured the even distribution of power to the watch escapement as the mainspring unwound. The watch's dial had an eccentric layout, with equal space devoted to the time dial and aperture for tourbillon. A sector for power reserve indication was incorporated at the top of the dial, and to its base a further aperture revealed the remontoire's fly regulator. Journe's highly individual style, exceptional skill and quality of production ensured that his brand quickly established a loyal fan base.

By the end of the twentieth century, the design of the watch appeared to have come full circle. Stylistic elements from the 1920s to the 1970s formed the basis for many models, and vintage designs that were either reinterpreted or reissued played an important part in the offerings of the major watch brands. However, the quartz crisis and its aftermath had forced the industry to innovate in order to survive, and a new wave of talent had introduced a fresh dynamic that often challenged the established traditions. Although a tremendous number of watch brands had disappeared during the difficult years of the 1970s and early 1980s, a new generation of watchmakers had been responsible for launching new brands, while the successful consolidation of many historic marques by the Swatch and Richemont groups had led to a regeneration of the market. At the dawn of the new millennium, demand for luxury watches continued to gain momentum and a new air of confidence pervaded – the mechanical watch's renaissance seemed all but complete.

BELOW George Daniels Millennium, made in 1999.
An 18 ct yellow gold automatic centre seconds wristwatch with Daniels's slim co-axial escapement
Diameter 37 mm

OPPOSITE F. P. Journe Tourbillon Souverain d'Égalité, introduced in 1999.
A platinum tourbillon wristwatch with constant-force remontoire and power reserve indication (cal. 1498)
Diameter 38 mm

JUMP HOUR AND WANDERING HOUR WATCHES

The 1990s witnessed a renewed interest in the development of watches with unusual time displays. In 1990 the watchmaker Breguet launched a limited-edition jump hour wristwatch. This watch was classically styled with a white enamel dial and a blued steel hand to indicate the minutes. An aperture above '60' displayed the hour in red Arabic numerals. Unusually, the disc that carried the numerals revolved once every 24 hours rather than twice, and was therefore calibrated from 1 to 24 rather than 1 to 12.

Audemars Piguet launched an entirely novel wandering hour wristwatch in 1991. Named the Star Wheel, the watch had a central three-armed wheel on which three transparent discs were calibrated with the hours from one to twelve o'clock. A sector at the top of the dial was calibrated for minutes. Only one disc at a time would follow the minute track – each hour index had a triangular indicator above it that pointed to the minute track as the current hour travelled across the minute sector. A highly unusual arrangement, it was a design that would be incorporated across a range of different

Audemars Piguet models, occasionally in combination with the additional complication of minute repetition.

In 1996 Cartier reintroduced a limited-edition Tank à Guichet model, a jump hour version of their Tank wristwatch, which had originally been designed in 1928. The reissued model was initially made in nine examples (three in pink gold, three in yellow gold, three in platinum) for the 'Magical Art of Cartier' auction held at Antiquorum Geneva in November 1996. In 1997, to celebrate the 150th anniversary of Cartier, a larger limited-edition series of Tank à Guichet watches was released. These models were all closely styled on jump hour watches of the Art Deco period; the 1996 series featured their winding crowns between the lugs above the twelve o'clock position, while those from 1997 could be found with their winding crown at three o'clock. This placement also followed the original Tank à Guichets, which were produced with crowns in either position.

A further variation on the jump hour theme was introduced in 1998 by Vacheron Constantin. Named

BELOW, LEFT Breguet Ref. 3420, introduced in 1990.
An 18 ct yellow gold automatic jump hour wristwatch (cal. 562)
Diameter 36 mm

BELOW, RIGHT Audemars Piguet Star Wheel, introduced in 1991.
An 18 ct yellow gold automatic wandering hour wristwatch (cal. 2124)
Diameter 36 mm

the Saltarello, this cushion form wristwatch combined vintage inspiration with modern design. There was a retrograde minute display, which formed an arc above which a conventional aperture displayed the jumping hours. As the minute hand reached '60' it would fly back to the start of the new hour. Although contemporary in design, the watch had a distinctive Art Deco inspired look, with stepped lugs and a bold, engine-turned dial with prominent sunray pattern.

TOURBILLONS

OPPOSITE AND BELOW Breguet Ref. 3350, introduced in 1990.
An 18 ct yellow gold tourbillon wristwatch (cal. 558)
Diameter 36 mm

The 1990s witnessed a dramatic increase in the range and availability of the tourbillon wristwatch. Long seen as one of the most desirable complications to be found in a watch, the tourbillon was invented by Abraham-Louis Breguet in 1801. Fittingly, the Breguet firm themselves began the new decade by introducing, in 1990, a tourbillon wristwatch model (Ref. 3350). With traditional Breguet styling, the watch had an engine-turned dial with a relatively small display for the minutes and hours, thereby allowing for a large aperture beneath, through which the tourbillon carriage was displayed. Tourbillons are mesmerising to see in action – a tourbillon watch has its escapement together with its balance mounted onto a tourbillon carriage, and this carriage rotates (in a wristwatch, usually one revolution per minute) while the balance continually oscillates and the escape wheel turns. Designed to eliminate the errors that occur when a watch is in a vertical position, the tourbillon complication is in fact more suited to the pocket watch than the wristwatch, but its dramatic motion is undeniably captivating and has ensured its enduring popularity in the wristwatch.

In 1991 Girard-Perregaux chose to mark their bicentenary with the introduction of a wristwatch version of their Three Bridge tourbillon. Ten years earlier, in 1981, Girard-Perregaux had begun to design and build a small series of twenty tourbillon pocket watches. These were based on an original Three Bridge tourbillon made by Constant Girard that had won first prize at the 1867 Universal Exposition in Paris. Development of a wristwatch version was begun in 1986 to ensure completion in time for the 1991 anniversary.[4] The linear design of the movement, with its prominent three bridges, appears beautifully simple, yet this masks its remarkable mechanical complexity. The partially skeletonised design was well suited to the early 1990s, a period when the popularity of the visibly displayed movement was rapidly growing.

One of the most impressive tourbillon watches of the 1990s was a model by A. Lange & Söhne named Pour Le Mérite. As one of the first watches released by the recently re-established German watchmaker, Lange's tourbillon not only asserted the firm's ambitions but enabled it to showcase its technical prowess. The dial

OPPOSITE Girard-Perregaux Three Bridge Tourbillon, introduced in 1991.
An 18 ct pink gold skeletonised tourbillon wristwatch (cal. 9600S)
Diameter 39 mm

BELOW A. Lange & Söhne Pour Le Mérite, first released in 1994.
A platinum tourbillon wristwatch with power reserve indication and sapphire crystal display back to reveal the movement (cal. L 902.0)
Diameter 38.5 mm

of the watch was perfectly balanced, with two subsidiary dials indicating seconds and power reserve, and a larger aperture beneath revealing the tourbillon carriage. Remarkably, the movement's going train was via a fusée and chain transmission, a feature that was otherwise largely consigned to the history books – this was almost certainly the first time such a feature had been designed for use in a wristwatch. The fusée and chain equalised the power of the mainspring to ensure even power distribution as the spring unwound. Fitted with a sapphire crystal display back, the back plate of the movement was partly cut away in order to show the fusée and its chain.

CHRONOGRAPHS

Chronograph models continued to be released in a wide range of styles during the 1990s. Although the chronograph function was incorporated into many of the period's most complex watches, such as those with perpetual calendars, models that were primarily devoted to the watch's timing abilities remained a popular genre during the decade.

In 1992, following three years of development, the International Watch Company launched a new split-seconds chronograph wristwatch named the Doppelchronograph. Styled in the manner of the firm's military watches, such as their famous Mark XI (see p. 182), the watch had a black dial with Arabic numerals, a triangular index at twelve o'clock and squares at the quarter hours. A large-sized model, the case measured 42 mm in diameter. The matt black dial included apertures for day and date indication, and three subsidiary dials displayed the constant seconds and registers for recording minutes and hours elapsed. An extra pusher to control the split seconds was incorporated to the left case side above the ten o'clock position.

A new quartz chronograph 'dress' model was released by Cartier in 1996 as part of their recently introduced Tank Française line of watches. Although based on the original Tank designs, the Française had a broader bezel to each side of the dial, with a curved upper case and flat back. The model was available with a specially designed bracelet that had satin-finished central links and polished side links. The dial was styled in a classic Cartier fashion with Roman numerals that stretched around its edge. Subsidiary dials displayed the date at twelve o'clock, and there were two further dials for registering minutes and hours while the chronograph was running.

BELOW Cartier Tank Française, introduced in 1996.
An 18 ct yellow gold quartz chronograph wristwatch with subsidiary dials for date, 30-minute and 12-hour registers (cal. 212 P)
Length 36 mm, width 28 mm

BELOW International Watch Co.
Doppelchronograph Ref. 3711,
introduced in 1992.
A stainless steel automatic split-seconds
chronograph wristwatch with subsidiary
dials for constant seconds, 30-minute
and 12-hour registers, and apertures
for day/date indication (cal. 79030)
Diameter 42 mm

At the Basel Watch Fair of 1998, Patek Philippe launched a new chronograph model, the Ref. 5070. Surprisingly, with the exception of the firm's perpetual calendar chronograph models, this was the first chronograph wristwatch to be manufactured by the watchmaker for almost 30 years. The watch's design was closely based on a wristwatch made between 1950 and 1952 under reference number 2512. This explains the 5070's classic, mid-century design; the case had a chamfered bezel and pronounced, downturned lugs with stepped edges. The dial, with its applied gold Arabic numerals and leaf-shaped hands, together with the style of the subsidiary dials and calibrations, were all typical of Patek Philippe's chronograph designs of the 1940s and '50s. However, although the Ref. 2512 wristwatch, which provided the inspiration for the Ref. 5070, was an oversized model, the series-produced vintage chronographs of the firm had been of modest size, ranging from around 33 mm to 37 mm. The 5070 was 42 mm in diameter, and while precedents had been set for larger watches by other watchmakers earlier in the 1990s, this was an unusually large model for Patek Philippe at the time of its release.

During the second half of the 1990s Rolex began introducing a range of opulent, gem-set versions of their Daytona models. These colourful watches were powered by the same Zenith El Primero-derived calibre that the watchmaker had first introduced to their chronograph range in 1988. Dial combinations ranged from models with gem-set indexes to dials covered with diamonds in a pavé setting. In addition to silvered, black and champagne dials, mother-of-pearl and mineral dials were also used. Some examples were produced with calibre-cut gem-set bezels in place of the traditional calibrated chronograph bezel. Hooded lugs on some models were also embellished with diamonds or other precious stones.

RIGHT Patek Philippe Ref. 5070,
introduced in 1998.
An 18 ct yellow gold manually wound
chronograph wristwatch with subsidiary
dials for seconds and 30-minute register,
outer tachymeter scale (cal. CH 27–70)
Diameter 42 mm

OPPOSITE Rolex Oyster Perpetual
Cosmograph Daytona Ref. 16599,
c. 1999.
An 18 ct white gold automatic
chronograph wristwatch with registers,
sodalite dial, diamond-set indexes,
sapphire-set bezel and diamond-set
hooded lugs (cal. 4030)
Diameter 39 mm

CALENDAR WATCHES

Breguet continued to expand throughout the 1990s, with new markets opening up for the brand in Asia and North America. The firm's calendar watches proved popular, the traditional styling of their dials being especially well suited to complex displays. Indeed, the historical 'Breguet' style would continue to influence the work of other makers, including that of Franck Muller, who launched an extraordinary array of highly complicated wristwatches during the 1990s. In 1992 Muller produced what was claimed to be the most complicated wristwatch in the world, using a movement by Louis-Elysée Piguet to which Muller added further mechanical functions. The wristwatch included a perpetual calendar, moon phases, monthly retrograde equation, *grande* and *petitie sonnerie*, minute repetition and temperature indication.[5] This model was closely styled on the aesthetics of watches by Abraham-Louis Breguet. In 1997 Muller introduced a small series of similarly complex watches with a new calibre, the cal. 97. The image opposite illustrates an example of the cal. 97 with an Art Deco

inspired case, a design period that greatly influenced Muller's work. Made in white gold, the case had large, hinged lugs inspired by forms from the 1930s.

At the Basel Watch Fair of 1992, Audemars Piguet presented a new, highly complex model that combined a perpetual calendar with chronograph and minute repetition. Aesthetically, the watch was still heavily influenced by the styles of the 1980s, with slim baton numerals and a rounded case and bezel. However, vintage design influences also showed, especially in the form of the lugs and the leaf-shaped hands, both elements of which harked back to the 1940s. Of particular note was the size of the watch's case, which measured 42 mm in diameter, making it an especially large watch for the period.

To mark the 125th anniversary of the International Watch Company in 1993, the watchmaker introduced its most complicated wristwatch to date. Named the Destriero Scafusia Ref. 1868, this model was also unusually large, with a case diameter of 43 mm and a particularly thick

OPPOSITE International Watch Co. Destriero Scafusia Ref. 1868, first introduced in 1993.
An 18 ct gold perpetual calendar minute-repeating tourbillon wristwatch with apertures for year indicator and moon phases, and split-seconds chronograph with 30-minute and 12-hour registers (cal. 1868)
Diameter 43 mm

RIGHT The sapphire crystal display back of the International Watch Co. Destriero Scafusia Ref. 1868

OVERLEAF, LEFT Patek Philippe Ref. 5016, introduced in 1993.
An 18 ct pink gold perpetual calendar tourbillon wristwatch with black dial, moon phases, minute repetition and retrograde date (cal. R TO 27PS QR)
Diameter 36 mm

OVERLEAF, RIGHT Patek Philippe Ref. 5035, formally released in 1996.
An 18 ct pink gold automatic annual calendar wristwatch with centre seconds (cal. 315 S QA)
Diameter 37 mm

profile of around 17 mm. The watch incorporated a tourbillon, perpetual calendar, moon phases, split-seconds chronograph with registers and minute repetition. At the time of its production it was the most complicated wristwatch ever produced in series. The watch incorporated 750 individually made and hand-finished parts which allowed the movement to control the model's 21 functions and displays. Although large in size, the design was heavily influenced by mid-twentieth-century case design, with a chamfered bezel, rectangular chronograph pushers and large, downturned lugs that had chamfered outer edges. A pronounced slide to the left case side activated the minute-repeating mechanism. The case back took full advantage of the recent trend for glazed covers, allowing the highly decorated movement to be viewed, including the impressive tourbillon carriage. The dial had a traditional silvered finish, and the shapes of the hands were also influenced by styles from the 1940s and early 1950s.

Patek Philippe offered a wide range of perpetual calendar watches throughout the 1990s. One of the most complex models offered during this period was released by the watchmaker in 1993 under reference number 5016. The 5016 was a minute-repeating tourbillon wristwatch

that also combined a perpetual calendar with retrograde date indication and moon phases. However, in 1996 the watchmaker also introduced a new 'annual calendar' model. While not a full perpetual calendar, the movement of this watch self-adjusted for the differing lengths of the months with the exception of February, thereby requiring adjustment only once per year. The calendar system required a less sophisticated and consequently less expensive arrangement than that of the perpetual calendar. Launched at the Basel Watch Fair of 1996, when sales of luxury watches were easing off following the boom years of the late 1980s and early 1990s, the model was offered at one-third of the price of Patek's standard perpetual calendar model.[6]

WORLD TIME WATCHES

During the 1990s there was a renewed interest in the world time wristwatch, with examples introduced by a number of different manufacturers. In 1990, Svend Andersen launched a model that was heavily influenced by the world time wristwatches that Patek Philippe had made from the late 1930s to the 1950s and which had incorporated the world time mechanism invented by Louis Cottier (see pp. 104–5). Andersen, who had previously worked at Patek Philippe before setting up his own watchmaking business, knew the world time model well, having serviced examples himself while working in Patek's Atelier des Grandes Complications during the 1970s.[7] Named the Communication, Andersen's world time wristwatch worked in a similar manner to Cottier's original designs: the user simply rotated the bezel until the current location/zone was shown at the twelve o'clock position, and with the hands then set to local time, the dial's outer 24-hour ring would continually indicate the hour in all zones around the world.

Vacheron Constantin, who had used Cottier's world time system during the 1930s, also launched a world time wristwatch based on the principles of the original models. Vacheron's new wristwatch was, however, contemporarily styled and was introduced as part of the brand's Phidias line. The case of the Phidias seamlessly merged with an integrated bracelet that was both bold and sleek. To the dial of the watch, a representation of the globe was marked with the lines of longitude and latitude. Vacheron's model also used a rotating bezel calibrated for locations around the world, each representing the different time zones. Once again, by moving the city/location representing the current time zone to the twelve o'clock position, the hour in all other zones was indicated to the 24-hour ring beneath.

A novel system of world time indication was introduced by Jaeger-LeCoultre to the dial of a new model named the Géographique. A long aperture above twelve o'clock allowed the user to select from a list of cities that represented the world's time zones – the selection was

BELOW, LEFT Svend Andersen Communication, introduced in 1990. An 18 ct yellow gold automatic wristwatch with world time indication (cal. 951) Diameter 32 mm

BELOW, RIGHT Vacheron Constantin Phidias, introduced in the early 1990s. An 18 ct yellow gold automatic wristwatch with world time indication (cal. 1180) Diameter 34.5 mm

made by turning the crown at the left case side above the ten o'clock position. At the base of the dial, a secondary time zone dial indicated the time in the city currently shown in the aperture, the hour hand moving automatically as the city disc was turned. A smaller 24-hour subsidiary dial, to the left side of the secondary time zone dial, indicated whether the hour shown in the second time zone was a.m. or p.m. Local time continued to be shown by the standard hour and minute hands to the centre of the main dial. The watch also had a fan-form sector for power reserve and a further subsidiary dial for date. This system was designed to enable the user to view the current time in any zone across the world quickly and easily. Shown at the Basel Watch Fair of 1990,[8] the aesthetic styling of the model retained the rounded bezel and case sides and discreet lugs favoured during the previous decade.

Another form of time zone indication continued to be available in the form of the twin-dial watch. During the 1990s, Cartier offered a dual-time version of their classic Tank Cintrée. Dividing the dial in half, the upper and lower time zones were powered by separate manually wound movements. The use of twin dials was a form that had appeared in previous decades, and the rectangular case of the Cintrée lent itself especially well to the concept, allowing two square dials of equal size to be used to fill the entire surface area of the dial.

GRANDE AND PETITE SONNERIE

During the 1990s, as complication wristwatches became more and more popular, watchmakers vied with one another to produce ever more complex models. However, not all the complication watches of the period were immediately visible as such. Although repeating watches that chimed the time on demand were often incorporated with a host of other mechanical functions, a number of firms continued to offer the minute-repeating wristwatch without additional mechanical complications, the only sign of their complexity being a discreet slide to the side of the case.

Although remaining rare, one form of complication that became more visible during the 1990s was the minute-repeating watch with *grande* and *petite sonnerie* – the so-called 'clock-watch'. Such watches may be set to chime the time in passing. *Grande sonnerie* watches will strike the hour automatically at the start of each new hour, then, on passing each quarter, the watch will once again strike the hour, together with the current quarter – this is usually composed of a single strike for each hour, while the quarters may be represented by a double strike using two hammers on two gongs. *Petite sonnerie* will normally strike each hour as it is reached and may additionally chime the quarters (although without the hour) as the minute hand reaches each quarter. Clock-watches will also usually incorporate repetition on demand, although unlike a standard minute repeater, the repetition is activated via a pusher or a short rather than long slide – this will release a pre-wound train, which then allows the watch to strike the time; this is in place of the longer slide used in a standard repeating watch, where the action of moving the slide winds the repeating work each time it is used.

In 1992 Philippe Dufour, an independent watchmaker based in the Vallée de Joux, Switzerland, presented an exceptional *grande sonnerie* wristwatch. The watch, which had taken two years to complete, was styled in the manner of a traditional pocket watch, with a white enamel dial, Roman numerals and blued steel hands. Slides or 'switches' within the case sides allowed the user to select whether or not the watch would be in striking mode and, if striking, whether the hours and/or quarters would sound. Although Dufour placed a glazed cuvette (cover) over the movement, the case had a solid hinged back, the maker preferring to conceal the movement from view, thereby making its reveal all the more special. Indeed, the movement was exquisitely finished with beautifully chamfered bridges bearing decorative Geneva stripes to their surfaces. The execution of the watch was an astonishing achievement – the experience that Dufour had obtained from restoring pocket watches in the 1980s, especially those with repeating work, had proved invaluable. Philippe Dufour was one of a small number of highly talented 'independents' whose watches would become increasingly sought after as the mechanical watch's renaissance continued throughout the 1990s.

OPPOSITE Philippe Dufour, introduced in 1992.
An 18 ct pink gold two-train wristwatch with *grande* and *petite sonnerie* and trip-minute repetition (cal. 12)
Diameter 41 mm

PANERAI AND OFFSHORE

During the 1980s the size of wristwatches had remained relatively modest, with circular-cased watches for men generally measuring between 34 and 36 mm. Trends for extremely large watches would develop in the years ahead, but most especially after the turn of the millennium. However, the early years of the 1990s began to see the introduction of some models with larger case sizes. In 1993, two brands released models that would challenge the sizing of watches and open the door to a new breed of outsized models.

In 1989 Emmanuel Gueit, a young designer working at Audemars Piguet, produced conceptual designs for an entirely new form of the brand's flagship model, the Royal Oak.[9] This new Royal Oak scaled up the original format dramatically and gave it a decidedly rugged look, helped by the fact that it was also a chronograph model. A thick and pronounced black gasket was visible between the screwed-down bezel and the main body of the case, while the crown and chronograph pushers, which were protected by silicon caps, were surrounded by substantial guards that protruded from the case. The dial had a hobnail finish across the surface, adding texture and further emphasising the watch's robust design. Most significant was the watch's size: measuring 42 mm in width and with a case depth of 15 mm, this was a vast wristwatch by the standards of the period. Named the Royal Oak Offshore, upon its release at the Basel Watch Fair of 1993 the watch had already earned the nickname 'The Beast'.[10]

OPPOSITE Officine Panerai Mare Nostrum Ref. 5218–301/A, introduced in 1993.
A stainless steel chronograph wristwatch with subsidiary dials for constant seconds and 30-minute register, bezel calibrated for tachymeter (cal. 3127)
Diameter 42 mm

RIGHT Audemars Piguet Royal Oak Offshore Ref. 25721ST, introduced in 1993.
A stainless steel automatic chronograph wristwatch with subsidiary dials for constant seconds, 30-minute and 12-hour registers, aperture for date, outer tachymeter scale (cal. 2126/2840)
Width 42 mm

On board an Italian Navy cruiser, in September 1993, the watch brand Panerai presented a series of three limited-edition watches. Based on models created by Panerai during the Second World War, these were extremely large models, the originals of which were designed for use by military divers and were intended to be worn on the outside of a diving suit. The models released were the Luminor, Luminor Marina and Mare Nostrum and were sized between 42 mm and 44 mm. The Mare Nostrum was a chronograph wristwatch with a broad, flat bezel and distinctive black dial that had bold luminescent numerals. However, it was the large cushion-form case of the Luminor watches that would become the signature style for future editions of the Panerai models. These watches had massive cushion-form cases and substantial guards that entirely covered the crown; the crown itself was locked in place by a lever within the guard. Both the Luminor and Luminor Marina had distinctive black dials with large Arabic and baton numerals, which were usually luminescent (although occasionally with luminescent accents above). Being of cushion shape and with a hefty crown guard, the 44 mm width of the Luminor watch case was even more pronounced. At the time of Panerai's relaunch in 1993, the Italian watch market was highly influential, and, despite a challenging economic situation during that year, the time was ripe for reinvigorating an Italian watch brand. Indeed, following their launch, the models were enthusiastically greeted by the collectors' market, and in 1997 the Vendôme Group (now known as the Richemont Group) purchased the Panerai brand. The following year, Panerai was formally launched on the world stage and would begin a dramatic rise to prominence within the first few years of its new ownership.

Both the Offshore and Panerai models would prove highly influential in the coming years. With their success, a new market for very large wristwatches was established. While the effects were not immediate, a trend for enlarging watches slowly began. Two decades after the introduction of the Offshore and Panerai models, the outsized watch case would come to dominate the market, with case widths of 40 mm and above being commonplace.

GLOSSARY

annual calendar This form of calendar *complication* will self-adjust for the varying lengths of the months throughout the year, with the exception of February, meaning that the date and month display will need adjusting just once per year.

automatic These watches incorporate an additional mechanism within their movement to ensure that a watch is automatically kept wound while being worn on the wrist. The majority of automatic watches have a **rotor** mounted to the back of the movement that travels around its circumference – the rotor's action engages the watch's automatic system, which in turn winds the *mainspring* to power the watch. In order to prevent a watch from being overwound when the mainspring is fully charged, a range of devices are used to block, lock or uncouple the winding system. Before the widespread use of rotors, the so-called **bumper automatic** movement was a common offering. In place of a rotor, bumper automatic watches used a pivoted weight that travelled around two-thirds of the circumference of the movement and buffered off springs at each end of the weight's arc of motion.

balance An oscillating wheel that, together with the balance spring, controls the speed at which the watch runs, thereby determining its timekeeping. Above the balance is the balance cock, a metal bridge that almost always has a regulating index to speed up or slow down the movement. Above the centre of the balance is the so-called 'end-stone': this is the jewel that caps the balance staff, and in some watches there is a shock resistance 'spring' that helps to absorb impacts to the watch. In the early part of the twentieth century, before the introduction of special balances and springs made of temperature-compensating alloys (such as Invar or Glucydur), balances were frequently made of two strips of metal fused together, usually steel and brass. These balances were cut near to their arms, allowing the free ends to move inward or outward as the temperature rose or fell respectively – this expansion and contraction of the balance's rim altered the moment of inertia of the balance as the rim's mass moved closer to or further away from the balance's centre. The elasticity of a non-temperature-compensated balance spring is greatly affected by changes in temperature, which will result in irregular oscillations of the balance with consequential impact on a watch's timekeeping. As the bi-metallic compensated balance expanded and contracted, so it would compensate for changes in the balance spring's elasticity.

bassine A traditional form of watch case comprising a hinged back with rounded edge and a rounded bezel that retains the watch's crystal.

bezel The part that holds a watch's crystal or glass in place, usually also incorporated into the overall design scheme. It takes various forms and may be detachable or moulded and fully integrated into the body of the watch. The most common styles of bezel are flat or chamfered/bevelled, rounded/convex or scooped/concave.

bombé A flowing form of *lug* design that has a distinctive faceted, flaring shape. It is relatively uncommon but, where found, examples tend to date to the mid-twentieth century.

bras-en-l'air Literally 'arms in the air', these watches used figures, animals or objects to indicate the time. They were operated via a pusher that, when depressed, would cause the arms or legs of a figure/animal or the extremities of an object to rise and indicate the time in hours and minutes against a scale calibrated on the watch's dial.

bumper automatic *see automatic*

calibre (cal.) Watch movements are usually defined by a calibre number. The same calibre may have several variants, sometimes indicated via suffixes to a base calibre number. Calibre numbers may also be prefixed by the movement manufacturer's stamp or logo. It was common practice for many watch brands to buy in movements, which were then often finished 'in-house'. For this reason, one may commonly find both the calibre number of a specialist movement manufacturer and the signature of a watchmaking 'brand' on the same movement. Where movements do not have a specific designation they may be referred to by their size using the *ligne* unit of measurement. *See also ligne*

calibré cut Precious stones cut in this manner are usually of faceted, tapered form and are specially cut to fit flush with one another, leaving no gapping.

The stones are most often of rectangular or keystone shape.

centre seconds a seconds hand that is mounted above the hour and minute hand to the centre of a watch dial. Centre seconds may also be referred to as **sweep seconds**.

channel setting To the viewer, precious stones mounted in this manner appear to be invisibly set; this is achieved by a groove cut into the sides of the stone that allows it to be slid onto a mount. On a watch, the mount may be concealed within the *bezel*, onto which the channel-set stones are set.

chapter ring This is the circular band on which the hour indexes of a watch may be displayed. A chapter ring is usually only mentioned when it is a clearly delineated section of the dial – perhaps sectioned via a specially printed ring or rendered in a different colour or tonal finish to the rest of the dial. In antique watches and clocks, the chapter ring was frequently a separate metal ring that was applied to the surface of the dial.

chronograph A standard time-telling watch with the addition of a timing/stopwatch function. A central chronograph seconds hand will be started, stopped and reset via a pusher or pushers. Most chronographs will have one or two **registers** in the form of subsidiary dials that will record time elapsed in minutes and sometimes hours as well. A **split-seconds chronograph** incorporates two central chronograph hands: one, the *fly-back*, is mounted above the other and can be independently stopped, reset or realigned to the main second hand, allowing multiple events to be timed. When a split-seconds chronograph is started using a pusher, both central seconds hands will begin moving together; a separate pusher allows the fly-back to be stopped independently and it may be left in this position until the main second hand is stopped separately, or it can be made to rejoin the main chronograph hand. When both hands are together and stopped, they can be reset to the zero position.

chronometer This has two different meanings:

    1. Originally, a chronometer referred only to watches that incorporated a chronometer

escapement. Such watches contain a **detent** within the escapement: a piece of steel mounted with a jewel which unlocks the escape wheel. This form of escapement has the greatest degree of 'detachment', meaning that friction is reduced to a minimum, ensuring the escapement moves as freely as possible. The English watchmakers John Arnold and Thomas Earnshaw both introduced forms of the spring detent escapement, and it was Earnshaw's version that eventually proved the most successful. Watches of exceptional precision, chronometers were most commonly used for navigating at sea; much larger marine chronometers that were fitted in wooden boxes and mounted on gimbals were also used for the same purpose.

2. A chronometer may also refer to a watch that has been officially certified to chronometer standards, regardless of the escapement used within it. The observatories at Besçancon, Neuchâtel and Geneva as well as official testing/control stations at Bienne, La Chaux-de-Fonds, Le Locle, Saint-Imier and Le Sentier all provided rigorous testing for watches submitted for official examination whereby the watch movement's performance was officially checked and recorded. Similar tests were also offered at Kew in England. During the trials, the watch's movement was tested over a fifteen-day period in five different positions. To gain chronometer status, the daily deviation in timekeeping of the watch's movement had to fall within specified parameters. The agreed parameters were altered over the course of the twentieth century; however, in the 1960s they were set at a mean daily variation of no greater than −1 to +10 seconds per day. In 1973, these permissible rates were updated by the Contrôle Officiel Suisse des Chronomètres (COSC) to require a daily mean deviation of no more than −4 to +6 seconds. More stringent rules were applied to quartz watches.

clock-watch Watches of this type will strike the time rather like a clock. As the minute hand reaches the new hour, the watch will chime the hour, usually on a coiled gong (although early watches could incorporate a bell). Clock watches are usually of two main types, either *grande sonnerie* or *petite sonnerie*, although they will frequently have settings allowing the user to select *grande*, *petite* or *silence*. **Grande sonnerie** watches will strike the hour automatically at the start of each new hour, then, on passing each quarter, the watch will once again strike the hour, together with the current quarter – this is usually composed of a single strike for each hour, while the quarters may be represented by a double strike using two hammers on two gongs. **Petite sonnerie** will normally strike each hour as it is reached and may additionally chime the quarters (although without the hour) as the minute hand reaches each quarter. Clock-watches will also repeat on demand, known as **trip-repeating**: unlike a standard *minute repeater*, the trip repetition is activated via a pusher/button rather than a slide. The pusher will release a pre-wound *train*, which then allows the watch to strike the time.

co-axial escapement A modern form of watch *escapement* invented by the English maker George Daniels. Its genius lies in the reduction of friction, which almost entirely removes the need for lubrication, thereby improving efficiency and extending servicing intervals. Daniels completed designs for the co-axial by 1974 and later acquired a patent for the invention in 1980.

complication Any function that is in addition to time-telling itself. This can be as basic as a date indication or as complex as a chiming or timing feature. Watches with multiple functions may be described as having 'complications'.

cuvette A cover that is placed over a movement and beneath the main case back. Usually intended to provide extra protection against the ingress of dirt and dust, these covers also help to provide additional strength to the case itself. Occasionally, cuvettes are glazed and may be used for exhibition purposes.

deck watch A watch of high precision that was used both on ships and submarines as an observation

and/or navigation tool. Deck watches were also used as an additional time source by which the ship's marine *chronometer* might be checked.

detent escapement *see chronometer*

ébauche A 'blank' movement before finishing. An ébauche may simply be a movement's base plates or it can already contain a number of components such as the spring barrel, regulator and ratchet wheel. Many watch companies did not manufacture their own ébauches, instead buying them in from specialist makers before finishing the movements themselves 'in-house'.

equation of time This is the difference between apparent *solar time* (the time as indicated on a sundial) and *mean time* (the average of solar time). Since the Earth has an elliptical orbit, the difference between mean and solar time ranges from +14 minutes, 59 seconds to −16 minutes, 15 seconds. Solar time agrees with mean time on or about 15 April, 14 June, 1 September and 24 December.

escapement The part of a movement that checks and releases the *train*, thereby transmitting an impulse from the *mainspring* to the watch's *balance*. The escapement takes various forms; however, the **lever escapement** is found in the vast majority of twentieth-century mechanical watches and was invented by the English watchmaker Thomas Mudge in 1754. *See also co-axial escapement*

fly-back The most common form of the fly-back is used for timing short intervals. This feature acts in a similar way to a standard *chronograph* seconds hand; however, unlike a chronograph seconds hand it is continually running, and depression of a pusher merely resets the hand to the twelve o'clock/zero position, whereupon it simultaneously restarts. A fly-back hand may also be found on a *split-seconds chronograph*; however, in these watches, the fly-back hand sits above the main chronograph seconds hand and can be stopped independently and made to 'fly-back' to twelve o'clock or forward to realign with the main chronograph seconds hand.

fly regulator *see remontoire*

friction fitting Case backs that are friction fitted are often referred to as 'snap-on' backs. Such case backs are usually detached with a case knife and rely on close-fitting rims to the back and body of the case that adhere to one another with friction, ensuring that they cannot become detached in everyday use.

fusée This component is designed to compensate for the varying force of a *mainspring* as it unwinds, thereby ensuring the even transmission of power to the watch's going *train*. The fusée is spirally grooved and conically shaped and is connected to the spring barrel by means of a chain. When the mainspring is fully wound, it turns the fusée and uncoils the chain from the smallest part of the fusée – requiring the greatest strength; by contrast, when the spring is almost spent, it pulls on the widest part of the fusée, which requires less energy to turn. Improvements in achieving constancy in the power of the mainspring meant that, by the early twentieth century, the fusée and chain form of transmission in watches was largely obsolete.

grande sonnerie *see clock-watch*

guilloché This decorative technique is achieved by using a special lathe known as a rose engine that can build up multiple contrasting finishes of engine-turned decoration. Applied to case backs, dials and sometimes *bezels*, guilloché decoration may be covered in translucent enamel to further enhance its decorative effect.

half-hunting case(d) In common with *hunting-cased* watches, the half-hunter has a cover over the dial but with the addition of a glazed aperture to the centre that allows the time to be read without opening the cover itself. The smaller aperture allowed for a stronger glass than that covering the dial beneath, making breakage less likely.

hands Made in a variety of different shapes throughout the twentieth century, some of the most common are:

>   *alpha*: of fine triangular-type taper leading to a sharp point at the tip.
>   *baton*: straight-sided hands of even width throughout their length, although the tips are usually pointed.

>   *dauphine*: of fine triangular form with a central facet running throughout the length. The hands terminate in a sharp point at their tip.
>   *épée*: sword-shaped hands that taper outwards from the centre of the dial before terminating in a short chevron shape at their tips.
>   *feuille*: leaf-shaped, these are slim hands that have a bowed centre.
>   *filigree*: usually made in gold and with the appearance of finely worked wire decoration; usually broader at the base with fine, sharp tips.
>   *moon* or *breguet*: most commonly found in blued steel or yellow gold, these hands often have a leaf-shaped body with a cut-out roundel towards their ends, terminating in a sharply tapered tip.
>   *skeletonised*: usually of broad form, the hour hand frequently with a bulbous head; both minute and hour hands may have wire crossings either to strengthen or decorate, or to help retain luminous paint.

hermetic This refers to a form of watch that features a double casing that is designed to protect the crown from the ingress of dirt and moisture. An inner case is usually hinged into an outer casement and may be 'swung out' for winding and hand-setting. The outer case is made of two parts: a solid body and separate screw-down *bezel*; the bezel invariably has a knurled finish for the owner's fingers to grip when opening and closing the watch.

hunting case(d) A watch with a hinged cover over the dial, usually opened via a pusher through the winding crown.

jacquemart An automaton figure that appears to strike a bell in time with the striking of a watch's bell or gong.

lapel watch A form of watch designed to fit through a buttonhole. These are usually composed of a small dial that protrudes on a short stem from the main body of the case and its movement. The effect is to display the dial while concealing the main body of the case beneath the buttonhole.

lever escapement *see escapement*

ligne Often represented by the triple prime symbol, ‴, a *ligne* is an old unit of measurement that was in use before the adoption of the metric system and is still employed by watchmakers to express the size of a watch movement. Watch movements are often defined by their *ligne*, especially when no calibre number is known or given; 1 *ligne* = 2.2558 mm.

lugs These protrude from the watch case and are joined to one another by either a removable spring-loaded lug pin or a fixed, solid metal bar. The pin or bar holds the watch's strap/band or bracelet in place.

mainspring This provides the mechanical watch's power. The spring is wound usually via an external crown or, on earlier watches, via a key. The power of the spring is released through the watch's train of wheels, which ultimately terminates in the *escapement*, which together with its *balance* controls the speed at which the mainspring's energy is released from the watch.

mean time This is the standard time shown on clocks and watches. The 24-hour day is the average of all the solar days in the year. *See also equation of time; solar time*

minute repeater Usually activated via a slide fitted to the case side of a watch. The slide will wind a short *train* that, when released, powers a striking mechanism that sounds the time, usually on coiled gongs within the movement. The hours are sounded first (a single tone for each hour), followed by the quarter hours (usually with a double tone) and finally the minutes (rapid single tones, usually of a higher pitch to the preceding strikes). **Quarter-repeating** watches operate in the same manner but, as their name suggests, strike only the hours and quarters.

open face(d) A watch without a cover to the dial such that the face is immediately visible to the viewer.

perpetual calendar This form of calendar *complication* ensures that the correct day, date and month will be displayed regardless of the number of days in a month. The perpetual calendar will also self-adjust for the extra day in February during a leap year.

petite sonnerie *see clock-watch*

power reserve indication Also referred to as 'up-and-down' indication, this usually takes the form of a fan-form sector displayed on a watch dial with its own hand to indicate the amount of power left in the *mainspring*.

pulsometer A scale incorporated on a chronograph dial that may be used by doctors. The dial will be marked with the number of pulsations for which it has been calibrated. If graduated for 30 pulsations, the doctor can start the chronograph as they begin counting their patient's pulse and stop it again after feeling the subject's thirtieth pulse; the now static chronograph seconds hand will display the patient's pulse rate per minute against the pulsation scale printed at the edge of the dial.

purse watch Rather than being of standard pocket watch design, the purse watch is usually oblong or square in shape and almost always has a cover to the dial. Purse watches were made for both men and women and were especially popular during the latter part of the 1920s and the 1930s.

quarter repeater *see minute repeater*

register *see chronograph*

remontoire A spring or other device that is wound by the *train* and discharged at regular intervals. A **fly regulator** will act as an air break to control the speed at which the remontoire rewinds.

rotor *see automatic*

sidereal time Traditionally the standard of time used by astronomers, sidereal time is based on the amount of time it takes the Earth to turn on its axis: by measuring the Earth's transit of a fixed star, one is able to measure the actual time it takes for the Earth to turn on its axis. This period of time is known as a sidereal day, which is approximately 23 hours, 56 minutes and 4.1 seconds.

simple calendar A watch that incorporates a simple calendar does not recognise the differing lengths of the months, and the date and month will therefore need to be manually adjusted for those months of fewer than 31 days.

skeletonised Movements that have been 'skeletonised' allow the viewer to see through them from one side to the other. Such watches usually dispense with the dial so that the skeletonised work of the movement may be appreciated from the front of the watch; in such examples, the indication of hours may be lacking or, instead, engraved to the *bezel* or marked on the crystal of the watch.

solar time The time as indicated on a sundial. A **solar day** is the time between two successive passages of the sun over the meridian. *See also equation of time*

sphere watch A watch of globular form.

split-seconds *see chronograph*

subsidiary dial A small dial contained within the main dial of a watch that displays additional functions, often seconds or calendar indications such as date, month or day.

tachymeter A scale calibrated – usually for miles or kilometres – on the dial of some *chronographs* that allows the user to calculate the speed of a travelling object over a set distance. If a car is timed over a measured mile or kilometre, the user may begin their chronograph at the starting point and stop it once the measured distance has been travelled; the now static chronograph seconds hand will point to the tachymeter scale and show the speed in miles or kilometres per hour.

telemeter A scale calibrated on the dial of some *chronographs* that allows the user to calculate the speed of an object or event that emits both sound and light – for example, if the chronograph is started when a flash of lightning is seen and stopped when the thunder is heard, reading the chronograph seconds hand against the telemeter scale will show the distance of the thunderstorm from the watch.

tonneau Of barrel shape; an oblong form with convex sides.

tourbillon A tourbillon watch has its *escapement* together with its *balance* mounted onto a tourbillon carriage, and this carriage rotates (usually once per minute in a wristwatch) while the balance continually oscillates and the escape wheel turns. Designed to eliminate positional errors that occur when a watch is in a vertical position, the tourbillon *complication* is in fact more suited to the pocket than the wristwatch, but its dramatic motion is undeniably captivating and has ensured its enduring popularity in the wristwatch. The tourbillon was invented by Abraham-Louis Breguet in 1801.

train This is composed of the wheels and pinions that connect the *mainspring* barrel to the watch's *escapement* and is often referred to as the 'going train'. In watches that have alarm or striking functions, an additional train called the 'strike train' will be incorporated.

trip-repeating *see clock-watch*

triple calendar A watch that displays the day, date and month. A watch referred to as a triple calendar is usually a *simple calendar*, for although *perpetual calendar* watches also display the day, date and month, this latter type is a more complex form of calendar watch and is therefore referred to separately.

units per hour *Chronographs* with their *bezels* calibrated for units per hour can be used to determine hourly production rates. In a factory, for example, a manager could use a chronograph with such a scale by starting the chronograph as production of an item began and stopping the chronograph when the product was complete. The then static chronograph seconds hands would indicate the number of units that could be produced during one hour's non-stop production.

NOTES

1900-1909

1 Georges-Frédéric Roskopf (1813–1889) was born in Germany but moved to La Chaux de Fonds in Switzerland in 1829. After completing a watchmaking apprenticeship and working for some years as a watchmaker, Roskopf set out to design a new watch for the working classes that would be simply finished, robust, reliable and cheap – priced at just 20 francs. The first of these watches were released in 1867 and, as an early measure of their success, Roskopf won a bronze medal at the Paris Universal Exposition that year.

2 D. R. Hoke, *The Time Museum Catalogue of American Pocket Watches*, Rockford, IL: Time Museum, 1991, p. 132.

3 Ibid., p. 106.

4 Ingersoll were selling watches for $1 by the end of the nineteenth century and the term 'dollar watch' has come to encompass this genre of cheap, machine-pressed watches.

5 M. Huber and A. Banbery, *Patek Philippe Genève: Wristwatches*, 2nd edn, Geneva: Patek Philippe, 1998, p. 63.

6 F. Chaille, *Girard-Perregaux*, Paris, Flammarion, 2004, p. 96.

7 K. H. Pritchard, *Swiss Timepiece Makers, 1775–1975*, vol. 1, West Kennebunk, ME: Phoenix Publishing, 1997, p. E49.

8 F. Chaille and F. Cologni, *The Cartier Collection: Timepieces*, Paris: Flammarion, 2006, p. 112.

9 Sotheby's London, *The Celebration of the English Watch*, Part III, 15 December 2016, p. 148.

10 T. Camerer Cuss, *The English Watch, 1585–1970*, Woodbridge: Antique Collectors' Club, 2009, p. 434.

11 K. H. Pritchard, *Swiss Timepiece Makers, 1775–1975*, vol. 2, West Kennebunk, ME: Phoenix Publishing, 1997, pp. L46–L47.

1910-1919

1 F. Chaille and F. Cologni, *The Cartier Collection: Timepieces*, Paris: Flammarion, 2006, p. 110.

2 F. von Osterhausen, *The Movado History*, Atglen, PA: Schiffer, 1996, p. 38.

3 'The Development of the Service Watch', *Horological Journal* vol. 60, no. 712, December 1917, p. 41.

4 M. Friedman and S. Vivas, *Audemars Piguet: 20th Century Complicated Wristwatches*, Le Brassus: Audemars Piguet, 2018, pp. 45–46.

5 'H. Williamson, Ltd.', *Horological Journal* vol. 58, no. 691, March 1916, p. 98.

1920-1929

1 Patek Philippe Museum, *Patek Philippe Watches*, vol. 2, Geneva: Patek Philippe SA, 2013, p. 121.

2 Data from the Swiss Chamber of Watchmaking, reproduced in E. Jaquet and A. Chapuis, *Technique and History of the Swiss Watch*, London: Hamlyn, 1970, p. 243.

3 J. Barracca, G. Negretti and F. Nencini, *Les Temps de Cartier*, Milan: Publi Prom, 1993, p. 132.

4 Patek Philippe Museum, *Patek Philippe Watches*, vol. 2, p. 274.

5 T. Camerer Cuss, *The English Watch, 1585–1970*, Woodbridge: Antique Collectors' Club, 2009, p. 425.

6 Ibid.

7 D. Boettcher, 'Double Case "Hermetic" Watches – Frederick Gruen (US) and Jean Finger (CH)', www.vintagewatchstraps.com/waterproof.php#Hermetic, accessed 3 June 2019.

8 J. Dowling and J. Hess, *The Best of Time: Rolex Wristwatches*, Atglen, PA: Schiffer, 2006, p. 42.

9 F. von Osterhausen, *The Movado History*, Atglen, PA: Schiffer, 1996, p. 74.

10 From an Ermeto advertisement, reproduced ibid., p. 81.

11 H. Hampel, *Automatic Wristwatches from Switzerland*, Atglen, PA: Schiffer, 1994, p. 11.

12 R. W. Pipe, *The Automatic Watch*, London: Heywood & Co., 1952, p. 6.

1930-1939

1 In value terms, this was a drop from 267 million francs in 1929 to just 71 million francs in 1932. Data from the Swiss Chamber of Watchmaking, reproduced in E. Jaquet and A. Chapuis, *Technique and History of the Swiss Watch*, London: Hamlyn, 1970, p. 243.

2 H. Kahlert, R. Mühe and G. Brunner, *Wristwatches: History of a Century's Development*, 5th edn, Atglen, PA: Schiffer, 2005, p. 20.

3 J. Dowling and J. Hess, *The Best of Time: Rolex Wristwatches*, Atglen, PA: Schiffer, 2006, p. 79.

4 For this early perpetual calendar watch by Thomas Mudge, see Sotheby's London, *Celebration of the English Watch Part II*, 7 July 2016, lot 28.

5 The first perpetual calendar wristwatch is believed to be one completed by Patek Philippe in 1925 (no. 97.975), today displayed at the Patek Philippe Museum in Geneva.

6 S. Perman, *A Grand Complication: A Race to Build the World's Most Legendary Watch*, New York: Atria, 2013, p. 219.

7 Patek Philippe Museum, *Patek Philippe Watches*, vol. 2, Geneva: Patek Philippe SA, 2013, p. 153.

8 Dowling and Hess, *The Best of Time*, p. 112.

9 F. Chaille and F. Cologni, *The Cartier Collection: Timepieces*, Paris: Flammarion, 2006, p. 334.

10 D. Boettcher, 'The Omega Watches "Marine" and "Marine Standard"', *NAWCC Watch and Clock Bulletin*, January/February 2012, p. 37.

11 Ibid.

1940-1949

1 Chambre Suisse d'Horlogerie, 'Rapport' report 1980, calculated from tables reproduced in D. Landes, *Revolution in Time: Clocks and the Making of the Modern World*, London: Viking, 2000, pp. 424–25.

2 Ibid.

3 R. Meis, *A. Lange & Söhne: The Watchmakers of Dresden*, Geneva: Antiquorum, 1999, p. 220.

4 Ibid., p. 218.

5 N. Foulkes, *Patek Philippe: The Authorised Biography*, London: Penguin, 2016, p. 190.

1950-1959

1 Includes total exports of watches and finished movements; source: Chambre Suisse d'Horlogerie, 'Rapport' report 1980, calculated from tables reproduced in D. Landes, *Revolution in Time: Clocks and the Making of the Modern World*, London: Viking, 2000, pp. 424–25.

2 M. Friedman and S. Vivas, *Audemars Piguet: 20th Century Complicated Wristwatches*, Le Brassus: Audemars Piguet, 2018, pp. 131–32.

1960-1969

1 G. Rossier and A. Marquié, *Moonwatch Only: 60 Years of the Omega Speedmaster*, La Croix/Lutry: Watchprint, 2017, p. 27.

2 Ibid., pp. 26–27.

1970–1979

1   Includes total exports of watches and finished movements; source. Chambre Suisse d'Horlogerie, 'Rapport' report 1980, calculated from tables reproduced in D. Landes, *Revolution in Time: Clocks and the Making of the Modern World*, London: Viking, 2000, pp. 424–25.

2   R. Good, 'The Basle Fair: Year of the Quartz Crystal Watch', *Horological Journal* vol. 112, May 1970, p. 5.

3   As stated in the official Hamilton Pulsar Press Release reproduced in the *Horological Journal* vol. 113, July 1970, pp. 14–15.

4   Ibid.

5   Antiquorum in association with Omega, *Omegamania*, Geneva: Antiquorum, 2007, p. 374.

6   F. Chaille, *Girard-Perregaux*, Paris: Flammarion, 2004, pp. 119–20.

7   Bulova advertisement, *Horological Journal* vol. 112, March 1970, p. 9.

8   M. Friedman and S. Vivas, *Audemars Piguet: 20th Century Complicated Wristwatches*, Le Brassus: Audemars Piguet, 2018, p. 229.

9   Ibid.

10   Ibid.

11   F. Müller, *Piaget*, New York: Abrams, 2014, p. 193.

12   Corum, 'Introducing the Brand', www.corum-watches.com/en/the-watch-brand, accessed 22 January 2019.

13   Translated from a Spanish-language Tissot catalogue of 1969.

14   'Modern Horology: New from Basle – the Plastics Watch Has Arrived', *Horological Journal* vol. 113, no. 11, May 1971, p. 8.

15   E. Hornby, *The Adventures of Edward Hornby*, Wellingborough: Skelton's Press, 1984, p. 34.

16   Extract from an article by George Daniels written for Sotheby's catalogue of *Important Clocks, Watches, Wristwatches and Barometers*, London, 22 June 1999.

1980–1989

1   'Jewellery, Watches and Accessories', *Horological Journal*, July 1980, p. 21.

2   G. Viola and G. Brunner, *Time in Gold: Wristwatches*, Atglen, PA: Schiffer, 1988, p. 219.

3   Société Suisse pour l'Industrie Horlogère (Swiss Society for the Horological Industry), known as the SSIH, was a Swiss watch group formed by the board of trustees of Omega and Tissot during the turbulent economic years that followed the Wall Street Crash. The group recognised the shared interests and values of the two companies and, through the agreement, sought to strengthen their positions by working together in both the commercial and industrial fields, including the sharing of production techniques and calibres. In 1932 the specialist maker of complication movements Lemania joined the group.

4   Allgemeine Gesellschaft der Schweizerischen Uhrenindustrie (General Society of the Swiss Watch Industry), known as ASUAG, was formed in 1931 during the Great Depression that followed the Wall Street Crash and was supported by the Swiss government and Swiss banks. Two main subsidiary companies within ASUAG were Ebauches SA, which included manufacturers of movements and watch parts, and the General Watch Co., a subsidiary for manufacturers of complete watches. A vast array of companies were part of the group, and by the 1970s ASUAG was the largest producer of watch parts and movements in the world.

5   Société de Microélectronique et d'Horlogerie (Society of Microelectronics and Watchmaking), known as SMH.

6   Details supplied by M. Schmid and B. Müller for the auction catalogue *The History of Swatch Design: The Schmid & Müller Collection*, Sotheby's Geneva, November 2015, pp. 3, 10.

7   Ibid., p. 12.

8   R. Carrera, *Swatchissimo, 1981–1991*, Geneva: Antiquorum, 1991, p. 79.

9   'Limited Edition Pop Art', *Horological Journal*, May 1988, p. 18.

10   Ibid.

11   R. Carrera, *Swatchissimo*, p. 368.

12   An example of Keith Haring's watch was illustrated by C. Pollan in *New York Magazine*'s supplement *Christmas Gifts New York* (2 December 1985), captioned: 'Keith Haring Swatch watch is about $50 at Bloomingdale's ... Macy's ... and Saks Fifth Avenue'.

13   Carrera, *Swatchissimo*, p. 381.

14   F. Cologni, *Secrets of Vacheron Constantin*, Paris: Flammarion, 2005, p. 163.

15   Jaeger-LeCoultre general catalogue, 1993.

16   G. Pergola, S. Mazzariol and G. Dosso, *Rolex Daytona: A Legend is Born*, Prato: Vintage Watches, 2006, p. 238.

17   M. Friedman and S. Vivas, *Calendar Watches: Audemars Piguet*, Le Brassus: Audemars Piguet, 2018, p. 229.

18   Viola and Brunner, *Time in Gold*, p. 17; the authors quote a retail price in German Deutsche Marks of 400,000.

19   The year 1984 is that given on the cover of *Antiquarian Horology* vol. 17, no. 1, Autumn 1987.

20   J. Knudsen, *The Jürgensen Dynasty: Four Centuries of Watchmaking in Two Countries*, Woodbridge: Antique Collectors' Club(?), 2013, p. 325.

21   N. Foulkes, *Patek Philippe: The Authorised Biography*, London: Penguin, 2016, pp. 310–311.

1990–1999

1   T. Treffry, 'Alain Silberstein, Watch Architect', *Horological Journal* vol. 138, no. 4, April 1996, p. 126.

2   S. Urquhart, 'A Tribute to Dr George Daniels', written for the auction catalogue *The George Daniels Horological Collection*, Sotheby's London, 6 November 2012, p. 81.

3   F.-P. Journe, 'A Tribute to Dr George Daniels', written for *The George Daniels Horological Collection*, p. 85.

4   F. Chaille, *Girard-Perregaux*, Paris: Flammarion, 2004, p. 92.

5   A. Downing, 'Franck Muller: Contentious Watchmaker', *Horological Journal* vol. 140, no. 9, September 1998, p. 299.

6   A. Downing, 'Luxury Mechanical Watches in Trouble', *Horological Journal* vol. 138, no. 4, April 1996, p. 110.

7   Andersen Genève, 'Heures du Monde/Worldtime Watches', www.andersen-geneve.ch/world-time, accessed 26 January 2019.

8   'On Show at Basel', *Horological Journal* vol. 132, no. 11, May 1990, p. 369.

9   M. Friedman and S. Vivas, *Audemars Piguet: 20th Century Complicated Wristwatches*, Le Brassus: Audemars Piguet, 2018, p. 241.

10   Ibid.

BIBLIOGRAPHY

Barracca, Jader, Giampiero Negretti and Franco Nencini, *Ore d'Oro, 2: orologi da polso – passione e investimento / Ore d'Oro, 2: Wrist Watches – Investment and Passion*, Milan: Editoriale Wrist, 1987

Barracca, Jader, Giampiero Negretti and Franco Nencini, *Les Temps de Cartier*, 2nd edn, Milan: Publi Prom, 1993

Britten, F. J., *The Watch and Clock Makers' Handbook, Dictionary and Guide*, 10th edn, London: E. & F. N. Spon, 1902

Brunner, Gisbert, and Christian Pfeiffer-Belli, *Swiss Wristwatches: Chronology of Worldwide Success*, Atglen, PA: Schiffer, 1991

Brunner, Gisbert, Christian Pfeiffer-Belli and Martin Wehrli, *Audemars Piguet: Masterpieces of Classical Watchmaking*, 2nd edn, Le Brassus: Audemars Piguet, 2000

Camerer Cuss, Terence, *The English Watch, 1585–1970*, Woodbridge: Antique Collectors' Club, 2009

Carrera, Roland, *Swatchissimo, 1981–1991*, Geneva: Antiquorum, 1992

Chaille, François, *Girard-Perregaux*, Paris: Flammarion, 2004

Chaille, François, and Franco Cologni, *The Cartier Collection: Timepieces*, Paris: Flammarion, 2006

Chapuis, Alfred, and Eugène Jaquet, *The History of the Self-winding Watch, 1770–1931*, revd English edn, trans. R. Savarè Grandvoinet, Neuchâtel: Éditions du Griffon, 1956

Clerizo, Michael, *George Daniels: A Master Watchmaker and His Art*, London: Thames & Hudson, 2013

Cologni, Franco, *Jaeger-LeCoultre: The Story of the Grande Maison*, Paris: Flammarion, 2006

Cologni, Franco, *Secrets of Vacheron Constantin*, Paris: Flammarion, 2005

Daniels, George, *All in Good Time: Reflections of a Watchmaker*, revd edn, London: Philip Wilson, 2013

Dowling, James, and Jeffrey Hess, *The Best of Time: Rolex Wristwatches*, 3rd edn, Atglen, PA: Schiffer, 2006

Fallet, Estelle, *Tissot: The Story of a Watch Company*, Le Locle: Tissot, 2002

Foulkes, Nicholas, *Patek Philippe: The Authorized Biography*, London: Penguin, 2016

Friedman, Michael, and Sébastian Vivas, *Audemars Piguet: 20th Century Complicated Wristwatches*, Le Brassus: Audemars Piguet, 2018

Goldberger, John, *Longines Watches*, Bologna: Damiani, 2006

Hampel, Heinz, *Automatic Wristwatches from Switzerland*, Atglen, PA: Schiffer, 1994

Hornby, Edward, *The Adventures of Edward Hornby*, Wellingborough: Skelton's Press, 1984

Huber, Martin, and Alan Banbery, *Patek Philippe Genève*, Zurich: Ineichen, 1982

Huber, Martin, and Alan Banbery, *Patek Philippe Genève: Wristwatches*, 2nd edn, Geneva: Patek Philippe, 1998

Hoke, Donald Robert, *The Time Museum Historical Catalogue of American Pocket Watches*, Rockford, IL: The Time Museum, 1991

Isnardi, Alberto, *Tudor Anthology*, Novi Ligure: Isnardi, 2013

Jaquet, Eugène, and Alfred Chapuis, *Technique and History of the Swiss Watch*, revd edn, London: Hamlyn, 1970

Kahlert, Helmut, Richard Mühe and Gisbert Brunner, *Wristwatches: History of a Century's Development*, 5th edn, Atglen, PA: Schiffer, 2005

Knudsen, John, *The Jürgensen Dynasty: Four Centuries of Watchmaking in Two Countries*, Woodbridge: Antique Collectors' Club, 2013

Lambelet, Carole, and Lorette Coen, *The World of Vacheron Constantin*, Lausanne: Éditions Scriptar, 1992

Landes, David, *Revolution in Time: Clocks and the Making of the Modern World*, revd edn, London: Viking/Penguin Group, 2000

Lang, Gerd-R., and Reinhard Meis, *Chronograph: Wristwatches to Stop Time*, Atglen, PA: Schiffer, 1993

Loomes, Brian, *Watchmakers and Clockmakers of the World: Complete 21st Century Edition*, London: NAG Press, 2006

Loring, John, *Tiffany Timepieces*, New York: Abrams, 2004

Marchenoir, Julien, *Treasures of Vacheron Constantin*, Paris: Éditions Hazan, 2011

Marozzi, Daria, and Gianluigi Toselli, *Longines*, Bologna: Edizioni Giada, 1990

Meis, Reinhard, *A. Lange & Söhne: The Watchmakers of Dresden*, trans. Alan Downing, Geneva: Antiquorum, 1999

Mondani, Franca, and Guido Mondani, *100 Years of Rolex, 1908–2008*, Genova: Guido Mondani Editore & Ass., 2008

Müller, Florence, *Piaget: Watchmakers and Jewellers since 1874*, New York: Abrams, 2014

Osterhausen, Fritz von, *The Movado History*, Atglen, PA: Schiffer, 1996

Patek Philippe Museum, *Patek Philippe Watches*, 2 vols, Geneva: Patek Philippe, 2013

Pergola, Carlo, Stefano Mazzariol and Giovanni Dosso, *Rolex Daytona, dalla nascita al mito: un viaggio tra tecnica e stile / Rolex Daytona, a Legend is Born: A Journey through the Techniques and Style*, Prato: Vintage Watches, 2006

Perman, Stacy, *A Grand Complication: The Race to Build the World's Most Legendary Watch*, New York: Atria International, 2013

Pritchard, Kathleen, *Swiss Timepiece Makers, 1775–1975*, 2 vols, West Kennebunk, ME: Phoenix, 1997

Randall, Anthony, *The Time Museum Catalogue of Chronometers*, Rockford, IL: The Time Museum, 1992

Rossier, Grégoire, and Anthony Marquié, *Moonwatch Only: 60 Years of Omega Speedmaster*, revd edn, La Croix/Lutry: Watchprint.com, 2017

Rudoe, Judy, *Cartier, 1900–1939*, London: British Museum Press, 1997

Sala, Pietro Giuliano, *Universal Watch Genève: Chronographs and Complicated Wristwatches*, Cassina de Pecchi: Vallardi, 2010

Schmidt, Ryan, *The Wristwatch Handbook: A Comprehensive Guide to Mechanical Wristwatches*, Woodbridge: Antique Collectors' Club, 2016

Skeet, Martin, and Nick Urul, *Vintage Rolex Sports Models*, 3rd edn, Atglen, PA: Schiffer, 2008

Sotheby's London, *George Daniels Retrospective Exhibition, 18–23 July 2006: Sotheby's in Association with Bobinet*, exh. cat., Sotheby's London, 2006

Thompson, David, *Watches*, London: British Museum Press, 2008

Tölke, Hans-F., and Jürgen King, *IWC: International Watch Co., Schaffhausen*, Zurich: Ineichen, 1987

Viola, Gerald, and Gisbert Brunner, *Time in Gold: Wristwatches*, Atglen, PA: Schiffer, 1988

Wesolowski, Zygmunt M., *A Concise Guide to Military Timepieces, 1880–1990*, Marlborough, Wilts: The Crowood Press, 1996

JOURNALS

Horological Journal: vol. 58, no. 691 (March 1916); vol. 60, no. 712 (December 1917); vol. 112 (March 1970); vol. 113 (July 1970); vol. 138, no. 4 (April 1996); vol. 140, no. 9 (September 1998)

NAWCC Watch and Clock Bulletin, January/ February 2012

AUCTION CATALOGUES

Antiquorum Geneva, *Important Modern and Vintage Timepieces*, 11 November 2012

Antiquorum Geneva, *The Magical Art of Cartier*, Antiquorum/Étude Tajan, 19 November 1996

Antiquorum Geneva, *Omegamania: Thematic Auction*, 14–15 April 2007

Antiquorum Geneva, *The Quarter Millennium of Vacheron Constantin*, 3 April 2005

Antiquorum Hong Kong, *Important Collectors Wristwatches, Pocket Watches*, 23 April 2006

Antiquorum Hong Kong, *Important Modern and Vintage Timepieces*, 22 February 2014

Antiquorum New York, *Important Collectors Wristwatches, Pocket Watches*, 18 June 2008

Bonhams, *Fine Jewellery*, London, New Bond Street, 9 December 2010

Bonhams, *Fine Watches and Wristwatches*, London, New Bond Street, 20 June 2018

Bonhams, *The First World War Centenary Sale*, London, Knightsbridge, 1 October 2014

Bonhams, *Sports, Competition and Collectors' Motor Cars, F1 Memorabilia, Automobilia and Models*, Chichester, Goodwood, 24 June 2005

Bonhams, *Watches and Wristwatches*, London, Knightsbridge, 16 September 2014

Bonhams, *Watches and Wristwatches*, London, 22 November 2016

Sotheby's Geneva, *A Collection of 69 Exceptional 20th Century Watches*, 13 May 2003

Sotheby's Geneva, *Exceptional Wristwatches*, 17 May 2004

Sotheby's Geneva, *Important Watches*, various, 1999–2019

Sotheby's Geneva, *Important Watches Including the Highly Important Henry Graves Jr Supercomplication*, 11 November 2014

Sotheby's Geneva, *The Yellow Gold Calibre 89: Patek Philippe's Most Complicated Watch*, 14 May 2017

Sotheby's Geneva, *Magnificent Jewels and Noble Jewels*, 17 May 2011; 16 May 2017

Sotheby's Hong Kong, *Important Watches*, various, 2002–19

Sotheby's London, *The Celebration of the English Watch, Part I* (15 December 2015); *Part II* (7 July 2016); *Part III* (15 December 2016); *Part IV* (6 July 2017)

Sotheby's London, Fine and Important Watches auctions, including those held in conjunction with the Clock, Barometer and Scientific Instrument Departments 1997–2019

Sotheby's London, *Fine Timepieces Including George Daniels Masterpieces*, 19 September 2017

Sotheby's London, *The George Daniels Horological Collection*, 6 November 2012

Sotheby's London, *Fine Jewels*, 11 June 2015

Sotheby's New York, *Important Watches*, various, 2002–19

Sotheby's New York, *Masterpieces from the Time Museum*, 2 December 1999

Sotheby's New York, *Masterpieces from the Time Museum, Part Four, Vol. III*, 14–15 October 2004

Sotheby's New York, *Watches from the Collection of the Late Reginald H. Fullerton, Jr. and his Grandfather Henry Graves, Jr.*, 14 June 2012

Sotheby's New York, *Magnificent Jewels*, 19 April 2016; 8 December 2016

WEBSITES

www.ahsoc.org
www.antiquorum.swiss
www.blackbough.co.uk
www.bonhams.com
www.christies.com
www.hodinkee.com
www.nawcc.org
www.phillips.com
www.sothebys.com
www.vintagewatchstraps.com

ACKNOWLEDGEMENTS

Embarking on any project of this nature inevitably involves the help of a vast number of people, but first and foremost my sincere thanks go to Adam Withington, for without his unwavering support, encouragement and patience this book would never have seen the light of day. I am extremely grateful to my brother Oliver Barter, who together with the rest of the team at Prestel was instrumental in ensuring this book got off the ground: my editors Lincoln Dexter and Anna Godfrey, copyeditor Aimee Selby and production manager Friederike Schirge; and from Grade Design, Peter Dawson and Alice Kennedy-Owen; all of whom have worked tirelessly to make this book a reality.

Sotheby's have provided the vast majority of photographs for this book and I would like to offer them my sincere gratitude. Having previously worked at Sotheby's for several years myself, one of the great pleasures in writing this book has been the collaboration with colleagues old and new. Daryn Schnipper, who has written the foreword to this book, is one of the true greats of the watch world; now Chairman of Sotheby's Watch Division, she has been a friend and mentor to me for more than twenty years and her support for my work on this book has been nothing short of magnificent. The patience of those at Sotheby's who helped me retrieve archived images from auctions all over the world from the last two decades has been humbling, and I would like to offer my sincere thanks to all those whom I unrelentingly nagged for photographs, as well as to the Sotheby's Watch departments in London, New York, Geneva and Hong Kong. In addition to Daryn Schnipper, I would especially like to thank Joanne Albertyn, Caitie Barrett, Benoît Colson, Charlie Foxhall, Jennifer Laster, David Mountain, Geraldine Nager, Sarah Soulen, Janet Tham, Katharine Thomas, Barbara Waginski, Douglas Walker, Tiffany Yeung, and the Sotheby's Digital Images teams in London and New York. I am also extremely grateful to the legion of exceptional photographers at Sotheby's. Since this book includes many photographs of watches from auctions throughout the last twenty years, the images have been taken by several different photographers, but I would like to give special thanks to Jasper Gough, Amanda Harvey and Ed Parrinello, who between them have photographed many thousands of watches for Sotheby's sales over the years.

Other auction houses have also very kindly supplied images for this book, and I would like to thank Julien Schaerer of Antiquorum Geneva; Bryony Bedingham, Jonathan Darracott, Charles Dower and Penelope Morris of Bonhams; and Carl Palmegren of Bukowskis. Thank you also to the Faerber Collection; JD Clerc and Tim Fischer of galerie123.com; Sian Griffiths; Anthony Kingsley; Nathalie Marielloni; Stefano Mazzariol and Virginia Giansoldati of mazzariolstefanolibrary.com; and Stephen Russell Collection NYC.

Many watch houses have also been extremely generous with their time and supply of imagery and information for the book, and I would like to offer special thanks to the following *maisons* and individuals who have so patiently helped to field my barrage of requests: Raphaël Balestra, Dave Grandjean, Michael Friedman and Sébastian Vivas at Audemars Piguet; Paula Cost at Bulova; Jennifer Bochud and Stéphanie Lachat at Longines; Phillipa James at Movado; the International Press Office at Omega; Elia Cottier, Sylvie Dricourt and Peter Friess at Patek Philippe; Alain Borgeaud at Piaget; Dr Roger Smith OBE at Roger W. Smith; Faye Lovenbury at Seiko; Priscila Viana at Swatch; Lysiane Blanchet, Sigrid Offenstein and Christian Selmoni at Vacheron Constantin; and Catherine Cariou and Julien Marchenoir at Van Cleef & Arpels.

ABOUT THE AUTHOR

Alexander Barter has worked in the vintage watch industry for over two decades. He joined Sotheby's watch division in 1996, initially working in their London office before moving to Geneva. He has travelled extensively, viewing and appraising watches across the world. In 2005 he became Sotheby's Deputy Worldwide Head of Watches before leaving in 2009 to co-found his own company, Black Bough. Barter is a consultant to Sotheby's, a member of the Antiquarian Horological Society and a Freeman of the Worshipful Company of Clockmakers, the oldest surviving horological institution in the world.

IMAGE CREDITS

T = top; B = bottom; M = middle, L = left;
R = right; TL = top left; TR = top right;
BL = bottom left; BR = bottom right

© Antiquorum Geneva, www.antiquorum.swiss:
pp. 74L, 187M, 222L, 227L

© Audemars Piguet, www.audemarspiguet.com
(photographer Karin Creuzet): frontispiece,
pp. 42T, 42M, 42BL, 42BR, 65R, 67, 177, 240L,
240R, 290

© Black Bough, www.blackbough.co.uk: pp. 10L,
16L, 16R, 48T, 50, 72, 73, 73B, 76L, 76R, 79R,
87R, 91T, 91B, 99, 100, 120R, 124T, 126L, 126R,
130, 136L, 136R, 137B, 143R, 146L, 146R, 147L,
148T, 152R, 153, 155, 156L, 156R, 160L, 160R, 161T,
166, 178L, 178R, 181R, 196L, 196R, 217, 217R, 223,
226L, 227R, 246L, 246R, 247L, 247R.

© Bonhams, www.bonhams.com: pp. 48B, 54R,
152L, 207B, 237R, 316L

© Bukowskis, www.bukowskis.com: p. 171

© Galerie 123 Geneva, www.galerie123.com:
pp. 8, 80

© Compagnie des Montres Longines Francillon
SA, www.longines.com: pp. 28, 96, 97

© Omega, www.omegawatches.com: p. 118

© Patek Philippe, www.patek.com: pp. 44L, 44R,
69, 108TL, 108TR, 108BL, 108BR, 167L, 203R,
224, 285L, 285R

© Piaget, www.piaget.com: pp. 192 (Archives
Piaget), 194 (photographer Fabien Cruchon)

© Seiko, www.seikowatches.com: p. 199R

© Sotheby's, www.sothebys.com: front cover,
pp. 4, 7, 10 R, 11, 12, 13, 14L, 14R, 15L, 15R, 17, 18,
19T, 19B, 20T, 20B, 21L, 21M, 21R, 22L, 22R, 23L,
23R, 24, 25, 27T, 27B, 30, 31L, 32L, 32R, 33T, 33B,
34, 35T, 35B, 36L, 36R, 37T, 27R, 37B, 38L, 38R,
39L, 39R, 40, 41, 43, 45, 46, 47T, 47BL, 47BR,
49T, 54L, 55, 56, 57, 58T, 58B, 59L, 59R, 60, 61L,
61R, 62L, 63, 64L, 64R, 65L, 66T, 66B, 68L,
68R, 70, 71L, 71R, 74R, 78, 79L, 82, 84T, 84B,

85L, 85R, 86, 87L, 88T, 88B, 91M, 92, 93L, 93R,
94, 95T, 95B, 98, 101, 102, 103, 104L, 105, 107,
109T, 109BL, 109BR, 110, 111, 112TL, 112TR, 113,
114, 115, 117T, 117B, 120L, 121, 122L, 122R, 123,
127L, 127R, 128, 129, 131T, 131B, 132, 133L, 133R,
134T, 134B, 135T, 135B, 137T, 138, 139, 140, 141,
142, 143L, 144, 145, 148B, 149T, 149BL, 149BR,
154, 157, 158T, 158BL, 158BR, 159, 161B, 162, 163L,
163R, 164, 165, 167R, 168, 169, 170L, 170R, 172,
173, 174, 175, 176, 179T, 180T, 180B, 181L, 182,
183, 184, 185L, 185R, 186T, 186B, 187L, 188, 189R,
190–91, 195L, 195R, 197L, 197R, 198, 199L, 200T,
200B, 201, 202, 203L, 204, 205L, 205R, 206L,
206R, 207T, 208, 209, 210, 211L, 211R, 212, 213,
214, 215, 216, 219L, 219R, 220, 221, 222R, 226R,
228L, 228R, 229L, 229R, 230L, 230R, 231T, 231B,
232, 233T, 233B, 234L, 234R, 235, 236L, 236R,
237L, 238, 239, 241, 242L, 242R, 243, 244, 245,
248T, 238B, 252, 253, 254L, 254R, 255, 256L,
256R, 257T, 257B, 258L, 258R, 259, 260, 261,
264, 265L, 265M, 265R, 268L, 268M, 267R, 269,
270L, 270R, 271, 272, 273, 274, 275, 276L, 276R,
277, 278, 280, 281, 282L, 282R, 283L, 283R, 284,
286, 287, 288, 289, 292L, 292R, 293L, 293R,
294L, 294R, 295, 296L, 296R, 297, 298, 299,
300L, 300R, 301L, 301R, 302, 303, 304, 305L,
305R, 306, 307, 308, 309, 310L, 310R, 311, 312,
313, 314, 315, 316R, 317L, 317R, 319, 320, 321, 322

© Stefano Mazzariol,
www.mazzariolstefanolibrary.com: pp. 52,
75L, 75R

© Swatch, www.swatch.com: pp. 263L, 263M,
263R, 266, 267L, 267M, 267R

© Vacheron Constantin, www.vacheron-
constantin.com: 3R, 51, 62R, 83T, 83B, 90L, 90R,
104R, 124B, 125T, 125B, 187R, 189L, 279

© Van Cleef & Arpels, www.vancleefarpels.com:
pp. 116L, 116r

Vintage images: pp. 49B, 77, 89, 147R, 150, 179B,
218, 250

It should be noted that where the calibre number
or movement *ligne* size of a watch is known, this
has been included within the captions. As access
was not available to all of the watches in the book,
where it has not been possible to confirm calibre
or *ligne* size, this information has been omitted
from the captions. The dates provided in the
captions relate to the date of manufacture or sale
of the actual illustrated examples and, unless
specifically stated, do not necessarily relate to the
date of a model's first release.

INDEX

Italic page numbers indicate illustrations.

In respect to links in the book the Publisher expressly
notes that no illegal content was discernible on the linked
sites at the time the links were created. The Publisher
has no influence at all over the current and future design,
content or authorship of the linked sites. For this reason
the Publisher expressly disassociates itself from all content
on linked sites that has been altered since the link
was created and assumes no liability for such content.

Front cover: Patek Philippe Calatrava Ref. 96,
made in 1941 (see pp. 120–21).
© Sotheby's, photographer Jasper Gough

A CIP catalogue record for this book is available from the
British Library.

Editorial direction: Lincoln Dexter, Anna Godfrey
Copy-editing: Aimee Selby
Index: Christopher Phipps
Design and layout: Peter Dawson, Alice Kennedy-Owen,
gradedesign.com
Production management: Friederike Schirge
Separations: Reproline Mediateam
Printing and binding: DZS Grafik, d.o.o., Ljubljana
Paper: Profisilk

Printed in Slovenia

MIX
Paper | Supporting
responsible forestry
FSC® C106600
www.fsc.org

Penguin Random House Verlagsgruppe FSC® N001967

ISBN 978-3-7913-8011-7

www.prestel.com